*American Author Houses,
Museums, Memorials, and Libraries*

American Author Houses, Museums, Memorials, and Libraries

A State-by-State Guide

by
SHIRLEY HOOVER BIGGERS

McFarland & Company, Inc., Publishers
Jefferson, North Carolina, and London

Library of Congress Cataloguing-in-Publication Data

Biggers, Shirley Hoover, 1936–
    American author houses, museums, memorials, and libraries :
a state-by-state guide / by Shirley Hoover Biggers.
        p.   cm.
    Includes indexes.
    ISBN 0-7864-0777-8 (illustrated case binding : 50# alkaline paper) ∞
    1. Literary landmarks—United States—Guidebooks.   2. Authors,
American—Homes and haunts—Guidebooks.   3. Literary libraries—
United States—Guidebooks.   4. Literary museums—United States—
Guidebooks.   5. Authors, American—Museums—Guidebooks.   6.
Memorials—United States—Guidebooks.   I. Title.
PS141.B54   2000
810.9—dc21   99-59558

British Library Cataloguing-in-Publication data are available

Manufactured in the United States of America

*McFarland & Company, Inc., Publishers
  Box 611, Jefferson, North Carolina 28640
    www.mcfarlandpub.com*

For my husband, Charles Biggers, for his help with this book: trips to countless sites, photography at each one, and expertise in the computer. With especial gratitude for his delight in it all.

Table of Contents

"Nothing you ever read about them can make you know them until you go there.... You always find something of what made them the souls they were ... you see their sky and their earth."

—Sarah Orne Jewett (on visiting the homes of authors), July 30, 1898, in *Letters of Sarah Orne Jewett*, Annie Fields, ed., Houghton Mifflin Company, Boston and New York, 1911, p. 158.

Preface

My first pilgrimage to an author's home was with a group of students. On that bright autumn day in 1977, we toured Faulkner's Rowan Oak. Since then, I have often traced writers' footsteps through their homes and haunts. Always when I cross the threshold of a house museum dedicated to an author, a blend of exhilaration and awe goes with me. I leave with more insight into the writer's life, works, and historical era.

That initial house museum tour led to other regional explorations with my classes for gifted and talented students. Before long, my husband and I were spending our vacations searching out memorials to America's writers all across the country. Since no current and user-friendly guide to writer memorials was available, I decided to publish my research. This book is the result.

My early interest in the subject was limited to America's pantheon of illustrious writers. Through correspondence with state and county organizations, though, I realized that memorials to regional writers should be included, too. Likewise, I focused only on America's *belles-lettres*—its fine poetry, fiction, and drama—until research convinced me to include memorials to journalists, historians, and conservationists who made significant contributions to America's enduring body of works. Moreover, tributes to writers of our national songs have earned their place in this book as have memorials to the authors of America's beloved children's stories. Ultimately, the book became a comprehensive guide to all kinds of tributes to America's writers, living and dead, from colonial to contemporary.

Curators at author museums I could not visit provided not only the requested information but often much enthusiasm for the project as well. In that vein, many individuals have made an extra effort to fulfill my written or telephoned requests for information and pictures. Library resources launched many a search, and local and state historical societies have been most helpful. Along the way I have gained a great respect for their faithful guardianship of the nation's past. Several times I have also been inspired by the persistent efforts of one man or one woman to establish a writer memorial. My students and colleagues, friends, and family have all provided information on writers' memorials. Undoubtedly, the Internet is the most beneficial tool for tracking down author tributes. How did researchers ever do without the web, faxes, and e-mail?

In 20 years of exploring America's author memorials, I have noted a great variety among the homes of writers, and among the writers themselves. Some houses are humble cottages, like Sandburg's three-room birthplace. Others, such as Edith Wharton's mansion, are impressive estates. Geographically, writers' homes dot the vast spectrum of America's landscape, from Sarah Orne Jewett's house in Maine to the Florida backwoods region which inspired Marjorie Kinnan Rawlings' *The Yearling*. House museums from East to West include Hawthorne's birthplace on the coast of Massachusetts and Robinson Jeffers' Tor House on California's.

One house, the Whittier Homestead, has been officially welcoming guests since 1893 while the birthplace of Margaret Mitchell's *Gone with the Wind* opened to the public in 1997. The National Park Service administers some author houses; others are state historic sites. Many are city-operated, and more are maintained by historical societies and private foundations. By preserving the bricks and boards of writers' houses, these farsighted organizations also safeguard segments of the national cultural heritage.

America honors its writers (both past and present) in a myriad of tangible ways. One is to name literary centers and theaters for them. Some are long established, like the Eugene O'Neill Theatre Center; others are brand new, for example, The National Steinbeck Center. Some are yet to come, as is the case with the Eudora Welty Writers Center and the Arthur Miller Theatre. Libraries, college buildings, parks, and even bridges are named for writers. Across the land, plaques and sculptures commemorate the life and death of authors. Literary characters, like Huck and Tom, Old Yeller, and the Cat in the Hat, step off their pages to become bronze statues. These spin-offs and others, including 44 United States commemorative postage stamps, appear with the more traditional tributes in this book's contents.

Cultural tourism is becoming an important activity. A new millennium is a good time to take stock of our American literary heritage. International visitors, as well as American tourists, are seeking out the nation's literary landmarks. The United States is still a young nation by history's count, but one evidence of its coming of age is an increasing dedication to preserving and enjoying literary treasures.

This book is a reference to hundreds of places in the 48 contiguous states and Washington, D.C., honoring more than 200 American writers. Entries are arranged alphabetically by state, then by city or town. Directions and telephone numbers are provided in addition to hours and dates the memorial centers are open. Admission rates are listed. Of course, both times and charges are subject to change. May this book be a useful guide in your visits to America's monuments to its men and women of letters. Wherever you find the author memorials, you will be enriched by savoring, through them, America's majestic literary heritage.

Shirley Hoover Biggers
Spring 2000

ALABAMA

Montgomery

SCOTT AND ZELDA FITZGERALD MUSEUM

> 919 Felder Ave., Apt. A. Open: Wed.–Fri. 10–2, Sat. and Sun. 1–5. Free admission but donation requested. (334) 264-4222.

F. Scott Fitzgerald (1896–1940), novelist, and his wife, Zelda Sayre Fitzgerald (1900–1948), a Montgomery native, rented this house in 1931 and 1932. Fitzgerald had already published three novels, including *The Great Gatsby*, considered to be among the century's best written. The house has been divided into apartments, the bottom right unit housing the museum. The museum's focus is on the personal artifacts which were a part of private and public lives of the Roaring Twenties couple. Displayed are articles, letters, partial manuscripts, photographs, and Scott Fitzgerald's books, including *This Side of Paradise* and *Tender Is the Night*. Some of Zelda's original paintings are exhibited as well as a copy of her book, *Save Me the Waltz*. This is the only museum dedicated to either of the dazzling Jazz Age pair.

Monroeville

OLD COURTHOUSE

> Town Square. (334) 575-7433.

This restored 1903 building's courtroom is the model for the court trial setting in *To Kill a Mockingbird* by Harper Lee (1926–   ), whose father was a Monroeville attorney and the model for the novel's Atticus Finch. Each May a production of the two-act play adapted from the novel is presented to packed audiences in the courtroom. The courthouse was visited by the Hollywood producers as they designed the courtroom scene in the Academy-Award winning movie based on the novel. Gregory Peck came, too, as he prepared for the role of Atticus Finch, a portrayal that won Peck an Academy Award in 1962. *To Kill a Mockingbird* earned Harper Lee a

Literary Arts Series, 1996.

Harper Lee's courthouse in *To Kill a Mockingbird* is based on this one. At this site the museum now housed here annually presents the play based on Lee's novel.

1961 Pulitzer Prize. The novel was on the best seller list for eighty weeks. Monroeville, Harper Lee's hometown, is called Maycomb in her acclaimed and only novel, so far.

A new courthouse was built in 1963, and the old one now houses the Monroe County Heritage Museum. Among its programs is the production of *To Kill a Mockingbird* each year. Available at the museum is a guide to a walking tour of Monroeville, highlighting scenes of the 1930s when Harper Lee and her friend, the writer Truman Capote, were growing up there.

Tuscumbia

Ivy Green

> Birthplace of Helen Keller, 300 West North Commons. Open: Mon.–Sat., 8:30–4, Sun. 1–4. Closed New Year's Day, Easter, Labor Day, Thanksgiving, Christmas Eve, and Christmas Day. Small admission fee. (205) 383-4066.

Helen Keller's paternal grandparents built Ivy Green in 1820. Helen was born in 1880 in the small house on the grounds. The main house, built in the Southern Virginia cottage style, is furnished with Keller family pieces. The dining room, where Helen and her new teacher clashed, is a highlight of the house. Another is the upstairs rooms that Helen shared with Annie Sullivan when "Teacher" came to live at Ivy Green. The museum room in the back exhibits Helen Keller's Braille typewriter, her library of Braille books, and many photographs and records of achievements. *The Story of My Life* and the other three books by Helen Keller are all there, too.

In her autobiography, Helen Keller tells of a tree that she had climbed in the yard and was caught in a thunderstorm. A plaque at that ancient tree today marks its significance. Ivy Green's spacious gardens display plaques, statuary, and other international gifts honoring "America's First Lady of Courage." Until her death in 1968, Keller worked on behalf of the blind worldwide.

Ivy Green is Helen Keller's family home in Tuscumbia, Alabama. She grew up here after becoming blind, deaf, and mute from an illness at 19 months. Her centenary commemorative stamp was issued here June 27, 1980.

Helen Keller was born in this cottage at Ivy Green. Her crib and toys are on display at this shrine.

Called the little house or the garden cottage, the small structure near the main house was the bridal suite for Helen's parents. Helen's teacher, Annie Sullivan, took her young charge there in an attempt to penetrate her darkness. Helen's crib and toys are on display in the smaller of the two rooms. The birthplace cottage is a shrine to Helen Keller.

THE MIRACLE WORKER, OUTDOOR THEATRE

The Miracle Worker, written in 1960 by playwright William Gibson (1914–   ), is presented six summer weekend evenings. The play dramatizes Annie Sullivan's teaching the isolated child, Helen Keller, how to communicate. Since 1962, Helen's spirit has been set free anew with each performance on the stage adjacent to the famous backyard pump. In 1962 Anne Bancroft and Patty Duke received Academy Awards for their

A plaque at this pump immortalized in *The Miracle Worker* reads: "At this well Annie Sullivan revealed the mystery of language to seven-year-old Helen Keller."

movie roles in *The Miracle Worker. The Miracle Worker* became Alabama's official state outdoor drama in 1991. In 1996 during his first trip to Ivy Green, William Gibson saw his world famous play performed here where it all began.

ARIZONA

Flagstaff

ZANE GREY COLLECTION

Cline Library Special Collections and Archives, Northern Arizona University. (602) 523-5551.

In 1988 the Cline Library acquired the Collection of G.M. Farley, Zane Grey scholar. Approximately 70 titles by Grey make up the bulk of this 160 item portion of the Collection. Many of the books are first editions; most of the multitudes of titles are represented by various editions. The Collection also includes magazine with condensations of Grey's novels, posters of movies made from his books, and some personal belongings. A second Zane Grey Collection is comprised of Grey's correspondence, letters both from and to the author, dating from 1901 until 1937.

Prescott

SHARLOT HALL MUSEUM

415 West Gurley St. Hours: Apr. 1–Oct. 31, Mon.–Sat. 10–5, Sun. 1–5; Nov. 1–Mar. 31, Mon.–Sat. 10–4, Sun. 1–5. (520) 445-3122.

Sharlot Hall (1870–1943), poet and historian, began this museum of Arizona history in 1927 with her collection of artifacts and documents. In 1934 the museum's primary exhibit hall was built and named the Sharlot Hall Building. The Museum Center, the latest building at this museum now named for its founder, was completed in 1979. In its lobby the Center maintains an exhibit about Sharlot Hall, who became one of the first women elected to the Arizona Women's Hall of Fame. Two of her books are *Poems of a Ranch Woman* and *Cactus and Pine.*

ARKANSAS

Fayetteville

CHARLIE MAY FLETCHER PAPERS AND JOHN GOULD FLETCHER PAPERS

Special Collections, The University of Arkansas Library, Resources for Women's Studies.

Charlie May Simon Fletcher (1897–1977), children's author, published 29 major works, primarily prize-winning biographies.

Robin on the Mountain is a children's classic. This collection of her papers, 1945–1973, includes manuscripts pertaining to *Johnwood*, her autobiographical account of her marriage to writer John Gould Fletcher, several short stories, speeches, and correspondence. The Charlie May Simon Children's Book Award is presented annually to an author whose book is selected by Arkansas school children's choice.

John Gould Fletcher (1886–1950), poet and author, is represented in the Resources for Women's Studies because of an extensive correspondents' index listing numerous women with whom Fletcher and his wife, Charlie May Simon Fletcher, corresponded concerning literature, family matters, and mutual interests. In addition, his papers, from 1881 to 1960, include literary manuscripts, lectures and other professional and personal papers. The correspondence is augmented by microfilm of other Fletcher letters preserved elsewhere.

Little Rock

WILLIAM E. WOODRUFF HOME AND PRINT SHOP

The Arkansas Territorial Restoration, Department of Arkansas Heritage, 200 E. 3rd St., I-30 exit 141A. Hours: Mon.–Sat., 9–5; Sun. 1–5; Closed major holidays. (501) 324-9351.

William E. Woodruff established *The Arkansas Gazette* in 1819. His home, separate kitchen, and print shop are all part of this site. Arkansas events are presented in relation to national and world events on a time line that extends the length of the house.

THE PIKE–FLETCHER–TERRY HOUSE

The Decorative Arts Museum of the Arkansas Arts Center, 7th and Rock Streets. Open: Mon.–Sat. 10–5; Sun. and holidays, 12–5; closed Christmas. Free admission. (501) 372-4000.

This large Greek Revival style house was built in 1840 by Albert Pike (1809–1891). The pioneer settler was a poet and author as

General Pike, a poet, built The Pike–Fletcher–Terry mansion in Little Rock, Arkansas. John Gould Fletcher, another poet, lived here. Now it is the Decorative Arts Museum.

well as soldier and statesman. Pike's poetry, including *The Widowed Heart,* was published in three volumes after his death. The albert Pike Masonic Temple is nearby. In 1889 the house was sold to the Fletchers. John Gould Fletcher (1886–1950), Pulitzer Prize winning imagist poet, grew up in the Pike House and commemorated it with his poem, "The Ghosts of an Old House." His association with the Agrarians at Vanderbilt influenced him to write several important regional works. The house, deeded to the city, was renovated and restored to house the Decorative Arts Museum. A display in the house's upstairs hall details the history of the house with some information about its well-known inhabitants.

PIGGOTT

> The Hemingway-Pfeifer Museum and Education Center 1021 W. Cherry Street, Owned and Administered by Arkansas State University, Jonesboro. (870) 972-3940.

When Hemingway was married to his second wife, Pauline Pfeiffer, they lived for a time at her home in northeast Arkansas. During that time he was writing *A Farewell to Arms* in a barn/studio on the property. The property has been converted to a literary conference center.

——— CALIFORNIA ———

Big Sur

HENRY MILLER LIBRARY

> Highway One. Open: Thur.–Sun. 11–5. (831) 667-2574.

Henry Miller (1891–1980), prolific writer best known for *Tropic of Cancer* and *Tropic of Capricorn,* is memorialized at this library, the former home of his friend, Emil White. The house was converted to the Henry Miller Library in 1981 to promote Miller's works and to serve as a cultural and educational resource. Visitors see audio-video presentations of Miller and his literary and artistic companions. Miller's works, including rare editions, and the permanent collection of his paintings, are on exhibit. The library celebrates the region's history and culture by hosting musical, literary, artistic, and educational events and by offering workshops in the arts.

Carmel

TOR HOUSE

> Carmel Point just to the south of Carmel Village. Tor House faces Scenic Ave. and is bounded by Stewart Way and Ocean View Ave. Tours: Fri. and Sat. 10–4; Admission: Adults $7, college students, $4, and high school students, $2. Under age 12 not admitted for safety reasons. Tor House Foundation. (408) 624-1813.

Tor House was the home of poet Robinson Jeffers (1887–1962) from 1916 until his death. Tor House and Hawk Tower are built of granite boulders from the rocky shore below. Jeffers himself constructed the 40-foot tower as a gift to his wife, Una. Over the fireplace is carved Virgil's motto. Its English translation is "They make their own dreams for themselves." Hawk Tower has become a symbol of the poet's life and work. Nature in its harsher forms, wild birds, and rocky coasts were all part of his inspiration. Jeffers has been called the Laureate of the

Top: Tor House near Carmel, California, was Robinson Jeffers' home. From his sketch, the house was built to resemble a Tudor Barn. The stones came from the coast below. *Bottom:* Robinson Jeffers constructed Hawk Tower above Carmel Point. It was a gift for his wife who inscribed: *RJ, with his own hands, made me this Hawk Tower, 1924.*

Big Sur Coast of Monterey County. Visitors to Hawk Tower may sit in Jeffers' chair at his desk. There he created his long narrative poems, including *The Woman at Sur Point*, and his dramas with classical themes. The most acclaimed one is his adaptation of *Medea*. In 1973 the Robinson Jeffers commemorative stamp was issued.

Danville

TAO HOUSE, EUGENE O'NEILL NATIONAL HISTORIC SITE

> 1000 Kuss Road. Hours: Wed.–Sun. 8–4:30, all year. Free. Directions provided when required reservation is confirmed. (925) 838-0249.

With the stipend from his 1936 Nobel Prize for Literature, Eugene O'Neill (1888–1953), America's greatest playwright, purchased a 158-acre ranch in the hills above Danville and built Tao House. The exterior is Spanish Colonial style, and the interior design is Chinese. The O'Neills lived here from 1937 to 1944. At this refuge the dramatist wrote his final plays, *The Iceman Cometh, A Moon for the Misbegotten,* and *Long Day's Journey into Night.*

On exhibit are items related to the playwright and his wife, including their furnishings, paintings, photographs, and O'Neill's cherished player piano. The National Park Service has been restoring Tao House and grounds since 1980 and providing guided tours of the house and courtyard. Visitors may also take a self-guided tour of the grounds. Two and one half hours should be allowed for visiting this site. Reservations must be made in advance.

Fresno

WILLIAM SAROYAN THEATRE

> 700 "M" Street, Fresno Convention Center complex. (559) 498-4000.

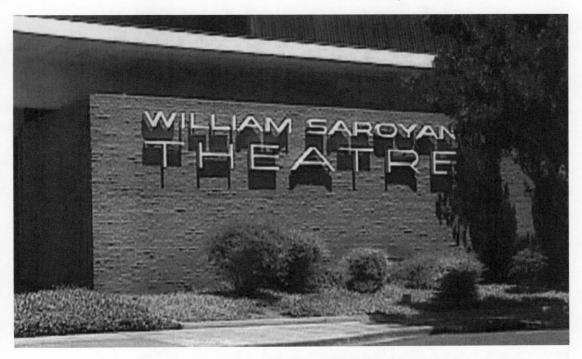

Fresno, California, honors its native son, William Saroyan, with this theatre dedicated in 1984. Saroyan received the Pulitzer Prize for his play, *The Time of Your Life.*

This bust of William Saroyan is in the lobby of the William Saroyan Theatre, Fresno, California.

William Saroyan (1908–1981), novelist, short story writer, and playwright, is memorialized here in his native city. Officially dedicated in 1984, the theatre is designed for theatrical productions, musical programs and assemblies. The theatre lobby features a bust of Saroyan, a portrait, and an enlargement of the commemorative U.S. postage in his honor. Fresno hosts an annual Saroyan Festival in the spring. Saroyan was awarded a Pulitzer Prize for his play, *The Time of Your Life* and an Academy Award for his screen writing for the film, *The Human Comedy*, from his novel of the same name.

Literary Arts Series, 1991.

Glen Ellen

JACK LONDON STATE HISTORIC PARK

2400 London Ranch Road. Hours: Daily: 10–5. Admission: $6 per car. (707) 938-5216.

Great American Issue, 1988.

Jack London (1876–1916), writer and adventurer, purchased Beauty Ranch in 1905, the year he published *White Fang*. Earlier novels, *The Call of the Wild* and *Sea-Wolf*, had already earned him success. In 1960 the state acquired the ruins of London's home, Wolf House, which burned in 1913, the cottage residence where London wrote, his grave, and the home his wife built after his death, House of Happy Walls. Since then the park has been expanded to 800 acres. House of Happy Walls is a museum housing many of London's works, photographs, and exhibits of the collections gathered in the Londons' world travels. Furniture designed by the Londons and custom-built for Wolf House is there as well as London's big roll-top desk and other items from his study. Trails lead to Wolf House and to the grave site.

Hemet

THE RAMONA PAGEANT

27400 Ramona Bowl Road. Last two weekends of April and first weekend in May, 3:30 P.M. Tickets: Adults $18–$25, Children $8–$23. (909) 658-2695.

Based on the classic novel *Ramona* by Helen Hunt Jackson (1830–1885), this pageant is the official California state outdoor play. Presented since 1923, it is also America's oldest outdoor drama. Garnet Holme (1873–1929), prominent outdoor dramatist, wrote the script and directed and produced the show until his death. Holme dramatized Jackson's story of the Indians' tragic treatment in southern California. The pageant is presented in a natural amphitheater in the San Jacinto Valley. Jackson set her novel inspired by real events there in the 1870s and 1880s. Sponsored first by the Hemet–San Jacinto Chamber of Commerce and later by the Ramona Pageant Association, it is produced by region volunteers.

Martinez

JOHN MUIR NATIONAL HISTORIC SITE

4202 Alhambra Ave. Open Wed.–Sun. 10–4:30, guided tours of Muir house at 2 P.M. Closed Thanksgiving, Dec. 26, and Jan. 1. Admission: $2 per adult or $4 per vehicle. Children 16 and under, free. (510) 228-8860.

The home of John Muir (1838–1914), conservationist and author, is in this 8.8-acre national park. Here Muir wrote to preserve America's wilderness and helped to foster America's National Park system. The Visitors Center presents Muir's life and work through the film, *Earth, Planet, Universe*. Tour booklets outline self-guided tours of the 1882 Muir house and orchards. Visitors see Muir's study where he wrote numerous books as well as articles for national newspapers and magazines. Among his many works are *My First Summer in the Sierra* and *The Yosemite*. The theme of these influential writings was the urgent need to preserve America's vanishing wilderness. His efforts resulted in the establishment of five national parks. In 1964 the John Muir commemorative stamp was issued. It pictures the conservationist and the Redwood Forest. In 1989, Muir's birthday, April 21, was proclaimed "John Muir Day" to be observed annually in California.

Oakland

JOAQUIN MILLER PARK

Joaquin Miller Rd. and Sanborn Dr. Open dawn to dusk. Suggested donation $2. City of Oakland Parks, Recreation and Cultural Services Department. (510) 238-3481.

Joaquin Miller, "Poet of the Sierras" (1839–1913), settled here in the hills above the city in 1886. He named his land "The Hights" and the home that he built in 1889 "The Abbey." It became a national historical landmark in 1963. Among the monuments at The Hights is the Browning Monument, a miniature castle made of native fieldstone. Erected in 1894, it is Miller's tribute to his friends, poets Robert and Elizabeth Barrett Browning. A tribute to the poet himself is a statue of Joaquin Miller on horseback, commissioned in 1942. This bold, weather-worn statue calls to mind his popular poem, "Kit Carson's Ride."

Today Miller's best known poem is "Columbus," written at The Hights. His *Songs of the Sierras* and *Songs of the Desert* are considered authentic and important documents of that part of American life which he embraced wholeheartedly. Perhaps Miller's most lasting contribution, though, is his work as an early environmentalist. He planted 75,000 trees, many still standing. In 1919 the city of Oakland purchased the estate.

WOODMINSTER AMPHITHEATER AND CASCADES

Joaquin Miller Park. (510) 531-9597.

Built in 1941 as a joint project by the Oakland Parks, Recreation and Cultural Services Department and the WPA, the site is a monument to California poets and writers. Woodminster means "cathedral in the woods." Since 1965 Woodminster Summer Theatre has presented musicals and other family entertainment at the amphitheater.

Pomona

LAURA INGALLS WILDER ROOM

Pomona Public Library, 625 S. Garey Ave. (909) 620-2017.

The original manuscript of *The Little Town on the Prairie* is held here. Although it is kept under glass, visitors can read the manuscript on microfilm. Also exhibited are the Sewell illustrated copies of the *Little House* books, a number of translated versions, and many different dolls representing Ingalls family members. A large wall map marks the various locations of the Laura Ingalls Wilders sites. For over 30 years the library has hosted the Annual Laura Ingalls Wilder Gingerbread Sociable.

Salinas

THE NATIONAL STEINBECK CENTER

One Main Street. Open daily 10–5, closed Thanksgiving, Christmas and New Year's Day. Adults $7, seniors and students with ID $6, children 11–17 $4, 10 and under free. Administered by the Steinbeck Foundation. (831) 796-3833.

This 37,000 square feet, nearly 12 million dollar facility opened in 1998. The life, writings, and philosophy of novelist John Steinbeck (1902–1968) are presented through innovative exhibits and interactive media presentations. Thousands of objects related to his life and art are on display, even "Rocinante," the 1960 truck that Steinbeck, accompanied by his poodle, drove across the country while writing *Travels with Charley*. Sound recordings and video clips summon stories from Steinbeck country: *Cannery Row, East of Eden, Of Mice and Men,* and *The Red Pony*. Visitors hear Steinbeck's taped 1962 Nobel Prize acceptance speech.

This author of the 1940 Pulitzer Prize winner, *Grapes of Wrath,* was born two blocks from the Center. The Salinas Valley was always Steinbeck Country in life and in his

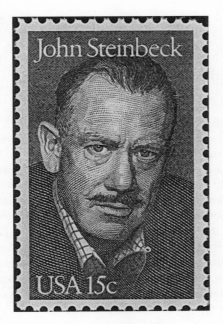

John Steinbeck, 1996.

works, but he was not always appreciated here. Steinbeck championed migrant farm workers in *Grapes of Wrath* and made enemies among the growers in his hometown. A generation passed before Salinas was ready to memorialize its world famous son. Steinbeck's ashes are in the family plot in Salinas.

San Buenaventura

ERLE STANLEY GARDNER COMMEMORATIVE SITES

Erle Stanley Gardner (1889–1970) created the character, detective Perry Mason, and wrote the first two of the 82 Perry Mason novels while practicing law here. The city, informally called Ventura, honors Gardner in several ways. At the corner of Main and California streets, the large building where Gardner had his office has been designated a historic site. It is marked with a bronze plaque linking it to the life and work of the author. In East Ventura a street was named for Gardner in the 1970s. At Fir and Main streets, the Elks Lodge maintains

a memorial to Gardner, a charter member. The Office of Cultural Affairs, (805) 658-4726, provides tours ($6) focusing on places associated with the 20 years that Gardner lived and worked in Ventura County.

San Francisco

SAN FRANCISCO STREETS HONORING AUTHORS

A project of City Lights Books, 261 Columbus Ave. (415) 362-8193.

In 1988 the city approved a proposal to rename 12 streets for famous authors and artists associated with San Francisco. All except two of the dozen were primarily writers. In addition, the City of San Francisco broke precedent in 1994 by naming a street for a living person, Lawrence Ferlinghetti. City street signs now honor 11 writers:

Ambrose Bierce Street runs behind the newspaper building where Bierce (1842–1914?) worked. It honors the author of macabre short stories and the *Devil's Dictionary*.

Richard Henry Dana Place, at Leavenworth Street's north end, is near the Historic Ships anchorage. Dana (1815–1882) wrote about the city in *Two Years Before the Mast*.

Dashiell Hammett Street—In the 1920s Hammett (1894–1961) lived on the street now named for him while he worked as a Pinkerton detective and plotted *The Maltese Falcon*. The novel's detective, Sam Spade, operated in the vicinity of this street.

Bob Kaufman Street—Kaufman (1925–1986) was a visionary poet especially popular in France. A long-time inhabitant of the North Shore, Kaufman once lived on Harwood Alley, the street which now bears his name. By mayoral proclamation, April 11, 1987, became Bob Kaufman Day in San Francisco.

Jack Kerouac Street—Kerouac, "King of the Beats" (1922–1969), frequented the area of Adler Alley, now renamed in his honor, while he wrote his major work, *On the Road*. His biographies describe his stays in North Beach, Russian Hill, and South of Market.

Jack London Street—London (1876–1916) was born in San Francisco. His first published story appeared in the city's *Overland Monthly* in 1898, beginning a career in which London became one of the highest paid and best-loved writers in the world. The street commemorating London is not far from his birthplace on Third Street, south of Market.

Frank Norris Street—Moving to San Francisco as a teenager, Norris (1870–1902) absorbed the aura of his new surroundings. *McTeague*, his masterpiece, is set in one of the neighborhoods he explored, Polk Street. The street re-named for Norris bisects Polk.

Kenneth Rexroth Place—Rexroth (1905–1982) is credited with making San Francisco a center for literary innovation in the 1950s. In the 1930s this prominent critic, poet, and essayist lived in North Beach, in the vicinity of the street renamed for him.

William Saroyan Place—*In Places Where I've Done Time*, Saroyan (1908–1981), playwright, novelist, and short story writer, wrote about the parts of San Francisco where he lived in the late 1920s. Characters in his play, *The Time of Your Life*, are said to have been inspired by people he met at a Pacific Street saloon, not far from the street now commemorating Saroyan.

Mark Twain Plaza—In 1863 Samuel Clemens (1835–1910) moved to San Francisco, where as Mark Twain he wrote for the *Golden Era*, an early San Francisco literary journal, and several newspapers. Mark Twain Plaza is near the site of the offices of the *Golden Era* and of the Turkish Baths where Twain met a man named Tom Sawyer.

Via Ferlinghetti—This North Shore alley now honors Lawrence Ferlinghetti (1919–   ), a leader in American poetry's revival in San Francisco in the 1950s. His poetry opposes violence—in art as well as in life. "Constantly Risking Absurdity" delineates Ferlinghetti's perception of the role of the poet.

LORRAINE HANSBERRY THEATRE

620 Sutter St. at Mason. Hours: Mon.–Sat. 12–5. Closed Sun. (415) 288-0320.

Devoted to producing African-American theatre, this professional theatre is named for playwright Lorraine Hansberry (1930–1965). In 1959 her play, *A Raisin in the Sun*, became the first on Broadway by a black woman. It won the New York Drama Critic's Circle Award as Best Play of the Year. *The Sign in Sidney Brustein's Window* closed on Broadway the night Hansberry died of cancer. The Lorraine Hansberry presents both new and classical works for the black community and the culture at large.

Stanford

SAROYAN COLLECTION

Department of Special Collections, Green Library, Stanford University Libraries.

In 1996 Stanford University acquired William Saroyan's library of journals, manuscripts, letters, and photographs. The archive reflects the spirit of Saroyan (1908–1981), the Armenian American whose fame began when his story collection, *The Daring Young Man on the Flying Trapeze*, was published in the 1930s.

COLORADO

Colorado Springs

HELEN HUNT JACKSON EXHIBIT

Colorado Springs Pioneers Museum. In the former El Paso County Court-house, 215 S. Tejon St. Open: Tues.–Sat. 10–5, Sun. (May–Oct.) 1–5. Free. (719) 578-6650.

On permanent display is part of the house of author Helen Hunt Jackson (1830–

1885). Reconstructed here, the salvaged rooms were moved from 228 E. Kiowa Street in 1961. The author's living and dining rooms and her study have been preserved in original condition. Her furnishings and other possessions are also part of the exhibit. A native of Amherst, Massachusetts, and a life-long friend of Emily Dickinson, Mrs. Jackson became concerned with injustices to Native Americans after moving west. Her first book on the subject was *A Century of Dishonor*. The second was her classic novel, *Ramona*.

Helen Hunt Jackson was buried at Helen Hunt Falls in the nearby Cheyenne Mountains.

CONNECTICUT

East Haddam

GILLETTE CASTLE

Gillette Castle State Park, 67 River Rd., off Rt. 82. Hours: Memorial Day–Columbus Day, Daily 10–5. Admission: Adults $4, Children 6–11 $2. (860) 526-2336.

William Gillette (1853–1937), playwright and actor, built this estate along the east bank of the Connecticut River. The site is the most southerly hill in a chain called the Seven Sisters. It overlooks the Chester-Hadlyme Ferry, one way to arrive at the Park. Construction on the granite and hand-hewn timber mansion resembling a medieval

Gillette Castle is William Gillette's 24-room mansion at East Haddam, Connecticut. The playwright and Sherlock Holmes actor lived here from 1919 until he died in 1937.

Gillette Castle's interior is characterized by its owner's innovative and eccentric touches. Built-in couches and furniture on tracks are two examples.

castle began in 1914 and was completed five years later. Gillette's creative genius is evidenced by eccentric mechanical devices in the two dozen rooms.

Gillette's acting career began when Mark Twain, his boyhood neighbor at Nook Farm, recommended him for a touring production of *The Gilded Age*. Soon, he was a playwright and a leading man in such plays as *The Professor* and *Secret Service*. Gillette was famous for playing Sherlock Holmes on the stage. He also wrote the plays *Sherlock Holmes* and *The Painful Predicament of Sherlock Holmes*. Gillette added the deerstalker cap, Inverness cape, and curved pipe to the Holmes persona.

Upstairs in this Rhenish fantasy, Sherlock Holmes and other theatrical memorabilia of all kinds are on display. Personal artifacts include scrapbooks and photographs depicting Gillette in his famous role as Sherlock Holmes and in a series of Civil War dramas which he also wrote. In 1945 the property which Gillette named "The Seventh Sister" became the Gillette Castle State Park.

Hamden

THORNTON WILDER HALL

Miller Cultural Complex, 2901 Dixwell Ave. Hamden Arts Commission. (203) 287-2546.

Thornton Wilder (1897–1975), novelist and playwright, lived many years in Hamden. He was memorialized here when the city built this complex in 1980 and named the auditorium for him. The dedication ceremony for the Thorton Wilder stamp was held here on his birth centenary.

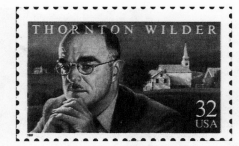

Literary Arts Series, 1997.

THORNTON WILDER MEMORIAL

Hamden Public Library, in the Miller Cultural Complex. Hours: Mon.–Thurs. 10–9, Fri.–Sat. 10–5:30. (203) 287-2686.

A corner in the library is devoted to Thornton Wilder. After his death at his Hamden home, his sister, Isabella Wilder, gave the furniture from his study to the library. The desk where he wrote some of his eight plays and seven novels is part of the exhibit. The counter serving as a room divider displays Wilder's works. They include *The Bridge of San Luis Rey*, which received the Pulitzer Prize for fiction, and his two Pulitzer Prize dramas, *Our Town* and *The Skin of Our Teeth*. A portrait and a bust of Thornton Wilder complete the library's Thornton Wilder tribute.

Hartford

THE MARK TWAIN HOUSE

351 Farmington Ave. Exit 46 off I-84. Right onto Sisson Ave. Right onto Farmington. Open: Memorial Day–Oct. 15 and Dec., Mon.–Sat. 9:30–5, Sun. 11–5. Last tour begins at 4 P.M. Oct. 16–Memorial Day Mon.–Sat. 9:30–5, Sun. 12–5. Closed Tues. Closed New Year's Day, Easter Sun., Thanksgiving and Dec. 24–25. Admission: Adults (ages 13–59): $7.50, Seniors (60+): $7, Children (6–12): $3.50. Group rates available. (860) 493-6411.

Samuel Clemens (1835–1910), who as Mark Twain became America's most famous

Famous Americans Issue, 1940.

writer, built this Gothic Revival house on seven acres of land. In the true Gilded Age style, it has 19 rooms, seven balconies, and seven chimneys. The years that Twain lived here with his family, 1874–1891, were his most productive as a writer. The seven major works written here include *The Adventures of Tom Sawyer, The Prince and the Pauper, Life on the Mississippi, Adventures of Huckleberry Finn*, and *A Connecticut Yankee in King Arthur's Court*. Increasing fame and prosperity allowed the author and his wife to decorate and furnish the house lavishly.

Hard times came to the Clemenses here, though. Mark Twain invested and lost thousands through investment in the Paige typesetter. The three ton machine is on display at the Visitors Center. The family moved to England to save money, and when the eldest Clemens daughter died at this house while on a visit back home, the family never entered their dream home again.

Today, 70 years after a group of Hartford citizens formed the Mark Twain Memorial and Library Commission to purchase and restore the property, that goal nears realization. The library, the dining room, and the drawing room have reclaimed their glory. The ornately carved bed that Mark Twain purchased in Venice again graces the master bedroom, and the billiard table presides once more in Twain's billiard room. The Mark Twain House is a registered

From hand carved wood in the foyer to the third floor billiard room's ceiling, Twain's unique Hartford, Connecticut, house is ornately designed, furnished, and decorated.

national historic landmark and the recipient of an award from the National Trust for Historic Preservation. Outstanding educational programs are offered throughout the year.

HARRIET BEECHER STOWE HOUSE

73 Forest Street. Tours of both the Stowe House and the Day House start from The Harriet Beecher Stowe Visitors Center, 77 Forest Street, I -84 Exit 46, R. onto Sisson. R. onto Farmington. R. onto Forest. Open: Year-round: Tue.–Sat. 9:30–4, Sun. Noon–4, Mon. Jun. 1–Columbus Day and December. Closed New Year's Day, Easter, Labor Day, Thanksgiving, Christmas Eve, and Christmas Day. Last tour before 4 P.M. daily. Admission Fee. Operated by the Harriet Beecher Stowe Center, a non-profit educational institution. (860) 522-9258.

Harriet Beecher Stowe (1811–1896), author, moved to this house in 1874. Already she was an established writer. Her *Uncle Tom's Cabin*, published in book form in 1852, had brought her international fame. Other novels, biographies, poetry, hymns, and children's stories were all part of her versatile output. Mrs. Stowe published another half-dozen books while living in this painted brick cottage that has characteristics of a romantic villa. It appears unassuming when compared to the houses of her Nook Farm neighbors, like Mark Twain.

The 17 rooms are decorated in a comfortable, not showy, style. The kitchen was designed in the efficient way advocated by Harriet and her sister, Catherine Beecher, in their popular 1869 book, *The American Woman's Home*. Much of the Stowe family's furniture is still in place: Harriet's dining table, her pink couch in the back parlor, her Minton tea set, and her bedroom furnishings.

Decorative items throughout her house

The last home of Harriet Beecher Stowe, author of *Uncle Tom's Cabin*, opened to the public in 1968 with an address by Archibald MacLeish, Pulitzer Prize poet.

are from her three trips to Europe. Her husband, Calvin Ellis Stowe, a seminary professor and Bible scholar, had retired when they moved to this house. His room contains copies of his work, *The Origins and History of the Books of the Bible*. Mrs. Stowe was also an accomplished gardener. Flower gardens surrounding her house still reflect her skill. Her paintings in three mediums are exhibited in the house, and she decorated the cottage-style furniture in her sitting room.

After her death her house was sold. Her grandniece, Katharine Seymour Day, purchased it in 1924 and began restoration. In 1968 the Harriet Beecher Stowe House opened to the public, one of the earliest Victorian house museums in the country. In 1995, Joan Hedrick, a Stowe Center trustee, was awarded the Pulitzer Prize in biography for her book, *Harriet Beecher Stowe: A Life*.

THE KATHARINE S. DAY HOUSE

> Included in the Stowe Center. See details of admission for the Harriet Beecher Stowe House.

Katharine Seymour Day (1870–1964) bought this house in 1939. She continued to live next door at the Stowe house and used her new property to store her mounting collection of documents and furniture which were to become the basis of the Harriet Beecher Stowe Center's library and museum collections. In 1962 Miss Day transferred ownership of this house to the Harriet Beecher Stowe Center, and it is now its headquarters. The underground library vault was added in 1977.

Katharine Day spent decades collecting books, artifacts, and memorabilia of members of her illustrious family and other Nook Farm residents. Photographs and framed documents on exhibit in the house attest to the stimulating intellectual environment of this neighborhood once known as Nook Farm. The interests of the residents ranged from politics and journalism to the suffrage movement and literature. A number of Nook Farm neighbors gained national ac-

claim: Isabella Beecher Hooker, William Gillette, Joseph Hawley, and Charles Dudley Warner. Two, Harriet Beecher Stowe and Mark Twain, achieved lasting fame worldwide. All of them are noted at the Day House.

The magnificent 1884 interior adapts well to its present purpose. The formal parlor is now the exhibition gallery, and an upstairs open central hall/sitting room is used by library/museum researchers as a reading room. The library focuses on nineteenth century cultural and literary history. Available by appointment to researchers of all ages, the library is open weekdays from 9 A.M. until 4 P.M. (860) 728-5507.

New Haven

THE JAMES WELDON JOHNSON COLLECTION

> Beinecke Rare Book and Manuscript Library, Yale University, 121 Wall Street. Hours for exhibition viewing: Mon.–Fri. 8:30–5, Sat. 10–5.

This collection was founded by Carl Van Vechten in 1941. It began as a tribute to Dr. James Weldon Johnson (1871–1938) and has expanded to encompass the accomplishments of many African-American writers and artists. In addition to Johnson's papers, the collection is a repository for manuscripts or correspondence of Arna Bontemps, Countee Cullen, Dr. W.E.B. DuBois, Chester Himes, Langston Hughes, Zora Neale Hurston, Claude McKay, Wallace Thurman, Poppy Cannon White, and Walter White. Van Vechten photographed all of these individuals as well as many other friends who were well-known African American performing artists. This collection, supplemented by photographs collected by Langston Hughes and Richard Wright, constitutes a significant visual record. Drawings, portraits, sculptures, commemorative medals, prints, and other works of art complete the collection.

New London

MONTE CRISTO COTTAGE

325 Pequot Avenue, I-95, Downtown New London exit. Hours: Memorial Day–Labor Day, Tues.–Sat., 10–5, Sun. 1-5, Admission. Owned and Maintained by The Eugene O'Neill Theater Center, Waterford, CT, the cottage is a registered national landmark. For information on fall hours, tours, and events, call (860) 443-0051, 443-5378.

Eugene O'Neill (1888–1953), America's greatest playwright, grew up in this house and returned intermittently until 1917 when he began to support himself as a writer. When Eugene's father, James O'Neill, a popular actor in *The Count of Monte Cristo*, bought the cottage in 1894, he named it for that play. Set on two lots overlooking the Thames River, the house had been built in the 1840s. James O'Neill joined an aban-

doned school house to it. Eugene was later to use the added-on room, called the living room, as the setting for two of his most acclaimed plays. The first was his only comedy, *Ah, Wilderness!*, inspired partly by family friends and neighbors of the O'Neills. The other was the tragic autobiographical drama, *Long Day's Journey into Night*. His detailed sketch of the two stage sets helped in the restoration after the Theatre Center purchased the cottage in the 1970s.

A multimedia presentation provides background on the house and the O'Neill family's life there. The often-present fog is used in the film as a symbol of young O'Neill's creativity and his restlessness. In the downstairs rooms, costumes, a model of the stage in *Ah, Wilderness*, and the table from the set of *Long Day's Journey into Night* are on display. On the walls are photographs of Eugene and his family, newspaper articles, posters, and his Nobel Prize diploma.

Monte Cristo Cottage was the only home Eugene O'Neill knew in his youth. Several of his plays are based on experiences of his family at the house.

Prominent Americans Issue, 1967.

The accompanying plaque explains that the sculpture was commissioned for the Eugene O'Neill Centennial and presented to the people of New London on October 16, 1988. The statue was inspired by a photograph of O'Neill as a boy on the New London waterfront in 1895. The plaque concludes with the statement that O'Neill was the first American dramatist to gain status with Shaw and Chekhov.

Waterford

THE EUGENE O'NEILL THEATER CENTER

305 Great Neck Road, (860) 443-5378.

Named for America's foremost playwright who as a child and young adult lived in neighboring New London, the O'Neill Theater Center was established in 1963. The Center is located on the shores of Long Island Sound on an estate which had been slated for destruction. From the O'Neill's origin, its unique mission has been to develop new playwrights and theatrical productions. Summer audiences, including the public, watch productions that are hit shows in the making. This internationally recognized non-profit organization has a part in identifying and refining the talents of dramatists who become candidates for Pulitzers, Oscars, Tonys, and even Nobel Prizes for literature. Among the programs sponsored by the O'Neill Center are the National Playwrights Conference, the National Theater Institute, and the National Music Theater.

The upstairs front bedrooms once used by Eugene and his brother James contain some items which belonged to the dramatist. His desk is there, along with a director's chair, his seaman's trunk, and a ship's 1911 payroll noting $14.84 for O'Neill. Those relics from his sailor days are reminders that the experience inspired some fine plays.

New London influences on his plays may be traced outside his immediate family and their home, too. The Greek Revival houses on Whale Oil Row may have been the model for the mansion in *Mourning Becomes Electra*. The elm trees of Pequot Avenue or possibly the two enormous old elms in the back yard at #325 likely reappeared in his classic tragedy, *Desire Under the Elms.* There can be no doubt that Eugene O'Neill's years at the Monte Cristo Cottage helped shape the art of America's only Nobel laureate for drama and only four-time recipient of the Pulitzer Prize for drama.

EUGENE O'NEILL CENTENNIAL STATUE

New London, near the railroad station and Fisher's Wharf Ferry.

The sculpture captures Eugene O'Neill at age seven. Wearing a school boy's cap, he is seated on a rock overlooking the harbor. Pen in hand, he is intent upon his tablet.

West Hartford

THE NOAH WEBSTER HOUSE

The Museum of West Hartford History, 227 South Main Street, I-84, exit 41, then follow the signs 1 mi. Hours: Sept.–June, daily except Wed. 1–4; July–Aug., Mon. Tues., Thurs., and Fri. 10–4, Sat.–Sun., 1–4. Admission: Adults

This harbor statue of the boy Eugene is an O'Neill Centennial memorial. It accentuates the early influence of the New London waterfront on the dramatist.

$5, Seniors and AAA members $4, Children 6–12 $1. Under 6 free. Tours by guides in historic dress. (860) 521-5362.

Noah Webster (1758–1843), author of the first American dictionary, was born and reared in this saltbox house. He attended Yale, Connecticut's only college at the time, during the years of the Revolutionary War. When he graduated in 1778, he began to teach school. Because he was critical of the textbooks which came from England, by 1783 he had written his own textbook, *A Grammatical Institute of the English Language*. It was commonly called the "blue-backed speller" because of its color. For the next 100 years children learned how to read, spell and pronounce words from that popular book. Early editions of the blue-backed speller are on exhibit at the author's birthplace.

In 1801 at age 43, Noah Webster started writing the first American dictionary. He wanted to standardize the spelling and pronunciation of words across the country. Although he wanted an American standard for English usage, he did not think that Americans must speak and spell just like the English. He introduced Americanized spellings for many English words, and he added American words which were unknown to the British. In 1828, after 27 years, the 70,000-word dictionary was completed. The museum exhibits early editions of that dictionary.

The Noah Webster House pays special interest to children's groups. They participate in colonial tasks such as flax breaking and wool carding while learning history. Year-round hands-on family programs, an autumn auction of celebrity-signed Merriam-Webster dictionaries and a December holiday open house are regular events.

DELAWARE

Dover

JOHN DICKINSON PLANTATION

Kitts Hummock Rd., 6 mi. south of Dover, off US 113. Open: Tues.–Sat. 10–3:30, Sun. 1:30–4:30. Closed Mon. and state holidays. Free, donations accepted. Operated by Delaware's Division of Historical and Cultural Affairs, Bureau of Museums and Historic Sites. (302) 739-3277.

This 1740 brick mansion is the boyhood home of John Dickinson (1732–1808), who was known as the "Penman of the Revolution." A statesman who favored reconciliation with England, Dickinson served in the Continental Congress. He presented his views in *Letters from a Farmer in Pennsylvania to the Inhabitants of the British Colonies.* He helped to frame the Constitution, and his letters in support of it, written under the name Fabius, contributed to its ratification. Samples of Dickinson's writing are on exhibit at the house, centerpiece of an 18-acre estate. The house is furnished with antiques of the period and family pieces.

A modern visitors center interprets the life of Dickinson, an early American Quaker patriot who freed his slaves. Farm outbuildings and a log dwelling add to the plantation interpretation. This site presents John Dickinson as governor of the state, contributor to the Constitution, and a popular writer.

DISTRICT OF COLUMBIA

Washington

FREDERICK DOUGLASS NATIONAL HISTORIC SITE

Cedar Hill, Anacostia, 1411 W Street, S.E. Off Martin Luther King, Jr., Ave. Open daily except New Year's Day,

Right: **Prominent Americans Issue, 1967.**

The original of this statue of Lew Wallace is in Statuary Hall of Fame in the Capitol Rotunda, Washington, D.C. This bronze replica stands on the grounds of his Crawfordsville, Indiana, home. General Wallace served in both the Mexican and Civil wars.

Thanksgiving, and Christmas. Spring–Summer, 9–5, Fall–Winter, 9–4; Tour $3. Operated by National Park Service. (202) 426-5961.

From 1877 until his death Frederick Douglass (1818–1895), orator, author, and editor lived in this Victorian house overlooking the Capitol. Douglass championed human rights throughout his long lifetime. His autobiography, *My Bondage and My Freedom* (1855), is a classic. The Visitor Center presents a film about Douglass, focusing on his life as a slave and his abolitionist work, including his newspaper, *The North Star*. On exhibit is a leather rocking chair from the people of Haiti, a memento of his

diplomatic service. Abraham Lincoln's cane given to Douglass by Mrs. Lincoln after the president's assassination is also displayed. The furnishings are original to the house.

NATIONAL STATUARY HALL

Each state is entitled to send statues of two outstanding citizens for display in Statuary Hall or elsewhere in the Capitol. Three of the 96 individuals honored here are authors. The *Ben-Hur* author, Lewis (Lew) Wallace, was honored by his home state, Indiana, with a bronze statue given in 1910. Oklahoma commemorated the other two with bronze statues: Sequoyah in 1917 and Will Rogers in 1939.

FLORIDA

Eatonville

ZORA NEALE HURSTON NATIONAL MUSEUM OF FINE ARTS

227 E. Kennedy Blvd., 10 mi. NE of downtown Orlando. Open: 9–4, Mon.–Fri., Free. Weekends by appointment (407) 647-3307.

Zora Neale Hurston (1891–1960), novelist, folklorist, and anthropologist, is memorialized here in her native community. Eatonville is popularly known as the first incorporated African–American municipality in the United States. Hurston's classic of black literature, *Their Eyes Were Watching God* (1937), is set in Eatonville. Works written by and about Zora Neale Hurston are exhibited in the museum. Since 1990 the Association to Preserve Eatonville Community, Incorporated, has sponsored the Zora Neale Hurston Festival of the Arts and Humanities. The festival occurs in January, Hurston's birth and death month. One festival event is the tour, Zora's Special Places, also available at other times by request.

Hawthorne

MARJORIE KINNAN RAWLINGS STATE HISTORIC SITE

Cross Creek, off State Road 325. Farm yard, groves, and nature trails open 9–5 daily year round, no charge; 1 hour house tours Thur.–Sun. at 10, 11, 1, 2, and 3 o'clock Oct.–July, $3 Adults, $2 Children. (352) 466-3672.

Marjorie Kinnan Rawlings' house at Cross Creek, Florida, was built of cypress and heart pine. Her book *Cross Creek* chronicles her life in the Big Scrub Country.

Marjorie Kinnan Rawlings wrote most of her ten novels on the screened verandah of her house at Cross Creek, Florida. *The Yearling* **is her most famous work.**

Marjorie Kinnan Rawlings (1896–1953), novelist, is commemorated at this site where she lived her last 25 years. Built of cypress and heart pine, the house is over a hundred years old. Here Mrs. Rawlings learned to appreciate the natural world around her. She became a serious citrus grower, and she found inspiration for her writing.

Visitors see the typewriter on the verandah where Rawlings wrote her books about the region around her. *The Yearling*, now a classic, is set in the area, and *Cross Creek* records her life in the rural north Florida community. Both were adapted into award-winning movies. Rawlings received the 1939 Pulitzer Prize for *The Yearling*. Listed since 1970 on the National Register of Historic Sites, the property is managed by the Florida Department of Environmental Protection, Division of Recreation and Parks.

Key West

THE ERNEST HEMINGWAY HOME AND MUSEUM

907 Whitehead St. Open: Daily 9–5. Admission: Adults $7.50, Children $4.50. Privately owned and operated. (305) 294-1136.

Built in 1851, this house was the home of Pulitzer and Nobel winning writer Ernest Hemingway (1899–1961). He and his second wife lived here from 1931 until 1940 when they divorced. Owned by Hemingway until his death, the house opened as a museum in 1964. Visitors see the writer's studio located on the second floor of the rear cottage. Among the works Hemingway wrote there are *For Whom the Bell Tolls* and "The Snows of Kilimanjaro." Trophies from the writer's big game hunting trips are exhibited in the

Top: This house in Key West, Florida, was the home of Ernest Hemingway during the 1930s. *For Whom the Bell Tolls* is one of his well-known books written here. *Bottom:* Hemingway's studio at Key West is on the second floor of the cottage behind the house. He wrote *To Have and Have Not* and "The Snows of Kilimanjaro" here.

Literary Arts Series, 1989.

house as are other personal mementos. The famed six-toed Hemingway cats are in abundance. The house, constructed of native stone, is a national historic landmark.

Tallahassee

LOIS LENSKI COLLECTION

> The Special Collections Department, Strozier Library, Florida State University Libraries.

Lois Lenski (1893–1974), author and illustrator of over 90 children's books, gave a collection of her books, illustrations, and articles to Strozier Library in 1958. The original collection has grown through additional donated materials. Manuscripts, background materials, and scrapbooks of two outstanding Lenski books, *Strawberry Girl* and *Judy's Journey*, are of special note.

NIGHT BEFORE CHRISTMAS COLLECTION

> The Special Collections Department, Strozier Library, Florida State University Libraries.

This collection contains hundreds of editions of the famous poem, "A Visit from St. Nicholas." Included is *The New York Book of Poetry* (1837), the first public edition in which Clement Moore accepted authorship of the poem. The poem, which has been called by both titles, is thought to have been written in 1822. Parodies of the poem, music, greeting cards, and other related memorabilia are included. Many well-known American illustrators are represented in the extensive collection.

Winter Park

ROLLINS COLLEGE WALK OF FAME

> Campus Horseshoe, 1000 Holt Avenue. (407) 646-2202.

Since 1929 rocks or stones associated in some way with famous American writers have become a part of this campus walkway. They blend with stones associated with writers, religious leaders, educators, statesmen, scientists and other notables from around the world. Each stone is set in a concrete slab engraved with the name of the person it represents and the city and country from which it came.

Among the 525 individuals represented by a stone in the walkway are 16 American authors. The writers represented here by a stone or brick significant to their lives include Louisa May Alcott, James Fenimore Cooper, Stephen Crane, Emily Dickinson, Ralph Waldo Emerson, Benjamin Franklin, Robert Frost, Zora Neale Hurston, Helen Keller, Edgar Allan Poe, Will Rogers, Booker T. Washington, Edith Wharton, and Walt Whitman.

One recent addition to the walkway is a stone from Stamps, Arkansas, the hometown of poet Maya Angelou. Another is a stone from the Ludlow, Massachusetts, birthplace of Florida Poet Laureate, Edmund Skellings. The nearly 800-foot semi-circular walkway curves around the campus green.

GEORGIA

Atlanta

THE WREN'S NEST, JOEL CHANDLER HARRIS HOME

1050 Ralph David Abernathy Blvd. S.W. (Ashby St. Ex. from I-20). Open for tours: Tues.–Sat., 10–4, Sun. 1–4. Closed Major Holidays. Admission: Adults, $6, Seniors/Teens $4, Age 12 and under $3. Group rates available. Administered by the Joel Chandler Harris Association. (404) 753-7735.

Joel Chandler Harris (1848–1908), author and journalist, moved to this site in 1881. The National Historic Landmark was then a five-room "dogtrot" cottage with a basement kitchen and a simple side porch located on a five-acre farm. The Queen Anne Victorian structure was created by vast renovation and addition in 1884. The transformation reflects the owner's success with the *Uncle Remus Tales*, first published in the *Atlanta Constitution* and syndicated across the country. Harris was associated with the newspaper as editorial and essay writer for many years.

The Wren's Nest, called Snap Bean Farm until wrens built a nest in the mailbox, contains original Harris family furnishings. Books, photographs, and memorabilia including the writer's typewriter, glasses, and hat are on display. A diorama from Disney's *Song of the South* reminds visitors of that movie's Uncle Remus origins. Special storytelling sessions on Saturdays at 2:00 are another memorial to Harris, the consummate storyteller.

THE MARGARET MITCHELL HOUSE

Birthplace of *Gone with the Wind*, Corner of Peachtree and Tenth streets, just a few blocks from I-75/85. Tours Daily, 9 A.M.–4 P.M. Closed major holidays. Admission: Adults, $6, Seniors/Students, $5. Youth (6–17), $5. Children under 6, Free. (404) 249-7012.

Great Americans Issue, 1986.

The Tudor Revival mansion, a national historic landmark, opened in 1997. The costly restoration was financed by a grant from Daimler–Benz, the industrial group. Tickets are purchased at the Visitors Center at Peachtree Street and Peachtree Place. The tour begins with a movie about the life of Margaret Mitchell and the 12-year battle to preserve and restore the house. Viewers learn that Margaret Mitchell grew up in Atlanta hearing vivid stories of the Civil War's impact on Atlanta. The author is presented as a civic-minded individual who early worked for civil rights and who devoted much of her time to the American Red Cross during World War II. Set against Atlanta's historical landscape, exclusive photographs and archival exhibits in the museum examine Margaret Mitchell's life and her phenomenal novel.

The docent-led house tour is a 40-minute experience. The side of the house facing Peachtree Street has been restored to the original 1899 appearance as a private residence. The Crescent Avenue side of the house appears as it did after the house was converted to apartments. In 1925 Margaret Mitchell and her husband, John Marsh, moved to Apt. #1, which Mitchell called "the

Margaret Mitchell House, birthplace of *Gone with the Wind*, is at Tenth and Peachtree streets in Atlanta. Mitchell wrote the bulk of the epic novel in Apt. #1.

dump." There visitors see the living room alcove where Mitchell wrote the bulk of her epic novel and the manual typewriter she used for the 10-year project. A towel is handy to cover her work, kept secret from all except her husband. He had suggested that she write her own book when he tired of lugging library books home to her after she broke her leg. Published in 1936, *Gone with the Wind* received the Pulitzer Prize in 1937 and remains the world's best-selling work of fiction. One week after the book was released, the movie rights were purchased for the perennially popular film.

ATLANTA-FULTON PUBLIC LIBRARY

One Margaret Mitchell Square.

The Margaret Mitchell Collection includes her Pulitzer award, photographs, and memorabilia.

MARGARET MITCHELL'S GRAVE

Oakland Cemetery, 248 Oakland Ave. Center open Mon.–Fri., 9–4:30. (404) 658-6019.

Margaret Mitchell died on August 16, 1949, a victim of a traffic accident on Peachtree Street, three blocks from the house where she wrote her novel. She had never written another one, spending her time working for international copyright laws and otherwise dealing with the aftermath of *Gone with the Wind*.

Augusta

POET'S MONUMENT

Center of Green Street, between Seventh and Eighth streets.

Four Southern poets are commemorated here:

Paul Hamilton Hayne (1830–1886) was an established poet before the Civil War. When his Charleston home was burned, he came to Augusta and built a simple cottage in a pine grove, where he did some of his best work. "Vicksburg" is one of his Civil War poems.

Sidney Lanier (1842–1881) was a Confederate soldier whose imprisonment at a Federal prison camp ruined his health. His lyrical poetry celebrates the natural beauties of his native Georgia.

James Ryder Randall (1839–1908) worked for several Augusta newspapers. His lyric, "Maryland, O Maryland," written in 1861, was the unofficial anthem of the Confederacy.

Father Abram Joseph Ryan (1836–1886) worked for two periodicals in Augusta and served as chaplain with a Southern regiment from 1862 until the war ended. Called the Poet of the Lost Cause, Ryan wrote "The Conquered Banner."

POET'S CORNER

Magnolia Cemetery, 702 Third Street.

Paul Hamilton Hayne, Father Ryan, and Richard Henry Wilde (1789–1847), author of "The Lament of the Captive," are all buried here.

Eatonton

BR'ER RABBIT STATUE

Courthouse Square.

UNCLE REMUS MUSEUM

Turner Park, 3 blocks S. of Putnam County Courthouse on Hwy. 441. Hours: Mon.–Sat., 10–5 (Closed for lunch); Sun. 2–5; Closed Tues. Sept.–May.

Joel Chandler Harris, creator of the Uncle Remus tales (1848–1908), was born and reared in this town which commemorates him by honoring his literary creations. A monument to Br'er Rabbit memorializes a character in Harris' Uncle Remus stories. The Uncle Remus Museum, a log cabin made from two original Putnam County slave cabins, is reminiscent of the one occupied by Uncle Remus, Harris' lovable storyteller. The cabin's focal point is a large portrait of Uncle Remus and the "Little Boy." At one end of the cabin is a fireplace similar to the one where Uncle Remus told his tales to the "Little Boy." The child was the son of Joseph Addison Turner, Harris' first employer. While helping to print a newspaper on the Turner plantation, Harris learned from slaves the folklore which inspired his famous tales. Turner Park, site of the museum, is part of the homeplace of Joseph Sidney Turner, the "Little Boy" of the Uncle Remus tales.

Macon

THE SIDNEY LANIER COTTAGE

935 High St. Open: Mon.–Fri. 9 A.M.–1 P.M. and 2–4 P.M., Sat. 9:30 A.M.–12:30 P.M. Open daily 9–5 in March during Cherry Blossom Festival. Admission. Middle Georgia Historical Society. (912) 743-6028.

Sidney Lanier (1842–1881), poet and musician, was born at this home of his grandparents. The historical society purchased the house in 1973 and has completely renovated it. The upstairs is used for the historical society headquarters. First floor rooms have been restored with period furnishings. There is a portrait of Lanier, painted from a photograph in his student days at Oglethorpe University. After graduation he joined the Confederate Army and spent a year in a Union prison camp. Tuberculosis contracted there caused his early death. Lanier's novel, *Tiger-Lillies*, came from his war experience. A portrait of his wife, Mary Day Lanier, hangs in the parlor,

Sidney Lanier Issue, 1972.

and her wedding gown is in the museum. A framed copy of Lanier's "A Ballad of Trees and the Master" is on display, too. The poem reflects his deep religious feelings. A photograph of an exhibit at Duke University Chapel shows three great Southerners symbolically represented: Thomas Jefferson, Robert E. Lee, and Sidney Lanier. Another photograph was given by Johns Hopkins University, where Lanier was an English professor his last years. The picture is of the Lanier bronze statue at Johns Hopkins University. Engraved on the statue are Lanier's words: "These two figures of music and poetry have kept in my heart so that I could not banish them."

Sidney Lanier was also first flutist with the Peabody Symphony Orchestra in Baltimore. His flute is on display in the cottage's museum. Lanier's music and his poetry blend in his best-known poems. Two of them, "Marshes of Glynn" and "Song of the Chattahoochee," are set in Georgia and reflect his love for his native state.

The Sidney Lanier Cottage in Macon, Georgia, is the poet's birthplace. It faces a park named for Lanier with live oaks reminiscent of his poem, "The Marshes of Glynn."

Mary Day's wedding gown worn at her marriage to Sidney Lanier in 1847 is on exhibit in the museum room of the Sidney Lanier Cottage.

Milledgeville

THE FLANNERY O'CONNOR MEMORIAL ROOM

Special Collections, Ina Dillard Russell Library, Georgia College and State University, 230 W. Hancock. Open: Weekdays, 8–8, Research by appointment. (912) 445-4047, 445-0988.

Flannery O'Connor (1925–1964), novelist and short story writer, is honored here by her alma mater. The project was begun in 1971 by other alumni and friends. O'Connor's mother contributed most of the room's permanent furnishings from Andalusia, the O'Connors' nearby farm. The Victorian style pieces include bookcases, library table and chairs, settee and arm chair. The carpet design resembles the fan tail of the peacock, the bird used symbolically in O'Connor stories. Included in the collection are manuscripts and O'Connor's personal library. Adjacent to the room is The Flannery O'Connor Window. Displays here feature items from the O'Connor Collection on a rotating basis. One exhibit focuses on her years at the University of Iowa, where she attended graduate school and published her first short story, "The Geranium." Items in the Iowa focus relate to the university's 1998 dramatization of another O'Connor work, "Everything That Rises Must Converge." Flannery O'Connor moved to Milledgeville as a teenager and returned to live and write at Andalusia. Her two novels are *Wise Blood* and *The Violent Carry It Away*.

FLANNERY O'CONNOR GRAVE SITE

Memory Hill Cemetery, Liberty and Franklin streets. (800) 653-1804.

No signs lead to O'Connor's final resting place. Close to the fence and next to the grave of her mother, a flat marble slab marks the grave of Mary Flannery O'Connor. She died of lupus before she was 40 years old.

Moreland

ERSKINE CALDWELL BIRTHPLACE

Moreland Town Square. Open: Sat.– Sun. 1–4, and by appointment. Admission: Adults, $2, Children, $1. (770) 251-4438, 254-8657.

Erskine Caldwell (1903–1987), novelist, short story and non-fiction writer, was born in this house called "The Little Manse." At that time Caldwell's father was a Presbyterian minister in a community near Moreland. After the writer's death, the Moreland Town Council voted to purchase, relocate, and restore the house, then used for storing hay. In 1990 the building was dismantled and brought in segments from its original location three miles away to its present site. After careful restoration to its turn-of-the-century condition, The Little Manse opened to the public.

The museum showcases Erskine Caldwell's literary accomplishments. A video presentation introduces visitors to the writer. A varied collection on Caldwell is displayed, including his worn pocket dictionary and passport photograph. Caldwell's books are exhibited throughout the museum, along with posters from the several novels made into movies. Best-known titles are *God's Little Acre* and *Tobacco Road,* also a long-running Broadway play. A panel exhibit traces the author's controversial ideas about social issues in the American South.

LEWIS GRIZZARD MUSEUM

US 29 and Church St. Open: Wed. 12–4, Thur.–Sat. 10–4, and by appointment. Free. ($1 donations requested for scholarship.) The Lewis Grizzard Memorial Trust. (770) 304-1490.

Lewis Grizzard (1947–1994), syndicated columnist and author of Southern humor books, spent his childhood in Moreland. The museum dedicated to his memory is now housed in a former filling station, which shares its space with a shop. Family photographs and possessions of the writer are on display as are copies of all his books. The titles, such as *I Haven't Understood Anything Since 1962,* reflect Grizzard's brand of humor. Moreland also commemorates its famous son each October with the Lewis Grizzard Memorial Catfish Ride for bicyclists. Catfish, Grizzard's dog, often appeared in his writing and is featured on the museum's sign.

Savannah

CONRAD AIKEN MEMORIAL PLAQUE

200 Block, East Oglethorpe Avenue.

A plaque honoring Conrad Aiken (1889–1973), the Savannah-born writer, stands in front of two adjoining townhouses in which Conrad Aiken lived, one early and one late in his life. Almost all of his first ten years were spent at one house and his last ten years at the neighboring one. Aiken's childhood home was 228 East Oglethorpe Avenue. The offices of his father, a physician, were in the basement. Aiken's parents died in a suicide-murder at this house. The house is the setting for Aiken's short story, "Strange Moonlight." His autobiography, *Ushant,* published in 1952, refers to the house as well. In 1962 Aiken bought the adjoining house, No. 230 E. Oglethorpe, and lived there until his death. Neither house is open to the public.

FLANNERY O'CONNOR CHILDHOOD HOME

207 E. Charlton Street. Lafayette Square Hours: Sat. 1–5 P.M., Sun. 1–4 P.M. Admission: $2. (912) 233-6014.

Mary Flannery O'Connor, novelist and short story writer, was born in this house in 1925 and lived here until 1938. A relative owned the property, which Flannery O'Connor inherited in 1959. After O'Connor's death, the house was sold. The Flannery O'Connor Home Foundation purchased it in 1989. Today it is a memorial to Miss O'Connor and a literary center for Savannah. Literary activities, including programs, lectures, and public readings of the works of O'Connor and

This Savannah, Georgia, plaque commemorates the poet Conrad Aiken's career referring to his 1930 Pulitzer Prize. The marker quotes Aiken: "Born in that most magical of cities, Savannah, I was allowed to run wild in that earthly paradise until I was nine: ideal for the boy who early decided he wanted to write."

This Savannah townhouse is the birthplace of Flannery O'Connor who received the O. Henry
Award three times during her brief lifetime and the National Book Award posthumously.

other Southern writers are scheduled regularly.

When the O'Connors lived here, the four-story building was a single-family dwelling. Now basement and top floor apartments are rented to defray expenses. The living room has been returned to the style of a middle-class home in the 1930s. Contributed period furniture and antiques and recollections of the O'Connor family's guests provide authenticity to the living room. Prominent about the room are family photographs and a portrait of Flannery O'Connor as a young woman. She died in 1964.

In the dining room, a painting and an arrangement emphasize the peacock, a recurring symbol in O'Connor's writing. The sun room features a series of paintings symbolically illustrating various O'Connor stories, including "The Displaced Person" and "Everything That Rises Must Converge." "Friends of Flannery" created and maintain a small, walled-in South Carolina garden in the back. It is the back yard where old newspaper film shows five-year-old Flannery and her chicken that she taught to walk backwards. The Catholic school and cathedral that Flannery O'Connor attended are just across the square. They are reminders that O'Connor's Catholicism was an influence in her works as was this city, the most Southern of surroundings.

IDAHO

Moscow

CAROL RYRIE BRINK NATURE PARK

At the site of Paradise Creek Restoration Project. The Palouse-Clearwater Environmental Institute (PCEI). (208) 882-1444.

Dedicated in October 1995, the nature park honors children's author, Carol Ryrie Brink, born in Moscow in 1895. The park site was said to be one of Brink's favorite places in Moscow. Much of the park land was provided by the local school district to use for environmental studies.

SUN VALLEY/KETCHUM

Ernest Hemingway's last home honors him in several ways: A memorial overlooking Trail Creek was dedicated on July 21, 1966, the sixty-seventh anniversary of Hemingway's birth. A bronze bust of Hemingway is accompanied by a plaque with these words written by Hemingway in 1939 as a eulogy for a friend killed in a hunting accident.

Near Ketchum, Idaho, this memorial to Ernest Hemingway was erected on July 21, 1966. Inscribed on it is a eulogy that Hemingway once wrote for a friend.

Hemingway's last home is this 17-room concrete house in Ketchum, Idaho. It is open to the public for tours only on Hemingway's birthday, July 21.

Best of all he loved the fall
the leaves yellow on cottonwoods
leaves floating on trout streams
and above the hills
the high blue windless skies
…Now he will be a part of them forever.

Hemingway's last house where he took his life on July 2, 1961, was donated to and is managed by the Nature Conservancy office in Ketchum (208) 726-3007. It is open to the public only one day each year, Hemingway's birthday. On July 21 visitors may tour the house and join a community celebration. At the Sun Valley Lodge pictures of Hemingway and his family are displayed in hallways, along with the last letter he wrote before he died. Ernest Hemingway is buried in the Ketchum cemetery.

ILLINOIS

De Kalb

THE ALGER ROOM

Northern Illinois University Libraries, Rare Book and Special Collections. (815) 753-0255.

Horatio Alger, Jr. (1832–1899), author of "rags-to-riches" stories for young people, wrote more than 100 books extolling the principle of success through self-reliance and honesty. In 1994 the NIU Library was designated as the official repository of the

Horatio Alger Society. The Library is dedicated to preserving examples of the body of Alger writings. It also makes them available to Alger researchers and collectors.

Galesburg

CARL SANDBURG STATE HISTORIC SITE—BIRTHPLACE COTTAGE

331 E. 3rd St. Open Daily 9–5; Administered by the Illinois Historic Preservation Agency. (309) 342-2361.

At the dedication of this cast aluminum historical marker, it was called a capsule story of Carl Sandburg and his humble beginnings for all to read and reflect upon.

The tour begins at the visitors center with a film featuring Carl Sandburg, famed poet and Lincoln biographer. The 50-year-old museum is filled with Sandburg photographs, documents, and memorabilia. Much of it relates to Sandburg's young years in Galesburg, which he chronicled in his autobiography, *Always the Young Strangers*. His role as Lincoln biographer is also prominent in exhibits. A framed stanza from Sandburg's poem, "Cornhuskers," hangs in a conspicuous place. *Time*, *Newsweek*, and two issues of *Life* magazine with Sandburg covers are there, affirming the fame of this winner of two Pulitzer Prizes, for history and for poetry. Evidences of his international acclaim include a proclamation from the King of Sweden. Sandburg's parents were Swedish immigrants.

Next door is the modest cottage which

Charles August (Carl) Sandburg was born on a cornhusk mattress in the left front room. He lived here one year and returned to visit at ages 70, 75, and 80.

August Sandburg bought in 1873. His son, Carl, was born there on January 6, 1878. The restored three-room birthplace opened to the public on October 7, 1946. Among the bedroom's family pieces is the sewing machine owned by Carl's mother. The family's

Carl Sandburg Issue, Jan. 6, 1978 (with Sandburg's signature). Issued at Galesburg, Illinois.

table and chairs are back home in the kitchen.

Behind the home in a park-like setting, a flagstone path includes twenty stones engraved with quotations from Sandburg's poetry. The walkway leads to Remembrance Rock. There beneath the red granite rock lie Carl Sandburg's ashes, returned to his birthplace after his death in 1967, as he had requested. Ten years later, the ashes of his wife, Lillian, were placed beside them. The rock is inscribed with a line from Sandburg's only novel, *Remembrance Rock:*

> For it could be a place to come and remember.

Lewistown

EDGAR LEE MASTERS BOYHOOD HOME

306 N. Adams.

Masters moved to Lewistown as a young boy. His experiences along the Spoon River and in Oak Hill Cemetery helped to inspire his *Spoon River Anthology*.

This house was Masters' home after his family moved from Petersburg. It is not open to the public, but a commemorative plaque is on the site. Lewistown annually observes Edgar Lee Masters Day.

Macomb

THE GWENDOLYN BROOKS CULTURAL CENTER

Burns Residence Hall, West Adams Road, Western Illinois University. Office Hours: Mon.–Fri. 8–4:30; Center Evening Hours: Mon.–Thur. 4:30–10. (309) 298-2220.

In 1970 the center was dedicated in honor of the Poet Laureate of Illinois, Gwendolyn Brooks (1917–   ). The center's goal is to help achieve multi-cultural and multi-racial campus community spirit.

Oak Park

ERNEST HEMINGWAY BIRTHPLACE

339 N. Oak Park Avenue. Open: Wed., Fri. and Sun., 1–5, Sat. 10–5. Rates: Adults: $6, Seniors/Students: $4.50, Children 5 and Under: Free. The Ernest Hemingway Foundation of Oak Park. (708) 848-2222.

Ernest Hemingway (1899–1961), a leading twentieth century novelist and short story writer, was born in this grand Queen Anne house built by his maternal grandparents. In connection with the Hemingway centennial, the building has been restored. Period furnishings also help to establish the turn-of-the-century aura. Photographs of the writer's birth family, memorabilia, and a video presentation review Hemingway's early years and influences.

HEMINGWAY MUSEUM

200 N. Oak Park Ave. Same hours as the Birthplace. Admission fee includes both sites. The Museum also houses the Museum Shop operated by the Foundation.

The Hemingway Museum traces the young Hemingway until age 20. A video presentation highlights Hemingway's energetic high school years. Displays focus on his family relationships, schooling, passion for nature, and World War I experiences. Exhibited artifacts include the young writer's early diary and a letter from the hospital nurse whose relationship with the author inspired *A Farewell to Arms*. The jackets of Hemingway first editions are displayed along with passages from the Nobel laureate's works.

Petersburg

THE EDGAR LEE MASTERS MEMORIAL

Eighth and Jackson streets. Hours: 10–12 and 1–3, Tues.–Sat., June–Aug. 31. Other times by appointment. (217) 632-2187, 632-2780.

Poet and author Edgar Lee Masters (1868–1950) lived here during childhood. The house was located then on West Monroe Street. Restored and preserved as a museum by people of the community, the building was moved to its present location on city property, and the Edgar Lee Masters Memorial Museum was opened to the public in 1966. A front porch plaque quotes Masters: "Petersburg Is My Heart's Home." The period furnishings and clothing were donated largely by family members. Framed documents and photographs attest to Masters' many years as a successful Chicago

Edgar Lee Masters Memorial Museum in Petersburg, Illinois, is pictured on the first day of issue envelope (August 22, 1970) for the Masters commemorative postage stamp.

Edgar Lee Masters Issue, 1970.

lawyer and as a writer with a wide literary circle. Edgar Lee Masters' cherry desk is

here. Some of his 54 volumes of poetry, plays, novels, and biographies are in a nearby bookcase. Others overflow their bookcase on the upstairs landing.

Evidences of *Spoon River Anthology*, the poet's masterpiece, are everywhere in the house. When the collection of verse was published in 1915, it created a sensation. In Masters' instant best-seller, inhabitants of Spoon River speak from their graves. Most are fictional characters or composites, but several were real people. In 1976 the house was placed on the National Register of Historic Places.

OAKLAND CEMETERY

Southwest edge of Petersburg on Lake Petersburg Road.

Edgar Lee Masters' grave is clearly indicated. There are also prominent signs identifying the graves of seven actual persons included in *Spoon River Anthology*. Among them are Squire Davis Masters and

Oakland Cemetery, Petersburg, Illinois, was one of the two models for the Spoon River Cemetery immortalized by the poet Edgar Lee Masters.

Edgar Lee Masters in tribute to his grandparents placed the tablet on their rock tombstone. His grave is next to theirs in Oakland Cemetery in Petersburg, Illinois.

his wife, Lucinda, whose last name is Matlock in their grandson's book. The poet's grave, close to the bench, is near theirs. His epitaph reads in part:

> Good Friends, Let's to the Fields…
> After a little walk, and by your pardon,
> I think I'll sleep. There is no sweeter thing,
> Nor Fate more Blessed Than to Sleep…

Ann Rutledge's grave is near the poet's in Oakland Cemetery. A stone surmounting her grave is inscribed with one of Masters' Spoon River epitaphs. It identifies her as "Beloved of Abraham Lincoln." Markers linking the graves of four other actual individuals with *Spoon River Anthology* are easily seen in the cemetery. They are "Mitch" Miller, Hannah Armstrong, and Bowling and Nancy Green. Masters' Spoon River Cemetery is not an actual place but is widely considered to be a combination of Oakland and a Lewistown Cemetery.

Springfield

Vachel Lindsay Home

603 S. Fifth St. State Historic Site. Currently undergoing renovation, the house is temporarily closed to the public. Administered by the Illinois Historic Preservation Agency. (217) 785-7960, (217) 524-0901.

This sign in front identifies the site:

> Home of Nicholas Vachel Lindsay,
> Who won international fame in the early decades of the 20th Century
> for his style of syncopated, repetitive poetry written to be performed.
> He also wrote prose and was an artist, working primarily in pen and ink.
> Lindsay called his house His "Hereditary Castle." He was born there in 1879.
> It remained his only and beloved home until his death there in 1931.

Lindsay, whose upstairs bedroom overlooked the Governor's Mansion, wrote a

Vachel Lindsay was born and died at this Springfield, Illinois, house. In between he dispensed his "Gospel of Beauty," emphasizing social and spiritual democracy.

poem honoring Governor Altgeld, "The Eagle That Is Forgotten." The poet is also remembered for "Abraham Lincoln Walks at Midnight," describing Lincoln's mystical return to his old Springfield neighborhood. Another Lindsay poem commemorating the city is "On the Building of Springfield."

Built in 1846, the house had the same designer and builder as Lincoln's home. The Lindsay house was originally owned by Mrs. Lincoln's sister and brother-in-law. Their parlor was the setting of a gala reception for Lincoln before his inauguration. Purchased in 1879 by Vachel Lindsay's parents, the Lindsay home today has many original fixtures and Lindsay family furnishings. On exhibit are Vachel Lindsay's artwork and writings. In the front hall is a bronze bust of the poet, purchased by Springfield citizens and originally placed at the city's Vachel Lindsay Bridge.

In 1958 the house was bought by the Vachel Lindsay House Fund and was maintained by the Vachel Lindsay Association until 1990 when it was transferred to the state. The Association's Repertory Group performs in Lindsay's verse-chanting style. The first performance poem by Lindsay, who was called the Prairie Troubadour, was "General William Booth Enters Into Heaven," still one of his most famous works.

Renaissance Hotel's Lindsay's Gallery

This downtown hotel restaurant features wall exhibits of Vachel Lindsay's poetry, illustrated by his paintings.

Wall Art Project

North wall of downtown building at 107 N. 5th St.

Vachel Lindsay's *The Wedding of the Rose and the Lotus* has been reproduced here. Lindsay painted the watercolor to accompany his poem by that title. He recited the poem for President Wilson's cabinet to commemorate the Panama Canal's opening.

The Vachel Lindsay Bridge

South side of the city.

This bridge is one of several Lindsay commemorative sites in Springfield, Illinois. The poet also commemorated has native city with *The Golden Book of Springfield*.

VACHEL LINDSAY'S GRAVE

Oak Ridge Cemetery, 1444 Monument Avenue. (217) 789-2338.

LINDSAY INSCRIPTION

Illinois State Library, Capital and 2nd Street.

Vachel Lindsay's name is engraved at the top of the building along with the names of twenty-three other writers who are Illinois natives or residents at some time in their lives.

Lindsay's grave at Oak Ridge Cemetery, Springfield, Illinois. His last popular recital of his poetry was at his family's church in Springfield shortly before his death by suicide.

INDIANA

Bloomington

ERNIE PYLE HALL

Indiana University School of Journalism. (812) 855-9247.

Ernest Taylor Pyle (1900–1945), world-renowned war correspondent of the Second World War, is memorialized at the college he attended from 1920 to 1923. While at Indiana, Pyle was on the staff and served as editor of the Indiana University student newspaper. The 1944 Pulitzer Prize–winning reporter, called the "Hoosier Vagabond," was a widely read war correspondent. He was killed on a World War II battlefield in the South Pacific.

Crawfordsville

BEN-HUR MUSEUM/GEN. LEW WALLACE STUDY

501 West Pike St. Open: Apr. 1–Oct. 31, Tue.–Sun., 1–4:30. June–Aug. Wed.–Sat. 10–4:30, Tue. and Sun. 1–4:30. Admission: Adults: $2, 6–12: $.50, Children under 6: Free, Group Tours by appointment. Maintained and administered by the Crawfordsville Park and Recreational Department. (765) 362-5769, 364-5175.

Lewis Wallace (1827–1905), author, soldier, and statesman, designed and supervised the construction of this study on the grounds of his home. Completed in 1898, the study was intended to be, in the words

The Ben-Hur Museum houses Wallace's lifetime collections. Minister to Turkey and president of the Andersonville Trial, he was an artist, inventor, and a violinist.

of Wallace, "a pleasure house for my soul." Today the building is home to General Wallace's personal memorabilia, library, and items relating to the Broadway play and the movies adapted from *Ben-Hur*. That novel, the third and last written by Wallace, was published in 1880 while General Wallace was governor of New Mexico Territory.

Much of the novel was written at the author's favorite writing place, beneath an old beech tree on the grounds. The dying tree was removed in 1908, but visitors learn that its place is marked with a bronze statue, erected in 1910. The statue from which this one was cast is in the Statuary Hall of Fame in Washington, D.C. Listed on the National Register of Historic Places, General Lew Wallace's study is a National Historic Landmark.

Oak Hill Cemetery, on the north edge of Crawfordsville, is General Wallace's burial site. His grave is marked by a 35-foot obelisk.

Dana

ERNIE PYLE STATE HISTORIC SITE

1 mi. N. of US 36 on IN 71. Open: mid–March to mid–Dec., Tue.–Sat. 9–5, Sun. 1–5. (765) 665-3633.

The journalist Ernie Pyle was born in this small west-central town in 1900. His

Ernest Taylor Pyle commemorative stamp, 1971.

birthplace became a State Historic Site in 1976. The two-story frame house has been restored and furnished with Pyle family pieces.

On April 18, 1995, the fiftieth anniversary of the famed war correspondent's death, the Ernie Pyle Visitor Center was dedicated. Housed in two Quonset huts donated by the Army and erected by the Indiana National Guard, the Center is just west of the house. More than 3,300 pieces of memorabilia are on display. Among them is the typewriter the Scripps-Howard Newspaper Alliance reporter used before the war to write his columns on assignments across the Western Hemisphere. The jacket that he wore in North Africa while covering the Allied campaign is on exhibit. Visitors also see the shovel Pyle used to dig the foxholes where he wrote his battlefront stories.

A theater is included in the Visitor Center, and there is a library with an archives of Pyle's letters, photographs, and columns. The Ernie Pyle Visitor Center was financed by a $250,000 grant from the Scripps-Howard Foundation and funds raised by the Friends of Ernie Pyle, Inc.

Geneva

LIMBERLOST STATE HISTORIC SITE

200 E. 6th St., one block east of US 27. Open: Tue.–Sat. 9–5, Sun. 1–5. Closed mid–Dec. to mid–Mar. Free admission. (219) 368-7428.

Gene Stratton Porter (1863–1924), author, naturalist, and photographer, built this house of Wisconsin timbers in 1895. Here she wrote *Freckles*, *a Girl of the Limberlost*, and *Laddie*, her novels celebrating the outdoors. The rustic style of the house is a combination of arts and crafts and Queen Anne. Most of its fourteen rooms are framed in red oak paneling. Some original furniture was in the house when the state received it; other original pieces have been given since then. Gene Stratton Porter's moth collection is on exhibit.

When Limberlost Swamp was drained in 1913, the Porters sold Limberlost Cabin and built another house similar to it near Rome City. The Limberlost Conservation Association of Geneva obtained the cabin and donated it to the state in 1947. The Friends of the Limberlost present events at the cabin throughout the year. The site is administered by the Indiana Department of Natural Resources.

Greenfield

JAMES WHITCOMB RILEY BIRTHPLACE AND BOYHOOD HOME

> 250 W. Main St. Open: May 1–Oct. 31, Tue.–Sat. 10–4, Sun. 1–4, Closed Mon. and Major Holidays. Admission: Adults: $4, Children: $1. ($.50 with group), Under 6: free. (317) 462-8539, 462-8527.

James Whitcomb Riley (1849–1916), the Hoosier poet, was born in a two-room log cabin on this site. During his boyhood the house was expanded to its present form. In 1865, due to financial reverses, the Riley family was forced to leave their home. In 1893 James Whitcomb Riley fulfilled his vow to buy back the property someday. The poet's brother and his wife occupied the house. In 1935, the property was purchased by the City of Greenfield. The Greenfield Parks and Recreation Department maintains and operates the Riley Home and Museum. The Riley Old Home Association was formed in 1937. The organization refurbished the house and furnishes it with family pieces as they become available.

Young Riley's experiences at this house and its surroundings inspired many of his best-known poems, such as "The Old Swimmin' Hole" and "Little Orphant Annie." His poetry uses the dialect of the country folk he encountered in his boyhood and youth. The Riley Museum interprets Riley's life after the family moved from the house.

STATUE OF JAMES WHITCOMB RILEY

> Hancock County Courthouse.

In 1918 the sculpture of the poet was erected in front of the courthouse. The statue was paid for with contributions by school children across the country. During the yearly festival celebrating the poet's birthday, Greenfield's school children honor him by parading to the statue and placing flowers around the statue.

THE RILEY FESTIVAL

James Whitcomb Riley's October 7 birthday is celebrated each year in downtown Greenfield with a festival the first weekend in October. Poetry readings are included in the activities. At the 1998 festival, Indiana's governor proclaimed "The Year of Riley in Indiana" to be observed from October 7, 1998, to October 7, 1999, in observance of the Riley sesquicentennial.

Indianapolis

JAMES WHITCOMB RILEY MUSEUM HOUSE

> 528 Lockerbie Street. Open: Tue.–Sat.: 10–3:30, Sun.: noon–3:30. Closed first two weeks in Jan. and major holidays.

Famous Americans Issue, 1940.

Admission: Adults: $2, Students 7–17: $.50, 6 and under: free. (317) 631-5885.

When James Whitcomb Riley (1849–1916) moved to this house in 1893, he was already a successful poet and performer of his works. A collection of his poems, including "When the Frost Is on the Punkin" had been published to popular acclaim ten years earlier. Tired of hotels, the lifelong bachelor arranged with friends to share their home as a paying guest. The poet lived here his last 23 years, writing and entertaining visitors.

The two-story Italianate structure was built in 1872. In its era the Victorian house's elegant furnishings and innovative features reflected the best of city living. Riley's friends purchased the property from the owner's estate, formed the James Whitcomb Riley Association, and in 1922 opened the house as a public museum, only six years after Riley's death. Visitors to the perfectly preserved house see the rooms just as they were during Riley's occupancy. His books, guitar, and piano are all still in place.

In the upstairs hall the poet's desk and papers are exhibited. In Riley's bedroom, his cane, silk hat, and some clothing are on display. Riley died in this room and was buried in Crown Hill Cemetery, Indianapolis.

After establishing the Riley House as a memorial to the Hoosier poet, The James Whitcomb Riley Memorial Association built the James Whitcomb Riley Children's Hospital and donated it to Indiana University Medical School in 1924. The Association's third memorial, Camp Riley for Youth with Physical Disabilities, opened at Bradford Woods in 1955.

Rome City

THE GENE STRATTON PORTER HISTORIC SITE

Limberlost North, 1205 Pleasant Point. Open: Tues.–Sat.: 9–5, Sun.: 1–5. Closed mid–Dec. to mid–Mar. Free admission. (219) 854-3790.

Gene (Geneva) Stratton Porter (1863–1924), author and naturalist, designed this two-story house with an exterior of Wisconsin cedar logs. She moved here in 1914 from her home in Geneva. The author spent much of her time after 1919 in California, where several of her novels were adapted as films, but she returned regularly to this house. A group of local citizens purchased the property and gave it to the state of Indiana in 1946.

Visitors begin their tour at the new interpretive center in the reconstructed carriage house. Called the "Cabin in Wildflower Woods," the 16-room log cabin is located on the shore of Sylvan Lake. The house preserves Mrs. Stratton Porter's library, as well as her furniture and many of her personal belongings. On exhibit also is the extensive collection of nature photographs taken by Stratton-Porter. The 34 acre site contains both individual formal gardens and wild forest land.

IOWA

Burr Oak

THE LAURA INGALLS WILDER PARK AND MUSEUM

3603 236th Ave., just off US 52. Open: Daily May 1–Oct. 1. Admission is charged. (319) 735-5916.

This Museum is housed in the Masters Hotel, where Laura and her family lived for a year while her mother worked there. It is the only one of the author's childhood homes still standing on its original site. Guided tours of the restored 1870s inn include the room where the Ingalls family lived. Scrapbooks about the author and copies of her books in translations are on display. The site is administered by a non-profit association.

Cedar Falls

BESS STREETER ALDRICH BOOKSHELF

Cedar Falls Historical Society Museum. 303 Clay St.

The Bess Streeter Aldrich Bookshelf is maintained by the local chapter of the Daughters of the American Revolution. Aldrich, a children's author, was born in Cedar Falls in 1881 and educated here. As a young wife and mother she pioneered to Nebraska in 1909.

Webster City

KANTOR-MOLLENHOFF PLAZA

Twin Parks.

In 1976, as part of its bicentennial celebration, Webster City erected the plaza in honor of its two Pulitzer Prize winners, MacKinlay Kantor and Clark R. Mollenhoff. Beside the plaza's fountain is a bronze marker engraved in the center with likenesses of the two writers. A plaque on the left is inscribed with Kantor's

In 1883 this doll, Flossie, was given to Bess Streeter Aldrich, age two, in Cedar Falls. The doll is in the Bess Streeter Aldrich Museum in Elmwood, Nebraska.

In 1976 in the spirit of America's Bicentennial, Webster City, Iowa, dedicated a plaza at the park to its Pulitzer Prize authors: MacKinlay Kantor and Clark Mollenhoff.

speech at the dedication ceremony. A biographical sketch of Mollenhoff appears on the right plaque.

MacKinlay Kantor (1904–1977), novelist, was born in Webster City, where two of his former residences still stand. Kantor's birthplace, 1627 Willson Avenue, and his grandfather's house at 1718 Willson Avenue are both private, unmarked homes now. A number of the author's works were inspired by his native region. One of them, *Glory for Me,* was adapted into an Academy Award winning film, *The Best Years of Our Lives.* His Pulitzer Prize was awarded for *Andersonville.* MacKinlay Kantor Drive on the west side of town is another memorial to Webster City's native son. MacKinlay Kantor's gravestone at Graceland Cemetery bears this inscription; the last line is from his writings:

> Singer of Songs
> Teller of Tales
> "Forever Walking Free"

Clark R. Mollenhoff (1921–1991), investigative journalist, grew up in Webster City. In 1958 he was awarded the Pulitzer Prize for national reporting. His books include *Washington Cover-up, Despoilers of Democracy,* and *The Story of Jimmy Hoffa.* One of his last works is *Ballad to an Iowa Farmer and Other Reflections.* In this collection of poems, Mollenhoff, the Washington correspondent and Washington and Lee professor, honors his roots. Webster City has also honored this writer by naming a street on the city's east side Clark Mollenhoff Drive.

A third Webster City writer, Dr. Faye Cashatt Lewis (1896–1982), author and physician, is honored by a street named for her. Lewis Street is on Webster City's south side. In 1921 Dr. Lewis, then Faye Cashatt, was the first woman to receive a medical degree from Washington University in St. Louis. Dr. Lewis wrote several books on medical subjects and two autobiographical books. During World War II, when her physician husband was in the military, she wrote a newspaper column, *Purgatorials,* which sometimes relayed her husband's observations from the war front.

West Branch

HERBERT HOOVER PRESIDENTIAL LIBRARY AND MUSEUM

Parkside Drive. Open 9–5 daily except Thanksgiving, Christmas, and New Year's Day. (319) 643-5301, 643-2541.

The Rose Wilder Lane Collection in the Archives here documents the writer's life (1886–1968), her writing career, and her role as editor of the classic *Little House* series written by her mother, Laura Ingalls Wilder. Rose Wilder Lane was Herbert Hoover's first biographer. In 1919 she published *The Making of Herbert Hoover*.

KANSAS

Emporia

WILLIAM ALLEN WHITE MEMORIAL

William Allen White (1868–1944), editor and author, is possibly best known as a journalist although he also wrote books of fiction and nonfiction. White was awarded one Pulitzer Prize for an editorial and another, posthumously, for his autobiography. Like William Faulkner in Oxford, Mississippi, and Willa Cather in Red Cloud, Nebraska, the "Sage of Emporia" is closely linked with his home town. In 1955 the William Allen White Emporia Memorial Foundation established the memorial drive in gratitude for White's contributions to community pride in the town where he was born and died. These six commemorative sites are identified by signs with William Allen White's silhouette.

WILLIAM ALLEN WHITE'S HOUSE, 927 EXCHANGE

Owned by the White Corporation and open for tours only by special arrangement.

Built in 1885, the house is called "Red Rocks," because of its first floor construction of red sandstone. It was White's home from 1899 until his death. According to legend, six presidents stayed in the house during the 45 years White lived there. It is now a National Historic Landmark.

WILLIAM ALLEN WHITE ELEMENTARY SCHOOL, 902 EXCHANGE

Constructed in 1950, the school was named by its students. Photographs of White and his family are exhibited in the lobby. Visitors are welcome.

WILLIAM ALLEN WHITE MEMORIAL LIBRARY

Corner of 12th and Merchant streets, Emporia State University. Visitors are welcome. Call (316) 341-5037 for tours.

The W.A. White Collection contains the author's correspondence, manuscripts, photographs, and other materials. The Mary White Collection honors White's daughter, killed in an accident at age 16. The Collection contains picture books for children and Mary White memorabilia. The William Allen White Children's Book Award is given to the book selected annually by Kansas school children. The library exhibits the books honored each year since 1952 when the award was established. Among them are Elizabeth Yates, Wilson Rawls, E.B. White, and William O. Steele.

WHITE MEMORIAL PARK

6th and Merchant.

A midtown park honoring both William Allen White and his son, William

Lindsay White (1900–1973). Selected writings of both men are displayed. William Lindsay White became famous as a World War II war correspondent and author of books about the war. A bust of W.L. White is a prominent feature of this park next to the *Emporia Gazette*.

THE EMPORIA GAZETTE

517 Merchant. (316) 342-4800.

William Allen White purchased this newspaper in 1895 and eventually made it famous. Although the building's exterior has been remodeled through the years, its interior and the character of the newspaper remain intact. Visitors who have made prior arrangements may visit the building's small museum.

WILLIAM ALLEN WHITE BUST AND MEMORIAL

Peter Pan Park, S. Rural St. and Kansas Avenue.

There are no roads into this 52 acre park. Located at the lake's southeast point, the bronze bust was dedicated by former President Hoover in 1950. Plaques on both sides of the bust are engraved with White's famous editorial eulogy, "Mary White." The Whites donated the land for the park in memory of their daughter, who died at age 16 in a horseback-riding accident. The park's name was chosen because Mary White, like Peter Pan, never wanted to grow up. On the State Street side of the park is a statue of Peter Pan and Wendy, characters created by Sir James Barrie.

Independence

WILLIAM INGE THEATRE

Fine Arts Building, Independence Community College, College Ave. and Brookside Drive.

William Inge (1913–1973), playwright, is memorialized in his native city at his alma mater by a theatre and a festival. Each April since 1982 the William Inge Theatre Festival and Conference has been held on campus. The nationally recognized three-day event annually celebrates the works of Inge and one other distinguished American playwright. A festival feature is the presentation of a William Inge play such as *Bus Stop*, *Picnic*, or *Come Back, Little Sheba*.

WILLIAM INGE BOYHOOD HOME

514 North 4th Street.

The house is now owned by the William Inge Theatre Festival Foundation. A visit there is a part of the annual festival's program.

THE WILLIAM INGE COLLECTION

College Library, Academic Building. Open: Mon.–Thur. 7:30 A.M.–9 P.M., Fri. 7:30 A.M.–4:30 P.M.

Begun in 1965, this collection on William Inge has grown to be the most extensive one in existence. The core of the collection is comprised of 400 original Inge manuscripts. Also in the collection are Inge's published works, some in translations. Critical and biographical sources, clippings, and theatre programs are included as well.

Topeka

GWENDOLYN BROOKS PARK

37th St. and Topeka Blvd.

Gwendolyn Brooks, Pulitzer Prize winning poet, was born in 1917 in Topeka. In 1996 a city park was named in her honor. Ms. Brooks was present for the dedication.

Wichita

W.H. AUDEN PAPERS

Special Collections, Wichita University Library Archives, 1845 Fairmount. Hours: Mon. 8–7, Tues.–Fri. 8–5 and by appointment (316) 978-3590.

The Auden collection includes photographs, letters, and newspaper clippings related to the life and works of English-born poet, W.H. Auden (1907–1973). Included are manuscripts of two Auden poems, "Marginalia" and "The Aliens." Auden became a naturalized American citizen in 1946.

KENTUCKY

Bardstown

THE STEPHEN FOSTER STORY

My Old Kentucky Home State Park, US Hwy. 150. Open early June through Labor Day weekend. Hours: Tues.–Sun. 8:30 P.M., Sun. 2:00. Admission: $15. (800) 626-1563.

In this symphonic drama, Paul Green incorporates famous songs by Stephen C. Foster (1826–1864) into his depiction of a year in Foster's life. Since 1959, this musical has been performed in an outdoor theatre on the grounds of My Old Kentucky Home Plantation.

MY OLD KENTUCKY HOME
    PLANTATION

Open: Daily June through Labor Day, tours daily from 8:30 A.M. until 6 P.M. Off-season tours 9–5. Admission: $4. The Commonwealth of Kentucky. (502) 348-3502.

Originally known as Federal Hill, the plantation traces its name change to Stephen Foster's visit and the writing of his famous song, "My Old Kentucky Home."

Bowling Green

CENTER FOR ROBERT PENN WARREN
    STUDIES

1 Big Red Way, Kentucky Building, Western Kentucky University.

Founded in 1987, this center has an educational focus, as requested by Robert Penn Warren (1905–1989). A novelist and poet, he also taught at several colleges and co-edited college textbooks. The personal working library of the distinguished American man of letters is here, surrounded by the furnishings of his study. The wreath presented to Warren in 1986 as the nation's first poet laureate is on exhibit, as is his Medal of Freedom. The Center offers a fellowship in Warren studies and hosts a yearly program featuring outstanding Warren scholars. The April event is open to the public.

Guthrie

ROBERT PENN WARREN BIRTHPLACE
    MUSEUM

3rd and Cherry St. Open: Tue.–Sat., 11:30–3:30, Sun. 2–4; closed Mon. Free admission but donations appreciated.

This turn-of-the-century red brick "railroad bungalow" was the birthplace in 1905 of Robert Penn Warren, recipient of two Pulitzer Prizes for poetry and one for the novel *All the King's Men*. The house was purchased and renovated through community effort. It opened in May 1989, just months before Warren's death. The Warren

In 1989 Robert Penn Warren Birthplace House opened in Guthrie, Kentucky, shortly before Warren's death. He was a distinguished poet, novelist, and critic.

family has since provided an endowment for the birthplace museum.

Permanent exhibits relate to Warren's writings and to his life in Guthrie through his high school years. The museum provides programs on the life and works of the poet, novelist, critic, editor, and educator. Guided tours of the house can be expanded to include regional sites which inspired Warren's poems, such as "The Covered Bridge." The non-profit corporation, The Committee for the Preservation of the Robert Penn Warren Birthplace in Todd County owns and maintains the museum.

Greenup

JESSE STUART LIBRARY AND READING ROOM

> Jesse Stuart Lodge, Greenbo Lake State Resort Park. KY Hwy. 1S. Open year-round. (606) 473-7324.

Writings and personal mementos of Jesse Stuart (1906–1984) are on display here. The poet and author was a life-long resident of this region which also honors him in several other ways. Each September Greenbo Lake State Park hosts Jesse Stuart Weekend commemorating the author's life.

THE JESSE STUART STATE NATURE PRESERVE

> W-Hollow Road, on KY 1, north of Grayson. (502) 573-2886.

Acquired by a gift–purchase arrangement with author Jesse Stuart, this 733-acre Greenup county preserve was dedicated in 1979. Its hills and hollows are immortalized in Stuart's writings such as *Taps for Private Tussie* and *Head O'W-Hollow*. The preserve is used for recreation and environmental education.

Lexington

THE PAUL LAURENCE DUNBAR HIGH
SCHOOL

1600 Man O' War Blvd.

This school is representative of countless others across the country named for Paul Laurence Dunbar, the internationally known African-American poet.

Madisonville

JESSE STUART ELEMENTARY SCHOOL

1710 Anton Road. (502) 825-6033.

This Hopkins County school in the western part of the state was named for Jesse Stuart, Kentucky poet-laureate and author. Stuart's most famous book, *The Thread That Runs So True*, concerns his career as an educator in eastern Kentucky.

Paris

JOHN FOX, JR., MEMORIAL LIBRARY

Duncan Tavern Historic Center, 323 High St., on Town Square just west of the courthouse. Open: Tues.–Sat. 10–12, 1–4. Admission $3. The Kentucky Society of the DAR. (606) 987-1788.

The library at Duncan Tavern, headquarters of the Kentucky Society of the Daughters of the American Revolution, is named in honor of John Fox, Jr., who was born in Bourbon County in 1862. His novel, *The Little Shepherd of Kingdom Come*, was the first American novel to sell a million copies. Duncan Tavern is a three-story stone structure built in 1788 and furnished with rare antiques. The top floor, originally the ballroom, is now a museum. The bottom floor library has copies of all of the books by John Fox, Jr., scrapbooks, and other memorabilia. The author's desk and chair are in the collection, too.

——— LOUISIANA ———

Alexandria

ARNA BONTEMPS AFRICAN AMERI-
CAN MUSEUM AND CULTURAL
ARTS CENTER

1327 Third St. Open: Tues.–Fri. 10–4; Sat. 10–2. (318) 473-4692.

Arna Bontemps (1902–1973), noted writer in the Harlem Renaissance, was born in this recently restored house. Biographical information about the life and work of the poet and author of children's books is presented in Bontemps' childhood home. His outstanding full-length book, *The Story of the Negro*, received both a 1949 Newbery Honor Book and the Jane Addams Book Award. The museum displays personal items

and memorabilia donated by the Bontemps family.

Cloutierville

KATE CHOPIN HOUSE

243 Hwy. 495. Open daily 10–5. $3 Admission. (318) 379-2233.

Katherine O'Flaherty Chopin (1851–1904), prolific writer about Creole culture and women's rights, lived in this typical early-Louisiana house, now the Bayou Folk Museum. The national historic landmark was built by slaves between 1805 and 1813. Chopin immortalized the Natchitoches area with her short story collections, *Bayou Folk* and *A Night in Acadie.* The museum also celebrates Chopin's classic novel, *The Awakening.*

New Orleans

MADAME JOHN'S LEGACY

632 Dumaine Street, between Chartres and Royal in the French Quarter. Open: Tues.–Sat., 9–5, Admission: $3. Louisiana State Museum. (504) 568-6968, 800-568-4995.

George Washington Cable (1844–1925), writer and humanitarian, is known for his works set in Old French New Orleans. Although this house derives its name from Cable's story, "Tite Poulette," included in his 1879 book, *Old Creole Days,* Madame John's Legacy is not officially a memorial to the writer. Cable's interest in the house led him to use it as the setting of "Tite Poulette." He named his lovely heroine Madame John. She inherits the house, but her legacy turns into a tragedy. A number of other French Quarter buildings are also now called by the names Cable gave them in his stories.

Built toward the end of the eighteenth century, Madame John's Legacy is one of the oldest houses in New Orleans and is a typical example of Louisiana Creole architecture of the era. Besides the main building at the site, there is a separate kitchen with cook's quarters and a two-story garconniere, or apartment. Madame John's Legacy was given to the Louisiana State Museum in 1947 and was restored in 1974. Based on an inventory prepared in 1819, this National Historic Landmark is furnished authentically. The ground floor is used to relate the history of the house by owner-blocks. Upstairs rooms exhibit collections of folk art.

ST. MARTINVILLE

Longfellow Evangeline State Commemorative Area. St. Rt. 31, just North of town, 1200 N. Main. (318) 394-3754, (888) 677-2900.

This site's name comes from Longfellow's poem, "Evangeline," which describes the exile of the Acadians by the British during the French and Indian War. Longfellow takes his heroine to St. Martinville. The early silent film, "Evangeline," renewed the area's Acadian pride.

In 1934 Longfellow-Evangeline became the first park in the state system. When the Louisiana State Parks developed the concept of historic commemorative areas, each with a unifying theme, this site developed the focus of the history of the French-speaking peoples of the Bayou Teche. The Visitors Center displays excerpts from Longfellow's diary entries about his poem and interprets history of French-speaking cultures along Bayou Teche.

THE EVANGELINE OAK

Evangeline Oak Park, Bayou Teche Promenade, East Port St. and Bayou Teche. Always open.

A plaque beneath the tree explains its significance as the meeting place of the separated lovers, Evangeline and Gabriel, in Longfellow's narrative poem.

EVANGELINE MONUMENT

Perpetual Adoration Garden and Historic Cemetery, St. Martin de Tours Church Square, Main Street. Always open.

Dolores del Rio, star of the early film, "Evangeline," was the model for this sculpture of the Acadian heroine immortalized by Longfellow.

—— MAINE ——

Blue Hill

THE JONATHAN FISHER HOUSE

> Rt. 176 and 15, near turnoff to South
> Blue Hill. Open: July to mid–Sept.,
> Mon.–Sat. 2–5. Admission: $2. Jona-
> than Fisher Memorial. (207) 374-2459.

Parson Jonathan Fisher (1768–1847)
was also an author and artist. He began
building this house in 1796 as the parsonage
of the Congregational Church, where he was
the minister for 43 years. The substantial
1814 addition is the extant part. The house
museum provides a picture of the multi-
talented man. Fisher's library contains books
that he wrote on national history and poetry. His original wood engravings illustrate
his book, *Scripture Animals or Natural History of the Living Creatures Named in the
Bible, Written Especially for Youth.*

A two story addition is used as a display
room and museum. Numerous examples of
Fisher's genius are exhibited, including his
paintings, bookbinding equipment, and
hand-made furniture. Also featured is a 1948
biography, *Jonathan Fisher, Maine Parson,*
written by Mary Ellen Chase (1887–1973),
another Blue Hill author. The Fisher House
is on the National Register of Historic
Places.

Brooklin

E.B. WHITE TRIBUTE

> Friends Memorial Library. Open: Tues.,
> Fri., Sat 10–4, Thurs. 10–6. (207) 359-
> 2276.

E.B. White (1899–1985), essayist and
children's author, gave the original illustrations for *Stuart Little,* one of his classic children's books, to this library. This village was
his last home. The library owns first editions

of White's works, and its Circle of Friends
Garden is dedicated to the memory of E.B.
and Katharine White. A bronze plaque rec-
ognizes their dedicated support of the library.

Near Brooklin is the Whites' long-time
home, a farm above Blue Hill Bay. The
house with its attached barn is still there,
along with the little boathouse where *Charlotte's Web* and *Stuart Little* were written.
The farm is privately owned, but occasion-
ally the owners invite local schoolchildren
to the barn for a reading of *Charlotte's Web.*
Mr. White's rope swing, just as he described
it in the novel, still hangs over the north
doorway.

Brunswick

THE ROBERT P.T. COFFIN
COLLECTION

> Special Collections and Archives, the
> Library, Bowdoin College, 3000 Col-
> lege Station.

Robert P. Tristram Coffin (1892–1955),
Pulitzer Prize winning poet, was a Bowdoin
alumnus and professor. The Robert P.T.
Coffin Collection includes manuscripts of
his writings, some drawings, recordings of
Coffin reading his poetry, various published
materials, and his personal and professional
correspondence.

THE KATE DOUGLAS WIGGIN
COLLECTION

> Special Collections and Archives, the
> Library, Bowdoin College, 3000 Col-
> lege Station.

Kate Douglas Smith Wiggin (1856–
1923), author, was awarded an honorary degree by Bowdoin College in 1904, the year
after she published *Rebecca of Sunnybrook*

Farm. The Collection includes material dating from 1867 to 1985, mostly from 1891 to 1917. It contains correspondence, manuscripts, scrapbooks, and photographs. First editions and autographed presentation volumes are also included.

THE HARRIET BEECHER STOWE HOUSE

> An inn, 63 Federal Street. (877) 427-8693.

Built in 1807, this federal-style house has a long association with Bowdoin College. Harriet Beecher Stowe and her husband moved to the house in 1850 when Calvin Stowe joined the Bowdoin faculty. Stowe's masterpiece, *Uncle Tom's Cabin,* was completed here. The historic inn has five suites named for famous Maine authors and poets. In addition to Mrs. Stowe, they are Henry Wadsworth Longfellow, Edna St. Vincent Millay, E.B. White, and Sarah Orne Jewett. These literary namesakes are celebrated through the suites' decor. In addition, a number of other well-known Maine writers are honored in the historic section of the Stowe House.

Camden

EDNA ST. VINCENT MILLAY COMMEMORATIVE PLAQUE

> Camden Hill State Park. 2 mi. N. of Camden on Belfast Road, Rt. 1. Admission: Day use of the park, $2 adults, $.50 children 5–11, 4 and under free. (207) 236-3109.

A plaque at the summit of Mount Battie, centerpiece of the park, commemorates the panorama which inspired Edna St. Vincent Millay (1892–1950) to write her famous poem, "Renascence." The plaque was dedicated on the seventy-fifth anniversary of Millay's birth.

Edna St. Vincent Millay Issue, 1981.

THE EDNA ST. VINCENT MILLAY COLLECTION

> Camden Public Library, 40 John Street. (207) 236-3440.

Housed in the Archives Room, the special collection contains articles, books, and primary source materials pertaining to the world-famous Camden poet. The first lines of Millay's poem, "Renascence," are inscribed around the ceiling of the library's 1996 Centennial Wing.

EDNA ST. VINCENT MILLAY STATUE

At the harbor just down the hill from the library, a bronze sculpture of Millay faces the ocean.

EDNA ST. VINCENT MILLAY MEMORIAL

> Whitehall Inn, 52 High Street. (207) 236-3391.

A parlor in this inn is devoted to Edna St. Vincent Millay. In 1912 a talent show at

The first stanza of Edna St. Vincent Millay's "Renascence" encircles the Camden library's reading room. Millay wrote the poem as a young girl in Camden, Maine.

the inn was the occasion for the first public recitation of Millay's famous poem, "Renascence." The parlor displays photographs of the young poet, her 1909 diploma from Camden High School, scrapbooks, manuscripts of several poems, and other memorabilia.

Damariscotta

SKIDOMPHA PUBLIC LIBRARY

Barbara Cooney (1917–   ), children's writer and illustrator, was honored in her hometown by "Barbara Cooney Day" in 1997, sponsored by the library. A "Barbara Cooney

This sculpted Edna St. Vincent Millay overlooks the harbor where she sailed as a girl in Camden, Maine. The poet holds a book and bouquet behind her back.

Children's Corner" was announced then. Library building plans call for additional Cooney tributes in the new facility. *Miss Rumphius* and numerous other Cooney books have Maine settings. In 1996 Barbara Cooney was designated Maine's first "Living Treasure."

Gardiner

JULIA WARD HOWE, LAURA E. RICHARDS, AND EDWIN ARLINGTON ROBINSON TRIBUTES

Gardiner Public Library. Open: Mon., Wed., Fri. 10:30–5, Tues. 10:30–7:30, Fri. 9:30–5, Sat. 9:30–12:30; 152 Water St. (207) 582-3312.

Special collections are maintained here on the two Gardiner Pulitzer Prize winners. Edwin Arlington Robinson (1869–1935) received three Pulitzer Prizes for poetry. Laura E. Richards (1850–1943) received the first

Pulitzer awarded for biography. She also wrote several volumes of children's verse and a series of juvenile fiction. *Captain January*, Richards' best–seller, was adapted to two motion pictures. A memorial wall is dedicated to Laura E. Richards and her mother, Julia Ward Howe, author of "The Battle Hymn of the Republic." Included in the exhibit is a wooden tablet memorializing Laura E. Richards. She was a moving force behind both the creation of the public library and the monument to the memory of Edwin Arlington Robinson.

EDWIN ARLINGTON ROBINSON MONUMENT

Church Square on the Common.

Robinson is memorialized here in the town where he lived until he was 21. The monument's plaque quotes from Robinson's volume, *Tilbury Town*, considered to be modeled after Gardiner. The volume contains

This library honors the town's two Pulitzer Prize winners, Laura E. Richards and Edwin Arlington Robinson. The architecture is Romanesque with Flemish gables.

two of Robinson's most memorable verse creations, "Richard Cory" and "Miniver Cheevy."

Portland

THE WADSWORTH-LONGFELLOW HOUSE

The Center for Maine History. 485 Congress St. Open Daily: June 1–Oct. 31, 10–4, Dec. Special holiday hours. Admission: Adults $5, Children (under 12) $1. (207) 774-1822.

Henry Wadsworth Longfellow (1807–1882), poet and professor of languages, spent his boyhood in this house which was build by his maternal grandfather, Peleg Wadsworth, in 1785. It was occupied by the family until 1901, when it was given to the Maine Historical Society and opened as a museum. Furnishings and artifacts belonged to the three generations of family residents.

The "Rainy Day Room" derives its name from the poem Longfellow composed there in 1841 while looking out at the garden. No other American poet has enjoyed the popularity that Longfellow did, but in his youth he had declared his poetic career finished when the little room here that he had used for writing was turned into a china closet. This three-story brick building was the home of the poet from 1807 until 1826 when he went to Europe for study. In 1963 the house became a national historic landmark.

South Berwick

SARAH ORNE JEWETT HOUSE

5 Portland St., the center of town where routes 236 and 4 divide. Open: June 1–Sept. 15, Wed.–Sun. Tours each hour, 11–4. Admission: Adults $4, Sr. $3.50, age 12 and under $2. Society for the Preservation of New England Antiquities. (603) 436-3205.

Sarah Orne Jewett (1849–1909), novelist and writer of short stories and sketches, was born in this 1744 Georgian house built

The Wadsworth-Longfellow House in Portland, Maine, was the boyhood home of Henry Wadsworth Longfellow.

by her sea captain grandfather. In *Deephaven*, a collection of stories and sketches, she mentions the laborious task of the ship's carpenters who carved the house's woodwork. Those moldings and even some of the original wallpaper are still here. Before the house became a museum in 1931, relatives removed most of the family possessions. In the parlor, though, is a display of books and memorabilia belonging to Sarah and her sister Mary, who spent most of their lives in the house. The house is furnished now with period pieces reconstructing the original appearance.

Sarah Orne Jewett's works most often center around the daily life of small Maine villages she knew. She sometimes accompanied her father, a country doctor, as he visited patients in the rural areas. *Country By-Ways*, dedicated to Dr. Jewett, typifies her subject. Dr. Jewett was a Bowdoin College graduate. Women were not accepted there

Top: In South Berwick, a Maine village, this sign marks the home of Sarah Orne Jewett. The Society for the Preservation of New England Antiquities is the owner. *Bottom:* The Jewett House sits at the intersection of the town's two streets. The upstairs center window was a perfect vantage point from which Jewett observed and wrote.

until 1970, but in 1901 Sarah was the first woman to be granted an honorary degree from Bowdoin.

Visitors to the house today see Jewett's Eastlake desk in the wide upstairs hall and can look down at the spot which was the center of village life during Jewett's day. Down the hall at the back of the house is the writer's bedroom, the only room left intact. She chose the oak leaf wallpaper still there because its design reminded her of her initials. On the wall near her bed a pencil in its holder is handy, as always.

The house and the one next door, the Jewett-Eastman House, are both on the national register of historic places. The Jewett-Eastman house is now the village library, but Sarah spent part of her girlhood there. The third sister, Carolyn Eastman, lived there after her marriage. Behind the houses and the Jewett family plot in the cemetery a few blocks away, tall evergreens recall Sarah Orne Jewett's masterpiece, *The Country of the Pointed Firs.*

Wells

Rachel Carson National Wildlife Refuge

> United States Department of the Interior, Fish and Wildlife Service. (207) 646-9226.

This wetlands program to preserve wildlife habitat along waterfowl migration routes pays tribute to the work of Rachel Carson, author and environmentalist. Her book, *The Sea Around Us,* explores "the marginal world" included in the preserve.

MARYLAND

Baltimore

The Edgar Allan Poe House and Museum

> 203 North Amity. Open Wednesday through Saturday, 12:00–4:00. Fee: $3. Operated by the City of Baltimore. (410) 396-7932.

The sign in front explains this house's significance to Poe's life and work. From 1832–1835 Poe lived here close to the street he termed lowly with a lovely name. Poe received his initial recognition for his writing during his time here. His short story, "MS. Found in a Bottle" won the 1833 literary contest sponsored by the *Baltimore Saturday Visitor.* Poe is famed for horror and

The Edgar Allan Poe House and Museum in Baltimore. While Poe lived here, he was unanimously awarded a $50 contest prize in 1833, his first public attention.

detective stories, lyric poetry, and literary criticism.

EDGAR ALLAN POE GRAVE

> Westminster Church Cemetery, Green and W. Fayette Street.

Just inside the churchyard originally called the Western Burying Ground is Poe's final resting place. He died in Baltimore four days after being found unconscious on the street. Poe's tomb was constructed partly by pennies from Baltimore school children. On the churchyard wall near his tomb is a Poe memorial erected by the French Literary Society in 1921. Since 1949 roses and cognac have mysteriously appeared at the grave each anniversary of Poe's birth.

H.L. MENCKEN HOUSE

> 1524 Hollins Street. Open two weekends each month. Admission: $1.75. Baltimore City Life Museums. (410) 396-7997.

Author, editor, and critic Henry Louis Mencken and his family moved into this house in 1883 when he was three years old. "The Sage of Baltimore," as he was called, lived here until his death in 1956. Mencken was an authority on the American language, the subject of one of his best-known books. In the 1920s, due to the widespread influence of his satirical editorials and essays, the *New York Times* called him the most powerful private citizen in the United States. The restored house and garden became a national historic landmark in 1985.

FRANCIS SCOTT KEY MONUMENT

Intersection of Eutaw Place and West Lonvale.

This impressive bronze sculpture was erected in 1911 to commemorate the writing of *The Star-Spangled Banner.* The sculpture depicts the circumstances surrounding

The tomb of Edgar Allan Poe in Baltimore is a site of international importance. Poe's wife, Virginia Clemm Poe, and his aunt, Maria Clemm, are buried here, too.

The H.L. Mencken House in Baltimore was the writer's home from age three. His witty newspaper column aired outspoken views and gave him a national following.

the anthem's composition. Key and Colonel Skinner were aboard a sloop in the Baltimore Harbor, waiting out the British bombardment of Baltimore during the War of 1812. When daylight revealed the flag still flying at Fort McHenry, Scott, an amateur poet, was inspired to write the words which became the National Anthem in 1931.

Frederick

THE HOME AND MUSEUM OF CHIEF JUSTICE TANEY

121 South Bentz Street. Open June through Sept. from 10:00 A.M. to 4:00 P.M. Admission fee. Owned and maintained by the Francis Scott Key Memorial Foundation.

This house, built in 1799, is operated as a national shrine to the memory of Chief Justice Roger Taney and his brother-in-law, Francis Scott Key. In addition to memorabilia related to Taney's life and career, mementos of Francis Scott Key are on exhibit in the upstairs museum. A book of his poems, published in 1857, can be seen as can the emblem of the Navy's nuclear powered submarine, the U.S.S. *Francis Scott Key*. The 1814 magazine containing the first printing of "The Defense

Top: **Francis Scott Key commemorative stamp, 1948.** *Bottom:* **Baltimore's Francis Scott Key monument commemorates the national anthem's inspiration. The statue benefits from a millennium historical preservation project. Key is depicted standing in a rowboat while being rowed to shore from Ft. McHenry.**

of Fort McHenry," the original title of "The Star-Spangled Banner" is also displayed.

THE FRANCIS SCOTT KEY MONUMENT AT GRAVE OF FRANCIS SCOTT KEY

Mount Olivet Cemetery.

The monument was dedicated on August 9, 1898, and rededicated on the centennial of the event.

BARBARA FRITCHIE HOUSE AND MUSEUM

154 W. Patrick. Hours: Apr.–Sept. Mon., Thur., Fri., Sat., 10–4; Sun. 1–4. Oct.–Nov. Sat. 10–4. Sun. 1–4. Closed Dec.–Mar. Admission. (301) 698–0630.

The original house was destroyed in 1868, six years after the death of the legendary American heroine. This house, built in 1927, is a replica of Mrs. Fritchie's home where at age 95 she defied Gen. Stonewall Jackson. With his ballad published in the *Atlantic Monthly* a year after the heroine's death, Whittier immortalized the Civil War incident. A portrait of Whittier is on display.

A videotape presents Barbara Fritchie's life and times beginning with her birth in 1766, and spanning almost a century. Exhibits include Fritchie's furniture, needlework, and documents of her era. The Barbara Fritchie Monument is in Mt. Olivet Cemetery.

The Barbara Fritchie House in Frederick, Maryland, interprets the life of this loyal Unionist. Whittier's poem immortalized her defense of the American flag.

—MASSACHUSETTS—

Amesbury

THE WHITTIER HOME

86 Friend Street. Open: Tues.–Sat. 10–4, May 1–Oct. 31. Winter months by appointment only. Closed Sun.– Mon. Admission: Adults $3.50, Children $1. (978) 388-1337.

John Greenleaf Whittier (1807–1892), Quaker poet and abolitionist, sold his birthplace at Haverhill after his father died. He

The Whittier Home in Amesbury, Massachusetts, was John Greenleaf Whittier's home from 1836 until his death in 1892. Here he wrote his most famous poem, "Snowbound."

and three female relatives moved to this house just seven miles away. At that time, 1836, it was a four-room cottage. The family's main rooms remain much the same as they were when the Whittiers occupied them. Their parlor wallpaper is still there. Portraits of Whittier and his mother are on the walls. The engraving of Lincoln over the dining room fireplace was placed here by Whittier. He helped to form the political party which nominated Lincoln.

Whittier's two additions to the house were the upstairs bedrooms and the garden room where he wrote. The secretary desk he used is in the manuscript room. After the success of "Snowbound," published in 1866, the poet bought the desk now in the Garden Room.

The Manuscript Room is filled with documents and mementos from Whittier's public life. His dedicated efforts in the cause of abolition are noted by a Rogers grouping. The sculptured figures include a slave woman, Whittier, Henry Ward Beecher, and William Garrison. Letters from public figures and friends are on display.

Artifacts connected with Whittier's poetry and his personal possessions are exhibited. There is a table and spectacles which belonged to the daughter in the poem, "The Witch of Wenham." Whittier's top coat, dressing gown, and suitcase can be seen in his room. The grapevines and trees which the poet planted still thrive in the yard. The old summer kitchen was returned in 1907 to its original place, a corner of the lot. In 1918 the Whittier Home Association purchased the property for a memorial.

Whittier commemorated this Amesbury site in his poem, "The Captain's Well." A shipwrecked captain honored his parched pledge to build a public well if he lived.

Public Well near the Amesbury Middle School

A plaque provides background. This well was dug by Captain Valentine Bagley in 1796 and immortalized by John Greenleaf Whittier in 1890. Whittier's two-stanza poem is inscribed here also. The poem relates the vow that the captain made when shipwrecked. Parched with thirst, he promises to dig a well if he ever reaches home again.

WHITTIER'S GRAVE

Quaker section of the Amesbury Union Cemetery.

A sign marks the Whittier Path. In the family plot, marked by a blue spruce hedge, lies every member of the "Snowbound" family.

Amherst

THE DICKINSON HOMESTEAD

280 Main Street. Tour Schedule (slight variations from year to year) Mar.: Wed. and Sat. 1–4; Apr.–May: Sat. 1–4; June–Aug.: Wed.–Sun. Additional tours Sat. A.M. only, 10:30 and 11:30; Sept.–Oct.: Wed.–Sat.; Nov.–Dec. (except Thanksgiving week) 1–4. Closed mid–Dec. to Mar. 1; Admission: Adults $4, Students $3, Children 6–11 $2, Under 6 free. (413) 542-8161.

Emily Dickinson (1830–1886), America's premier woman poet, was born here in her grandfather's stately house. Samuel Fowler Dickinson built the house in 1813. Except for the fifteen years (1840–1855) when her family lived on North Pleasant Street in a house no longer standing, the Homestead was her lifelong home. In recognition of the ever-increasing stature of Emily Dickinson's poetry, the Dickinson Homestead was designated a National Historic Landmark in 1963.

A few pieces of original furniture are in the house. One is the Dickinson cradle used by all three children: Austin, the eldest; Emily next; and then Lavinia. When Austin married, he moved next door. His home, "The Evergreens," recently underwent restoration and reopened on a limited basis in the summer of 1999. The Dickinson sisters remained at the Homestead until their deaths.

This elevated sign in the Amesbury Union Cemetery symbolizes the popularity of John Greenleaf Whittier. Graves of all the "Snowbound" family are near the poet's.

The Dickinson Homestead in Amherst, Massachusetts, was the birthplace of Emily Dickinson in 1830.

Emily Dickinson Issue, 1971.

Increasingly reclusive by 1868, Emily was still active about the houses and grounds. She baked, and she cultivated plants in her garden and conservatory, which had been added to the house but is no longer there. Her lovely flower gardens still grace the spacious grounds, however. She also read the many books and periodicals which came to the house. Her 1,000 extant letters show that Emily Dickinson maintained a lively and extensive correspondence with family and friends.

On the sill of her bedroom window sits a basket with a cord tied to its handle. Visitors to her upstairs front bedroom hear the legend that Emily used the basket to send down treats for waiting neighborhood children. Also on exhibit in the bedroom is one of the white dresses which Emily took to wearing. And, most significant, there is her writing table. It was here that Emily quietly wrote nearly all of her almost 1,800 poems, although fewer than a dozen were published in her lifetime. After Emily's death, her sister, Lavinia, discovered hundreds of Emily's lyrical poems tucked away. It was she who started the publication process.

After Lavinia's death in 1899, Martha Dickinson Bianchi, Austin's daughter, inherited the Homestead. In 1965 the trustees of Amherst College bought the property. (Emily's grandfather, father, and brother had been connected with the college.) Special events at the Dickinson Homestead include an Emily Dickinson Poetry Walk in the spring and an Open House in honor of Emily's December birthday.

A POETIC DIALOGUE

Two nearly life-sized silhouetted figures created by Michael J. Virzi sit beneath a tree just a block or so down Main Street from the Homestead. Commissioned by Amherst Public Art Commission, 1995.

Emily Dickinson and Robert Frost carry on a private poetic conversation. It is fanciful, of course. Although Frost was a long-time visiting lecturer at Amherst, he was only 12 when Dickinson died. Plaques set in the rocks where the silhouettes are seated provide background on the two poets and draw some parallels between their work. Two poems are also inscribed on the plaques, Frost's "The Road Not Taken" and Dickinson's "I Had a Jewel in My Fingers."

EMILY DICKINSON GRAVE SITE

> West Cemetery, Off Triangle Street— almost within sight from Homestead's back yard.

The Dickinson family plot is enclosed by a fence. Attached to the gate is a plaque:

In Memoriam Emily Dickinson Poetess
Erected by The Dickinson Kinsfolk
August 28, 1952

The epitaph on Emily Dickinson's tombstone is two words: "Called Back." Apparently

Plaques beside this poetic pair of silhouettes reveal that Dickinson and Frost wrote poetry in Amherst about the simplest and deepest aspects of human life.

they were taken from the last letter the poet wrote. To her two cousins in Cambridge, it said: "Little Cousins, Called Back Emily."

JONES LIBRARY

43 Amity Street. Open: Mon.–Sat. 9–5, and on Tues. and Thurs. until 9:30 P.M. The Special Collections Department is open Mon.–Fri. from 10–5, and Sat. 11–1 and 2–5. (413) 256–4090.

Jones Library is the main branch of Amherst's public library system. The Special Collections Department houses exhibits and other material on authors associated with Amherst: Emily Dickinson, Robert Frost, Robert Francis, and Julius Lester. In addition to various of Emily Dickinson's letters on exhibit, her poem discovered in 1997 is also displayed. Jones Library purchased the poem at Sotheby's Auction for $24,150.

Boston

HEMINGWAY ROOM

John F. Kennedy Library and Museum, Columbia Point, south of downtown, close to I-93. Hours: 9–5, Closed Thanksgiving, Christmas, and New Year's Day. Admission fee. (617) 929-4523.

The Ernest Hemingway Collection was assembled by Mary Hemingway from three sources where her husband had stored papers, paintings, and other belongings. The locations were Hemingway's Havana home, Sloppy Joe's Bar in Key West, and the Ritz Hotel in Paris. The Hemingway Room was dedicated by Patrick Hemingway and Jacqueline Kennedy

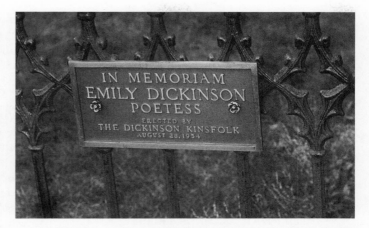

Top: This plaque is on the gate to the Dickinson family plot where the poet is buried. West Cemetery, visible from Emily's home, may have inspired her death poetry. *Bottom:* Jones Library, housed in a homelike stone building, is Amherst's public library. Its Special Collections focus on Amherst authors and Pioneer Valley history.

Onassis in 1980. Trophies from a Hemingway safari, the head of an antelope shot by Hemingway and a lion shot by Mary, also found a home in the Hemingway Room. A synchronicity brought the Hemingway Collection to the Kennedy Library and Museum. It should be noted here that America's thirty-fifth President, to whose memory this library is dedicated, was himself a writer. John F. Kennedy's *While England Slept* became popular in 1940. His *Profiles in Courage* received the 1957 Pulitzer Prize for Biography.

ROBERT McCLOSKEY TRIBUTE

Make Way for Ducklings sculpture. Public Garden, across Charles St. from Boston Common. Free. (617) 323-2700.

Author and illustrator Robert Mc-Closkey (1914–   ) set the children's classic *Make Way for Ducklings* in urban Boston. Nancy Schon's sculpture, based on Mc-Closkey's drawings and story, commemorates the Public Garden's sesquicentennial and honors Mr. McCloskey. Mrs. Mallard (38 inches tall) leads her eight ducklings (12–18 inches each) down a pathway of old Boston Cobblestone. A plaque explains:

> This sculpture has been placed here as a tribute to Robert McCloskey whose story "Make Way for Ducklings" has made the Boston Public Garden familiar to children throughout the world. 1987

Barbara Bush presented a replica of this sculpture to Raisa Gorbachev in 1991. In Novodevichy Park the sculpture sits on a pathway of Boston cobblestones linked with black basalt stones like ones in nearby Red Square. The plaque in Moscow reads:

> This sculpture was given in love and friendship to the children of the Soviet Union on behalf of the children of the United States.

This sculpture, inspired by Robert McCloskey's book, *Make Way for Ducklings,* **is in the Boston Public Garden, Boston, Massachusetts.**

WILLIAM HICKLING PRESCOTT HOUSE

55 Beacon St. Open: Apr.–Oct. Wed, Thurs., Sat., 12–4; Nov.–Mar. Wed. 12–4. Closed holidays. Admission $4. National Society of Colonial Dames of America, Massachusetts Headquarters. (617) 742-3190.

William Hickling Prescott (1796–1859), historian, purchased this 1808 Georgian house on Beacon Hill in 1844. The National Society of Colonial Dames of America in Massachusetts restored Prescott's study at the top of the house. Here he wrote his carefully documented books, including *The History of the Conquest of Mexico.* Because Prescott's eyesight was extremely poor, he used a noctograph to keep from running lines together. The instrument is displayed on the writer's small English desk.

Cambridge

LONGFELLOW NATIONAL HISTORIC SITE

105 Brattle Street. Closed for rehabilitation until Spring 2000, when six tours daily, Wed.–Sat., 10:00–4:30, May–Oct., will resume. Admission. The museum library remains open for research. Appointment required. The National Park Service. (617) 876-4491.

Henry Wadsworth Longfellow (1807–1882), poet, scholar, and educator, lived in this Georgian mansion from 1837 until his death. Built in 1759, it was General Washington's headquarters from 1775 to 1776. As a new Harvard professor, Longfellow rented rooms here at the Craigie House, as it was then called. When he married in 1843, the

Longfellow House in Cambridge, Massachusetts, was the poet's home for 45 years. General Washington used this house for his headquarters early in the Revolutionary War.

UNITED STATES POSTAGE

1 CENT — CENT 1
HENRY W. LONGFELLOW

Famous Americans Issue, 1940.

house was a wedding gift from the bride's father, Nathan Appleton. For 90 years after the poet's death, his family preserved the property and its collections of decorative and fine arts and his personal library and papers. Almost all of the furnishings are original to the house, most linked to Henry Wadsworth Longfellow's nearly half-century here.

The study is preserved as Longfellow left it. Its art pieces, books, and mementos reflect his international tastes. The inscription on the inkstand reads: "Saml Taylor Coleridge: his inkstand." Here Longfellow wrote his popular narrative poems celebrating early America, including "Evangeline," which appeared on his fortieth birthday. "The Children's Hour" was written for his two sons and three daughters. When the chestnut tree immortalized in "The Village Blacksmith" was cut down, the Cambridge school children financed a chair made from the wood. Presented to the "children's poet" on his birthday in 1879, the chair sits beside the fireplace today. In 1962 the Longfellow House was designated a National Historic Landmark and in 1972 a unit of the National Park Service.

MARGARET FULLER MEMORIAL

Mount Auburn Cemetery, 580 Mount Auburn St. (Rt. 16). Open: May 1–

Oct.1, 8–7 daily; rest of the year 8–5; office closed Sun. and holidays. Free admission. (617) 547-7105.

Margaret Fuller (1810–1850), writer, is memorialized here by a monument on Pyrola Path. While on assignment to report on the Italian Revolution, she married an Italian nobleman and gave birth to a son. All three died in a shipwreck; only the child's body was recovered. The tribute to Margaret Fuller Ossoli reads in part:

By Birth a Child of New England.
By Adoption A Citizen of Rome
By Genius Belonging to the World.

Other renowned American writers whose graves are in Mt. Auburn include Dorothea Dix, Oliver Wendell Holmes, Julia Ward Howe, Henry Wadsworth Longfellow, Amy Lowell, James Russell Lowell, Bernard Malamud, and Francis Parkman.

Chicopee

BELLAMY HOMESTEAD

Mass Pike, Ex. 5, 91-93 Church St. Open by appointment. (413) 594-6496.

The home of Edward Bellamy (1850–1898), novelist and sociologist, was purchased in 1975 by the Edward Bellamy Memorial Association. It maintains displays of Bellamy memorabilia for research and study of Edward Bellamy books and papers. In 1988 the association sponsored a centennial celebration of the Bellamy classic, *Looking Backward*. The house, also headquarters for the Chicopee Historical Society and Chicopee Arts Council, is a National Historic Landmark.

Concord

ORCHARD HOUSE, HOME OF THE ALCOTTS AND LITTLE WOMEN

399 Lexington Road, off Rt. 2A, 1 mi. east of Concord Center. Open: Apr. 1–Oct. 31, Mon.–Sat. 10–4:30; Nov. 1–Mar. 31, Mon.–Fri. 11–3, Sat. 10–4:30, Sun. 1–4:30. Closed: Jan. 1–15, Easter, Thanksgiving, Christmas. Admission: Adults $5.50, College students and seniors $4.50, Youths 6–17 $3.50. (978) 369-4118.

Louisa May Alcott (1832–1888), author, moved to this house with her family in 1858. Here they remained for 20 years. Her father, Bronson Alcott, joined two eighteenth-century houses together, accounting for Orchard House's unusual shape. They named it for the 40 apple trees on the place. One survives today. Only three of the four sisters to become famous in *Little Women* came here to live. Elizabeth, the third child and the musical one, had died at age 22 a few months before. She is remembered at Orchard House by her melodeon and her portrait above it.

Orchard House today is a testimonial to the remarkable Alcotts. Bronson Alcott's study reflects his life's work as educator and philosopher. Emerson, Thoreau, and other prominent Transcendentalists were frequent visitors here. On display is a bust of Alcott sculpted by Daniel Chester French in 1879. The kitchen, the domain of Mrs. Abigail Alcott, displays family housewares. It is thought that Louisa bought the soapstone sink; the waterboiler or "set kettle" was installed by Bronson, and the clothes drying rack was his design. A wooden board decorated with a hot poker by May Alcott is on display. Louisa's book makes light of her sister's pygrography experiences. Visitors learn that the dining room was used as a stage for

Orchard House was the home of the Alcott family in Concord, Massachusetts. Louisa May Alcott wrote *Little Women* here in 1868.

the sisters' performances. A trunk and its costumes survive. Audiences at the plays were seated in the adjoining parlor. In 1860, the marriage of the eldest, Anna, a talented actress, took place in the parlor.

May, the youngest daughter, was a talented and trained artist. Her drawings are on display in her bedroom. A studio was added to the house in 1865 as May's workshop and classroom. There she taught young Daniel Chester French, who became the famed sculptor of *The Minute Man* and the *Lincoln Memorial*. Today the studio is used for the museum's changing exhibits.

It is the room of Louisa, the writing daughter, that is the highlight of the house. An 1872 photograph of the room shows the bookcase, round table and the round chair where Louisa sits before her desk. The photograph does not include the fireplace with its picture of an owl above the mantle. The painting was May's tribute to her sister,

whom she called a "wise old owl." Not much has changed in the room since Louisa May Alcott wrote *Little Women* in ten weeks at the desk between the windows. That was in 1868; the book about the Alcott family has never been out of print.

In the backyard at the Orchard House stands the Concord School of Philosophy, established by Bronson Alcott in 1879. It closed in 1888 after his death. Since 1976 it has again hosted a summer lecture and conversation series. In 1911, Harriet Lothrop, a children's author and Concord neighbor, bought Orchard House to establish a Louisa May Alcott memorial. The next year the museum opened under the direction of the Louisa May Alcott Memorial Association.

EMERSON HOUSE

28 Cambridge Turnpike. Hours: mid–Apr. to mid–Oct., Tues., Fri., Sat., 10–4:30, Sun. 2–4:30. Ongoing 30-

The Emerson House in Concord, Massachusetts, became a center for the philosophers and writers who created the American literary renaissance. Emerson moved there in 1835.

Famous Americans Issue, 1940.

minute tours. Admission: Adult $4.50, Student $3. Senior $3, Under 7 free. (978) 369-2236.

Ralph Waldo Emerson (1803–1882), poet, essayist, and founder of Transcendentalism, moved with his new wife and his mother to this colonial house in 1835. Built a few years before, it was originally an L-shaped structure. The Emersons added the present parlor and the bedroom above it to form the traditional square. In 1857 third floor attic space was converted to a den. It was used primarily by grandchildren and other young guests.

The Emerson home became the center of intellectual life in Concord and, in many ways, the center of the American literary renaissance. Emerson's study was the setting for stimulating discussion by distinguished visitors. This is the only room where the contents have been altered much. Because the house had once been damaged by fire, there was concern for the safety of the study's valuable contents in a frame house. Consequently, both furnishings and books have been removed; the furnishings are at the Concord Museum, and most of the books and papers are at Harvard University. Books and furnishings in the study now were taken from other parts of the house. A unique round table here revolves so that its drawers may be opened readily.

Visitors see "The Pilgrim's Chamber," Emerson's name for the downstairs guest room, which also served as a birthing room for the four Emerson children. A drawing hanging in the room depicts the back yard study built for Emerson by Alcott. It proved more beautiful than practical and was soon removed. References to Emerson's now celebrated neighbors, especially Thoreau, are frequent in the course of the tour. A family friend, Thoreau lived here during two winters while Emerson was away on his lecture circuit. The guide speaks also of renowned individuals from other nations who were a part of Emerson's wide circle, as well. Above the parlor sofa hangs a steel engraving, a gift from Thomas Carlyle.

Always an appreciator of nature, Mr. Emerson planted a great many trees. The grounds now are kept looking as much as possible as they did when he was alive. His habit was to take long, meditative walks through the meadows behind his house to Walden Woods, afterwards returning home to write his reflective works. The meadows are still there. In 1930 after the death of the last child, Dr. Edward Emerson, the Ralph Waldo Emerson Memorial Association was formed to administer the Emerson House.

THE OLD MANSE

269 Monument St., ½ mi. north of Concord center (Monument Square). Hours: mid–Apr. to Oct. 31, Mon.–Sat., 10–5, Sun. and holidays, 12–5. Admission fee. (978) 369-3909.

The Old Manse's gambrel roof and saltbox lean-to blend with its otherwise Georgian exterior. This house is unique in that it is associated with several authors but was primarily a minister's residence. It was built in 1770 for the Rev. William Emerson, who was also a patriot. From his grounds he encouraged the Colonials as the American Revolution began adjacent to his property. The next year, 1776, he died while serving as a chaplain in Washington's army. In 1835 his grandson, Ralph Waldo Emerson, wrote his

Hawthorne called this house the Old Manse because it was the home of ministers, but it was his book, *Mosses from an Old Manse*, that immortalized the house.

first and most influential book, *Nature*, in this house. The little corner room on the second floor was his study while staying with his grandmother and step-grandfather, Ezra Ripley.

Important as Emerson's book was and lengthy as the stay of the Emerson-Ripley family in the house was (159 years), it was Nathaniel Hawthorne (1804–1860) who gave the house its lasting name and who is the literary figure most closely associated with it. In 1842 Hawthorne and his bride, Sophia Peabody, began a three-year idyllic stay here in their rented first home. They chose for their bedroom a second floor front room, refurbished with fresh paint and wallpaper, and called it "the golden room." Today it is known as the Hawthorne bedroom although furnished with Emerson and Ripley family pieces. At least one piece, a daybed, belonged to Phebe Emerson Ripley.

The dining room contains some of the house's oldest furniture, such as the table and chairs from the 1720s. However, for literary pilgrims the most interesting part of the room is the windowpane where Sophia Hawthorne used her diamond to etch two notations. One reports that her painting of Endymion was done in that room. The other, dated a year later in January, 1845, announces that her first-born, Una Hawthorne, stood on this windowsill and delighted in the icy trees outside, "tho only ten months old."

It was the study, though, where the Hawthornes left their most indelible mark, both figuratively and literally. Hawthorne, like Emerson seven years before him, had found the room to suit his composition purposes. Using the small wooden standing desk still to be seen there, he wrote most of his collection of stories, *Mosses from an Old Manse*. Again, a window is the main attraction; Nathaniel and Sophia inscribed comments there in turn, all dated 1843.

The Old Manse was purchased by the Trustees of Reservations in 1939. Surrounding land is kept as natural meadows. An open field connects the property with the North Bridge, site of the Concord Battle in 1775. Ezra Ripley gave land to the town to erect a monument. At the dedication of that first monument on July 4, 1837, Emerson's "Concord Hymn," composed for the occasion, was sung.

MINUTE MAN NATIONAL HISTORICAL PARK

174 Liberty Street, North Bridge of the Concord River, National Park Service Visitor Center. (978) 369-6993.

The Minute Man statue was sculpted by Daniel Chester French, who was only 23 years old at the time of its completion. The monument commemorates the citizen-soldier of 1775. It was commissioned for the Centennial of the North Bridge battle. On the statue's base appears the first stanza of Emerson's poem, "Concord Hymn."

THE WAYSIDE

455 Lexington Road. Hours: Daily except closed on Wed., June–Oct. 9–5. Admission: age 17 and older $3. The National Park Service, Minute Man Park. (508) 371-2483.

In 1965 this historic house became part of Minute Man National Historical Park. It was a natural union considering that Samuel Whitney, Muster Master of the Concord Minutemen, lived here at the start of the American Revolution. The arrangement marked the first literary site to be acquired by the National Park Service. It could be called three literary sites in one, the home of the Alcotts, the

The first stanza of Emerson's "Concord Hymn" is inscribed on the base of this statue: "By the rude bridge that arched the flood,/ Their flag to April's breeze unfurled, Here once the embattled farmers stood/ And fired the shot heard round the world."

The Wayside in Concord was the home of three literary families. All left their mark. Their home and works represent 300 years of America's history.

Hawthornes, and the Lothrops. The Wayside has been restored to its early 1920s appearance.

The Wayside Barn is used for ticket office and exhibit area. A lifelike sculpture of Louisa May Alcott in swashbuckler costume is part of the current exhibit. Bronson Alcott is represented in the exhibit also. The philosopher is seated, book in hand. Hawthorne is there, too, standing at his desk in his tower study. Harriett Lothrop has a place of honor in the gallery also. The gracious lady sits in a high-backed wicker chair. The exhibits honor all three literary families who owned The Wayside. All of them left their mark.

When Bronson Alcott (1799–1888), bought this house in 1845, it was a four room colonial farmhouse. He added an outbuild-ing to each of the house's ends. Alcott named this house, the first one he had ever owned, "The Hillside." At first all four Alcott daughters shared the upstairs east chamber. The next year, 13-year-old Louisa got her own bedroom. Here she had the privacy for serious writing, but there was also time for fun. Visitors today see the girls' attic playroom. The sisters also enacted *Pilgrim's Progress* on the colonial staircase in the front entry. The barn, which was on the other side of the house when the Alcotts lived there, was the scene of the Alcott girls' theatricals. Although Louisa wrote *Little Women* at Orchard House, Hillside was the setting for the real life happenings she immortalized.

Nathaniel Hawthorne (1804–1864), bought the house from Alcott in 1852 and renamed it "The Wayside." Hawthorne had

Opposite: **At the Wayside Barn exhibit Louisa May Alcott enacts a male role in the Alcott sister the-atricals. She immortalized their playacting in *Little Women*.**

put into the books, & so I
made my fortune out of my
seeming misfortunes; I
speak of myself because what
one has lived one really knows
& so can speak honestly."

– Louisa May Alcott, Letters, February 5, 1884

L. M. Alcott.

LOUISA MAY ALCOTT

Although best known for her children's
books, Louisa was also the author of
many short stories, "blood-and-thunder"
tales, and novels. Before she was
recognized as an author, she helped
support her family in other ways, often
working away from home. Louisa took
her experiences, including many from
her childhood at The Wayside, and
created from them the most popular and
enduring novel of a family – *Little Women*.
Mothers and daughters all over the
world have found that it captures most
realistically their closest relationships.

returned to Concord an acclaimed novelist. Four of his novels had been published in three years, including his masterpieces, *The Scarlet Letter* and *The House of the Seven Gables.* He was financially able to alter the house to meet the needs of his family, which now included three children. In addition to a bedroom over Alcott's west wing, Hawthorne added a three story tower at the back. Above the windows and doorways of all four new rooms are pointed gables, Hawthorne's architectural motif. The "sky-parlor" is Hawthorne's third floor tower study. Still here is the stand-up writing desk which he himself built. Hawthorne wrote his last book, *Our Old Home*, here and left two novels unfinished at his death.

In 1870 Hawthorne's heirs sold The Wayside, but in 1879, the youngest Hawthorne child, Rose, and her husband, George Lathrop, bought the house. A token of their tenure stands before the fireplace in the sitting room. Rose painted a scene on the fire screen there and inscribed on it a passage from her father's story, "Fire Worship," in *Mosses from an Old Manse.*

In 1883 the third literary family, the Lothrops, bought the Wayside from the Lathrops, along with some of the Hawthorne family furniture. Daniel Lothrop, a Boston publisher, and his wife, Harriett, made only one structural change to the house, a piazza on the west side. Mrs. Lothrop (1844–1924), as Margaret Sidney, wrote most of the dozen books in her popular children's series, *The Five Little Peppers*, at The Wayside. Margaret, the Lothrops' only child, born here in 1884, was also the only author's child born at The Wayside. In a curious way her childhood is commemorated here. Louis Meynelle's painting, *Whittier with the Children*, hangs at The Wayside today. The painting was used as the frontispiece of Margaret Sidney's 1893 book with the same title. The little girl sitting on Whittier's lap is Margaret Lothrop. A shadow box on the sitting room mantle displays Lothrop family mementos. Lothrop pieces furnish the house.

From the beginning the Lothrops were dedicated to preserving The Wayside's heritage. One of Mrs. Lothrop's celebrations contributed significantly to that goal. This Hawthorne centenary plaque placed at the back of The Wayside property explains:

THIS TABLET PLACED
AT THE CENTENNIAL EXERCISES
JULY 4, 1904
COMMEMORATES
NATHANIEL HAWTHORNE
HE TROD DAILY THIS PATH TO THE HILL
TO FORMULATE
AS HE PACED TO AND FRO
UPON ITS SUMMIT
HIS MARVELOUS ROMANCES

When Harriett Lothrop died in 1924, her daughter, Margaret Lothrop, became The Wayside's last private owner. In 1932 she moved back to her birthplace and devoted herself to preserving the house. Through her efforts, The Wayside was designated a National Historic Landmark in 1963. The property was opened to the public in 1971.

The Concord Museum

200 Lexington Road. Hours: Jan.– Mar.: Mon.–Sat. 11–4, Sun. 1–4; Apr.– Dec.: Mon.–Sat. 9–5, Sun. 12–5. Closed Thanksgiving, Christmas, New Year's Day and Easter. Admission: Adults $6. Seniors $5, Students $4, and Children $3. (978) 369-9763, 369-9609.

Among the museum's renowned collections is the world's largest collection of Thoreau possessions. Henry David Thoreau (1817–1862), essayist and poetic naturalist, was a Concord native. An excerpt from his journal is seen at the museum: "I think I could write a poem to be called *Concord*." A life-long Concord resident except for his

Opposite: **Vivid graphics in the Wayside Barn link the house's several author/owners. Here Hawthorne writes at the standing desk in his Tower study at the Wayside.**

Henry David Thoreau Issue, 1967.

Harvard years, he was well acquainted with the river, hills, and fields his journal entry

goes on to extol. The holdings of the museum include the furniture Thoreau used at his Walden cabin. Thoreau's bed, desk, and chair are all here. During the famous two-year stay at Walden Pond, he drafted his first book, *A Week on the Concord and Merrimack Rivers*, and filled his journals with the material for his masterwork, *Walden*. He also began his influential essay, *Civil Disobedience*. At Walden Pond Thoreau made productive use of this furniture.

THOREAU PLAQUE

> Site of old Concord jail, Main Street, near the Lowell Road intersection.

A plaque at the site identifies the site's significance:

> HENRY DAVID THOREAU
> was imprisoned for one night in a jail on this site, July, 1846 for refusing to recognize the right of the state to collect taxes from him in support of slavery—an episode made famous in his essay
> "Civil Disobedience"

As a protest of slavery, Thoreau once refused to pay a tax. The result was a jail stay and his essay, *Civil Disobedience.* **A Concord, Massachusetts, plaque marks the event.**

The Night Thoreau Spent in Jail, a play by Jerome Lawrence (1915–   ) and Robert E. Lee (1918–1994), dramatizes the celebrated event. First presented in 1970, it has been called one of the most widely produced plays of our time.

SITE OF THOREAU CABIN AND REPLICA OF CABIN WITH THOREAU STATUE

> Walden Pond State Reservation. 915 Walden St., Route 126. Hours: Mon.–Fri. 7 A.M.–7:30 P.M.; Sat.–Sun. 5 A.M.–7:30 P.M. Admission: Parking is $2 per vehicle per day.

Henry David Thoreau's sojourn at Walden Pond from 1845 to 1847 is commemorated in several ways here. In 1922 area landowners granted 80 acres to the state to preserve Walden by restricting activity on the premises. In 1945, the centennial year of Thoreau's move to Walden, his cabin's chimney foundation was discovered and excavated. In July 1947, the Thoreau Society dedicated the inscribed fieldstone that marks Thoreau's hearth site today. A cairn commemorates the site, and the cabin's 10 × 15 dimensions are outlined. A map marking the foot path to the cabin site is available at the park entrance. A replica of Thoreau's cabin and a bronze statue of Thoreau stand close to Gate 3 near the main entrance to Walden Pond.

AUTHORS RIDGE

> Sleepy Hollow Cemetery, Bedford Street, The Pritchard Gate. Well-marked signs to Authors' Ridge. Hours: Dawn to Dusk daily. (978) 371-6299.

The final resting places of the Concord writers are close together here. Thoreau was the first of the Concord literati to be buried here. A large monument at the family plot lists names and dates of birth and death for the family with simple individual stones inscribed with initials only. The Alcott plot is nearby. Louisa's grave is marked by an

The Concord literati took walks in the area before it became a cemetery. Now they are buried near each other at Concord's Sleepy Hollow Cemetery.

American flag signifying her service as a Civil War nurse. Lead poisoning contracted then eventually caused her death. Louisa May Alcott died only two days after the death of her father. Nathaniel Hawthorne's tombstone is engraved with one word, "Hawthorne." The Hawthorne family plot has only memorials for Sophia Hawthorne and daughter Una. Both are buried in England. The Emerson plot is farther down the ridge. Ralph Waldo Emerson's rose stone tombstone is large and impressive. His wife, Lidian, and his daughter, Ellen Tucker Emerson, are interred on either side. Daniel

The bronze tablet on Emerson's massive tombstone of rose quartz reads: "The passive master lent his hand/ To the vast soul o'er which him planned."

and Harriett Lothrop's graves are also on the ridge. Harriett's pen name appears on her tombstone, too.

EMERSON STATUE

> Concord Free Public Library, Academy Lane at Main Street.

A life-size statue of Ralph Waldo Emerson sits majestically in the library's entrance. Its sculptor is Daniel Chester French. The library's collections contain the manuscript materials of the Concord writers.

A colorful quilt hangs on the wall in the children's section of the library. It celebrates children's classics by quilt blocks with designs of their characters.

This sculpture of Emerson is the work of Daniel Chester French. Emerson, the Sage of Concord, was the magnet by which other writers were drawn to Concord.

This quilt in the children's section of the Concord Free Public Library commemorates children's authors by illustrating their creations.

Cummington

THE WILLIAM CULLEN BRYANT HOMESTEAD

207 Bryant Road, off Route 112. From junction of Rt. 9 and Rt. 112, take Rt. 112 south 1.5 miles. At the five-way intersection, go straight on Bryant Road 0.2 mi. to the Homestead. Open: Last weekend in June through Labor Day: Fri.–Sun. and holidays. Labor Day through Columbus Day: Weekends and holiday only, 1–5. Admission: $5. (413) 634-2244.

William Cullen Bryant (1794–1878), poet and newspaper editor, spent his boyhood in this house, the original part of which was built in the 1780s. Bryant enlarged the house for a summer retirement home, adding a first floor and elevating the two original floors. Now 23 rooms, the structure is Victorian with gambrel roofs. The Homestead is filled with family furnishings and antiques from several generations.

As a boy on his Grandfather Snell's farm, Bryant loved the beautiful Berkshire setting and showed an early talent for poetry. "The Embargo," published when Bryant was thirteen, previewed his political crusading. His masterpiece, "Thanatopsis," was largely composed when he was only seventeen. The Homestead's setting inspired his romantic nature poetry. "Inscription for the Entrance to a Wood" celebrates a grove close by. At a nearby stream, his poem, "The Rivulet," is noted by a commemorative marker:

> From this pristine natural setting and the surrounding countryside,
>   Bryant drew much of the inspiration for his beauty.

Called the father of American poetry, Bryant was a major poet by 1821. His best poetry, though, was written by 1825 when he left the Berkshires for New York City. After fifty years as the influential editor of *The New York Evening Post,* Bryant bought

The Bryant Homestead in Cummington, Massachusetts, is on a hillside above the Westfield River valley. This Berkshire setting inspired much of Bryant's nature poetry.

back the homestead in 1865 and began additions and renovation. He lived here summers until his death. Six trips to Europe are noted by his leather-bound trunk on display. The Turkish room exhibits mementos from one journey. A porthole window set in an exterior wall was his conditioning against seasickness. Two wooden dumbbells reflect Bryant's fitness regimen; he also took long walks in the countryside. Today his berry-picking hat hangs ready for an outing.

Bryant's additions to the Homestead included a wing duplicating an earlier one. It had been his father's office; the new area was Bryant's study. Here he translated Homer's *The Iliad* and *The Odyssey* in his last years. The Homestead, acquired by the Trustees of Reservation in 1929, was designated a national historic landmark in 1963.

WILLIAM CULLEN BRYANT
  BIRTHPLACE

> Potash Hill Road, directly across the road from Dawes Cemetery.

Slightly over a mile from the Bryant Homestead a six-foot stone obelisk marks his birthplace. It also states that he is buried in Roslyn.

Falmouth

THE CONANT HOUSE, KATHARINE
LEE BATES ROOM

> 65 Palmer Avenue, on the Village Green. Open for Tours: 2 P.M.–5 P.M. mid–June to mid–Sept. Closed Mon.–Tues. Falmouth Historical Society. (978) 548-4857.

This room is dedicated to Katharine Lee Bates (1859–1929), author of "America the Beautiful." The exhibits include her travel books and her children's classic, *Sigurd: Our Golden Collie.* Her poetry is there, too, as well as photographs and memorabilia. The memorial is temporarily housed at the Conant House until the Katharine Lee Bates Birthplace Museum opens. The Historical Society owns the property, which is rented to a tenant. Miss Bates, a Wellesley College professor, wrote her patriotic anthem in 1893 while visiting Pike's Peak. The song first appeared in print on July 4, 1895.

In addition to this room and her birthplace on Main Street, which has a memorial plaque in front, Miss Bates is memorialized at several other sites in town. A street is named for her, and a life-size bronze statue stands on the Falmouth Main Library grounds. "The Shining Sea" Bike Path honors a line from her most famous poem. Katharine Lee Bates is buried at Oak Grove Cemetery, about a half-mile from her birthplace.

Great Barrington

MONUMENT MOUNTAIN

> Monument Mountain Reservation, Route 7, between Stockbridge and Great Barrington. Open daily year round, free. The Trustees of Reservations. (413) 298-3239.

Every August, the Trustees of Reservations sponsor a hike to Monument Mountain's summit. The event commemorates the historic first meeting of literary giants Herman Melville and Nathaniel Hawthorne. It was an event that is said to have changed the course of American literature. The occasion was a summer picnic hosted by Oliver Wendell Holmes. Melville, Hawthorne, and Holmes hiked the three miles to the mountain's summit. Melville bestrode a rock where he delivered William Cullen Bryant's poem, "Monument Mountain." The party toasted Bryant. Soon afterward, Melville moved to Pittsfield, near where Hawthorne was living, and their literary friendship began. The annual August outing follows the pattern of that significant picnic in 1850.

Hampden

LAUGHING BROOK EDUCATION CENTER AND WILDLIFE SANCTUARY

The Burgess House, 793 Main Street. Open May–Oct. Sat.: Free with sanctuary admission: Adults $3, Senior and Age 3–12 $2. Massachusetts Audubon Society. (413) 566-8034.

Thornton W. Burgess (1874–1965), children's author and naturalist, bought this place in 1925 for a summer residence and lived here permanently after 1957. After his death, the Massachusetts Audubon Society purchased the property and established the Laughing Brook Nature Center in 1968. Burgess wanted to preserve the setting of his hundreds of stories as a mecca for the children of three generations who had written to him of their love for his works.

His stories show animals like Mrs. Hootie Owl and Reddy Fox living in the fields and forests and behaving like people. Laughing Brook, his name for his home, supplied an ideal setting for his works with its green meadows and forest, brook and purple mountains, as well as an old orchard. His earlier books were in series, such as *Mother West Wind*. His autobiography, *Now I Remember: Autobiography of an Amateur Naturalist,* was published in 1960.

The Storyteller's House, as it is now called, is a circa 1790 Cape Cod home. Tour guides there provide background on Mr. Burgess and his Laughing Brook days. One of the many children's activities at the center is Story Trails. Special locations at Laughing Brook are matched with a favorite nature story of Thornton W. Burgess.

Harvard

FRUITLANDS

102 Prospect Hill, 30 mi. W. of Boston, 6 mi. from junction of Rt. 495 and Rt. 2. Hours for the four museums of

This traditional colonial farmhouse at Fruitlands once sheltered a small group of idealists. The ell at the right side houses artifacts, including Bronson Alcott's plow.

American Art and History: mid–May to mid–October: Tues.–Sun., also Mon. holidays, 10–5. Admission charged. (508) 456-3924.

Fruitlands Farmhouse is now a museum of Transcendentalism. It contains letters of the movement's founders, Alcott, Emerson, and Thoreau. Bronson Alcott's books are in the study. He moved his family here in 1843 to begin an experiment in communal living. The short-lived utopian community practiced a strict vegetarian diet, and even the children participated in the philosophic discussions. Ten-year-old Louisa May Alcott recorded her skeptical reactions in a diary on exhibit.

Haverhill

WHITTIER FAMILY HOMESTEAD AND BIRTHPLACE OF JOHN GREENLEAF WHITTIER

305 Whittier Road, on Rt. 110, 1 mi. east of Exit 52 off I-495. Hours: May 1–Oct. 31, Tues.–Sat. 10–5, Sun. 1–5; Nov. 1–Apr.30, Tues.–Fri. and Sun. 1–5, Sat. 10–5, or by appointment. Admission: Adults $3, Children $1. Group Tours by prior arrangement. Owned and operated by the Haverhill Whittier Club. (978) 373-3979.

This home of the Whittier family for five generations is the birthplace of John Greenleaf Whittier (1807–1892), poet, newspaper editor, and abolitionist. The house appears much as it did when Whittier was growing up here. The Homestead, the first part of which was built in 1688, is an old New England working farm. Family furniture and possessions, especially the belongings of Greenleaf's mother, Abigail, are everywhere throughout the house. Abigail's chair and flax-spinning wheel and her wedding china are here, as well as a quilt she made. Dining room furniture is intact, table and chairs and lowboy. Braided rugs have survived, and a chest and cradle, too. So have Uncle Mose's musket and powder horn, and Aunt Mercy's favorite rocker. The home-

The oldest part of the Whittier Homestead dates to 1688. This back view of the house illustrates the custom of painting only the front white to economize.

stead's interior still reflects Whittier's description in "Snowbound." The kitchen's ample fireplace hearth and the elevated Mother's bedroom are familiar sights to readers of the poem.

Outside scenes inspired the young poet, too. There is the doorstone where "the barefoot boy with cheeks of tan" ate from his wooden bowl. The 69 acres around the boy poet inspired "Fernside Brook," which still flows as he described it. A bee hive on the property today calls to mind Whittier's "Telling the Bees." As a young man Whittier wrote his first poem here at his grandfather's desk. In 1826 his first published poem appeared in the paper where William Lloyd Garrison was editor. It was Garrison who encouraged Whittier to become an abolitionist. After his father died in 1832, Whittier came home to run the farm, but finally had to sell it and move to Amesbury in 1836.

Many of Whittier's poems were written long after he moved away from his birthplace although inspired by his early years there. One poem prompted by an experience late in the poet's life, though, is represented by an object displayed at the Homestead. In Whittier's old age, all of his household had died. He stayed with cousins in Danvers during his last winters. Once during a deep snow, Whittier watched a young daughter of the family feeding the birds. "Red Riding Hood" is the poem that he wrote about the incident, and the scarlet cloak that the little girl wore that day is on display here.

After "Snowbound" was published, literary pilgrims began descending on the Homestead to see its setting. The memorial was opened to the public in 1893 after the house was purchased and presented to the Haverhill Whittier Club. The Whittier Homestead was listed on the National Register of Historic Places in 1975.

WHITTIER COLLECTION

> Haverhill Public Library, 99 Main Street, Downtown at the corner of Main and Summer Streets (Intersection of Rt. 125 and 97). Hours: Mon.–Thurs. 10–9, Fri.–Sat. 10–5:30, Sun. (Sept.–May) 1–5.

The library's first special collection began in 1887 when the Whittier Club of Haverhill began to collect every known edition of the poet's work and everything written about the poet to give to the library. Maintained and enlarged, the Whittier Collection is now one of the most complete accumulations of its kind. Available by appointment.

Lawrence

ROBERT FROST FOUNTAIN

Robert Frost and his wife Elinor White Frost were co-valedictorians of the class of 1892 at Lawrence High School. The school is no longer standing nor is the City Hall building where the ceremony was held. Across the street from the current Lawrence City Hall built on the site is the Robert Frost Fountain. It marks the location of the reception honoring graduates after the 1892 commencement exercises. The fountain, constructed in 1982 and 1983, is in the Campagnone Common on Common Street across the street from City Hall. The fountain recalls the poems "Birches," "Mending Wall" and "West Running Brook." The paths leading away from the fountain recall "The Road Not Taken."

THE ROBERT LEE FROST SCHOOL (KINDERGARTEN–GRADE 8)

> 33 Hamlet Street, South Lawrence.

Frost spoke at the dedication in 1962 of the original Frost School. After it burned, a

Opposite: **This fireplace at the Whittier birthplace in Haverhill, Massachusetts, was immortalized in Whittier's masterpiece, "Snowbound."**

The Robert Frost Fountain in Lawrence, Massachusetts, is on Common St. in the Campagnone Common. The fountain and encircling plaza recall four Frost poems.

new Frost School opened in 1986. An excerpt from Frost's "Black Cottage" is carved in a black granite slab set in a concrete bell tower at the school's front. In the school yard four other poems are inscribed on brass tablets set in concrete slabs. The school's Frost Memorial Window was created in part from glass saved from the First Unitarian Church which the Frost family attended in Lawrence. Murals inside the building illustrate familiar Frost poems painted by students on wood panels.

Lenox

THE MOUNT, HOME OF EDITH WHARTON

At the southern junction of rts. 7 and 7A, corner of Plunkett St. and Rt. 7. Open: Memorial Day–Nov.1, and weekends in May, 9 A.M.–3 P.M., last tour at

Edith Wharton Issue, 1980.

The Mount is Edith Wharton's architectural masterpiece. Its imperial appearance is enhanced by graceful landscaping, a French courtyard and Italianate terrace.

2 P.M. Admission: Adults $6, Sr. $5.50, Ages 13–18 $4.50, under 12 free. Edith Wharton Restoration. (413) 637-1899.

Edith Wharton (1862–1937), novelist and designer, built this American classical mansion in 1901–02, inspired by a seventeenth century English estate. The Mount's setting high on a hillside provides its name and highlights its grandeur. In 1897 Wharton co-authored *The Decoration of Houses,* expressing ideas on home design later applied at The Mount. Symmetry, proportion, and simplicity characterize the estate, including its majestic classical gardens. European influences are seen in the use of marble and terrazzo. Until restoration is complete, house tours are limited to the majestic first floor.

Wharton's grand library features a 1905 photograph of the novelist at her library desk after publishing her first best-seller, *The House of Mirth.* Actually she worked in her bedroom above the library. *Ethan Frome,* her best-known work, was written there. A steep hill in the village nearby is the model for its tragic climactic scene.

Shakespeare and Company's arrangement with Edith Wharton Restoration provides for theatrical productions at three theatres on the grounds. One of them, the Salon Theatre, presents one-act matinees, including adaptations of Wharton's stories. Audiences are served tea in the adjoining dining room.

The Whartons sold The Mount in 1911. Sixty years later it became one of the few National Historic Landmarks dedicated to women. At the Mount, Edith Wharton is represented in a lecture series, "Women of Achievement." Biographical, designing, literary, and historical facets of Edith Wharton are all a part of The Mount's guided tours.

TANGLEWOOD

Hawthorne Road, Hawthorne's Little Red House, on the grounds of Boston Symphony's summer residence. West Street/Route 183. Open part of every day in July and Aug. Free admission. (413) 637-1600. Main Gate.

This house is a replica of the one that Nathaniel Hawthorne and his family lived in on this site from the spring of 1850 to the autumn of 1851. It was rented from friends, the William Tappans, who had recently purchased the property and planned to build an estate there. In 1936 their daughter and granddaughter deeded that estate, Tanglewood, to the Boston Symphony Orchestra. Tanglewood is a mecca for thousands of concert-goers. Its name is Hawthorne's name for the place, preserved in *Tanglewood Tales*.

Hawthorne moved here after losing a

Top: Nathaniel Hawthorne Issue, 1983. *Bottom:* Tanglewood, near Lenox, Massachusetts, was Hawthorne's Berkshires home for 18 productive months. The house, destroyed by fire in 1890, was accurately rebuilt.

political appointment in Salem. At Tanglewood he wrote *The House of the Seven Gables* and *The Wonder Book*. The Tanglewood porch is the frontispiece of *The Wonder Book*. Tanglewood Music Institute uses the house now for a studio and classroom and maintains a Hawthorne exhibit here.

New Bedford

MOBY-DICK: THE MARATHON

New Bedford Whaling Museum, 18 Johnny Cake Hill. Hours: Open daily 9–5; (Thurs. until 8 P.M. Memorial Day–Labor Day) Closed Thanksgiving, Christmas, New Year's Day. Admission: Adults $4.50, seniors $3.50, Children (6–14) $3. (508) 997-0046.

Melville's sailing from New Bedford's port is commemorated annually at the New Bedford Whaling Museum with a round-the-clock-reading of *Moby Dick*. Prior to the marathon volunteers are scheduled to read a section of the novel. The event is held on the anniversary of Melville's January 1841 departure aboard the whaleship *Acushnet* for a three-year voyage to the South Seas. *Moby Dick* related exhibits cover one end of the museum. Across the street the Seaman's Bethel, described in the novel, also commemorates Melville in New Bedford.

Top: The New Bedford Whaling Museum's exhibits include a wall devoted to Melville's *Moby Dick*. "Moby-Dick: The Author" is among the displays. *Bottom:* Melville, as well as Ishmael, his narrator in *Moby Dick*, visited this chapel before he shipped out from New Bedford. Seamen's Bethel is open to the public.

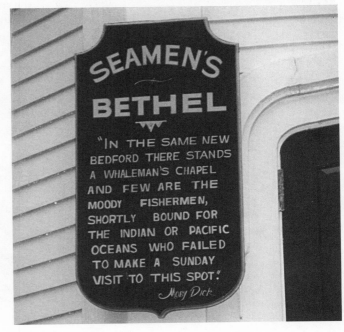

Pittsfield

HERMAN MELVILLE'S ARROWHEAD

780 Holmes Rd. Open: Memorial Day–Oct. 31, 9:30–5, last tour at 4:00. Admission: Adults $5, Sr. $4.50, Age 6–16, $3. Berkshire County Historical Society. (413) 442-1793.

Herman Melville (1819–1891), novelist and short story writer, moved to this house in 1850. Its name came from the Indian artifacts unearthed by Melville's plow. The federal-style building was originally a 1780s tavern and inn on the stage route. Although Melville moved to New York in 1863, Arrowhead remained in the Melville family until the 1920s. The house, yellow with green trim just as Melville had it painted, became a national historic landmark in 1963.

The farmstead has been partially re-

Herman Melville Issue, 1984.

stored to the Melville era. Much is here today to point to that productive time in the writer's career. The chimney room celebrates Melville's "I and My Chimney" written here. Alan Melville, the author's brother, inscribed the story on large tablets. They are above the mantle today. Melville wrote *Moby Dick* in his upstairs study here. From his north window he could see vast Mt. Greylock in the distance, looking like a great whale. He dedicated his novel *Pierre* to Mt. Greylock. The piazza that Melville built on the north side of the house is immortalized in his *Piazza Tales*. The piazza has been restored to Melville's original specifications.

The tour ends with a visit to the same red barn where Melville held long discussions with his new friend, Hawthorne, who was also living in the area. Today the barn is the museum shop. An excellent video shown there, "The Berkshire Legacy," discusses the artists who chose to live in the Berkshires. Contributions to America's heritage by Melville, Hawthorne, Edith Wharton, Daniel Chester French, and Norman Rockwell are explored. Melville recognized the

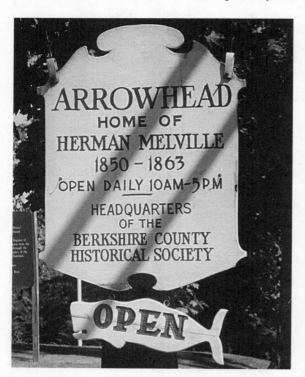

At Pittsfield, Massachusetts, Arrowhead's whale logo signifies the home of *Moby Dick*. The waving cornfield and distant Mt. Greylock suggested sea and whale to Melville.

Already famous when he bought Arrowhead, Melville wrote a number of his significant works at the eighteenth century federal-style farmhouse from 1850 until 1863.

influence on his writing of his late night discussions with Hawthorne in this old barn. He inscribed his masterpiece, *Moby Dick,* to Nathaniel Hawthorne.

and a vast repository of research materials. First editions of Melville's works are here along with papers and volumes from Melville's

THE HERMAN MELVILLE MEMORIAL ROOM

The Berkshire Athenaeum, Pittsfield's Public Library, 1 Wendell Ave. (413) 499-9486.

In 1953 this memorial room was established in recognition of Melville's 30-year association with Pittsfield, beginning at his uncle's farm in 1833 and including his Arrowhead years. The Herman Melville Memorial Room houses the world's largest collection of Melville personal memorabilia

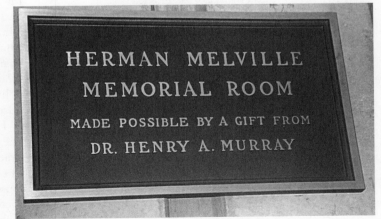

The national center for Melville studies is located in The Berkshire Athenaeum in Pittsfield, Massachusetts. Guided visits are offered to the Herman Melville Memorial Room.

The mahogany secretary at which Herman Melville wrote Billy Budd is in the Melville Room of the Berkshire Athenaeum, Pittsfield, Massachusetts.

library. Two personal treasures are the wooden sea chest with Melville's initials carved on the end and the tin bread box where his wife kept the manuscript of *Billy Budd*.

Salem

THE HOUSE OF THE SEVEN GABLES HISTORIC SITE

The Turner-Ingersoll Mansion and the Nathaniel Hawthorne Birthplace, 54

Turner St. Directions: I-95, Ex. 25A to Rt. 114 east to Salem Center. Follow Waterfront signs to Derby St. Hours: Open daily except Thanksgiving, Christmas and New Year's Day. July 1–Oct. 31, 9–6; Nov. 1–June 30, 10–4:30; Jan.–Mar. Sun. 12–4:30. Admission: Adults $7, Ages 6–17 $4, Under 6 free. Allow 1 hr. for tours. The House of the Seven Gables Settlement Association (978) 744-0991.

THE TURNER-INGERSOLL MANSION

Nathaniel Hawthorne (1804–1864) immortalized this house in his classic novel, *The House of the Seven Gables* (1851). A Salem native, he sometimes visited his older cousin, Susannah Ingersoll, here in the first quarter of the nineteenth century. Susannah, a local historian and storyteller, related the background of the house and their ancestors. Built in 1668, the house was ancient even then. Except for the Puritan style kitchen, the house appears much as it did at Hawthorne's visits. The furnishings are authentic to the period although few were owned by the Ingersoll family. However, the parlor's "Hawthorne corner" contains a desk and chair Hawthorne admired in the house. His checkerboard is displayed in the dining room cupboard.

The Judge's chair, a link to Hawthorne's novel, is there too. The dining room is called Hepzibah's Room because it matches the sitting room of Hawthorne's elderly character, Hepzibah Pyncheon. His Col. Pyncheon's reception room corresponds to this house's distinctive great parlor. An upstairs bedroom, the great chamber, is called Phoebe's room for the novel's heroine. Hawthorne fictionalized Susannah's accounts of events and people, but this house is the principal model for his Pyncheon

Left: Hawthorne's statue is in Salem, Massachusetts, his birthplace and the setting of his novel, *The House of the Seven Gables. Right:* In 1804 Nathaniel Hawthorne was born in this house in Salem, Massachusetts. It has been moved a few blocks to the House of the Seven Gables Historic Site.

House. Other features include the garret (Clifford's chamber in the novel) and the mysterious winding spiral of the secret stairway. Costumed guides conduct the tours of this National Historic Landmark.

NATHANIEL HAWTHORNE'S BIRTHPLACE

Nathaniel Hawthorne was born in this house on July 4, 1804. It was moved to the House of Seven Gables Historic Site in 1958 from nearby Union Street. The year of the house's construction is not certain; some say 1685, others no earlier than 1740. It is known, though, that by 1772 Captain Daniel Hathorne owned it. His grandson was Nathaniel, who later inserted a "w" into the surname. Nathaniel's father, a ship captain, was lost at sea when the boy was only four. He grew up in this house where his mother kept grieving. After college he returned home to live in seclusion in a little room under the eaves of the ancient house. For 12 years he struggled here to perfect his writing skills. His "dark years" ended in 1837 with the publication of *Twice-Told Tales.*

Sandwich

THORNTON W. BURGESS MUSEUM

4 Water Street, on Shawme Pond, in historic center of Sandwich Village, on Cape Cod. Open: Apr.–Dec., Mon.–

Sat. 10–4, Sun. 1–4. Winter hours vary. Admission by donation. The Thornton W. Society. (508) 888-6870.

Thornton W. Burgess (1874–1965), children's author and naturalist, is memorialized here in one of Sandwich's old homes. He was born and reared in this village. Burgess is known internationally for his children's stories teaching lessons of conservation and appreciation for wildlife. The museum displays books and memorabilia from the author's life and works, including his animal adventure series. Exhibits of the region's natural history also can be seen. In summer the museum hosts Burgess Animal Story times.

GREEN BRIAR NATURE CENTER AND JAM KITCHEN

6 Discovery Hill Road, off Rt. 6-A, East Sandwich. Hours: Apr.–Dec. Mon.–Sat. 10–4, Sun. 1–4. Winter hours vary. Admission by donation. The

Top: Thornton W. Burgess Museum, in Sandwich, Massachusetts, is dedicated to the life and works of Thornton Burgess, children's author, naturalist, and Sandwich native. *Bottom:* Thornton W. Burgess Museum also operates the Green Briar Nature Center in East Sandwich to further the Burgess devotion to wildlife and the natural environment.

Thornton W. Burgess Society, a non-profit, educational organization. (508) 888-6870.

Smiling Pool and the old Briar Patch, immortalized in the Thornton W. Burgess stories for children, are preserved here in a quiet corner of Cape Cod. Live animals, an award-winning wildflower garden, and nature trails are all a part of the 57-acre Briar Patch Conservation Area. The Green Briar Nature Center is a sanctuary in all seasons. It offers year-round natural history classes, nature walks, lectures, and workshops. Products of the 1903 Jam Kitchen on the property help to fund The Thornton W. Burgess Society.

Springfield

DR. SEUSS NATIONAL MEMORIAL

Quadrangle Park, Springfield Library and Museums Association. 220 State St. Free admission. Scheduled for completion in late 2000. (800) 625-7738.

An open-air memorial honors author and illustrator of children's books, Theodor Seuss Geisel (1904–1991). The author, better known as Dr. Seuss, was born in Springfield. His first book, *And to Think That I Saw It on Mulberry Street*, was inspired by his early neighborhood. At the Seuss memorial, the complete text and pictures of that 1938 book are featured in a bas relief. Centerpiece of the six bronze sculptural works is *Ted and the Cat*, a composite sculpture of Ted Geisel and his alter ego, the Cat in the Hat. Horton, the Lorax, and Yertle are all three

around, too. The Story-Telling Place is a big chair set against an oversized book containing every word of *Oh, the Places You'll Go!*

Sudbury

LONGFELLOW'S WAYSIDE INN

Wayside Inn Rd., Rt. 20, Free self-guided or pre-arranged guided tours, Closed Dec. 25 and July 4; Non-profit educational Wayside Inn Trust. (978) 443-1776, (800) 339-1776.

Immortalized by Longfellow's *Tales of a Wayside Inn* in 1863, this "ancient ... hostelry" changed its name accordingly. Longfellow's poetic tales were set at an inn then called The Red Horse. "Paul Revere's Ride" is the best-known poem included. Today the site is a working inn and a museum. In addition to its name, the inn's Longfellow memorials include a bust of the poet and the Longfellow Garden. The inn is a national historic site.

1950s Pane, Celebrate the Century Series, 1999. Description on stamp's reverse side also honors this 1957 book.

MICHIGAN

Ann Arbor

ARTHUR MILLER THEATRE

University of Michigan campus.

Plans are underway for the Arthur Miller Theatre honoring America's most distinguished living playwright and one of

the University of Michigan's most famous graduates. Arthur Miller sanctioned the tribute from his alma mater. Miller, a 1938 alumnus, also received an honorary degree from the university in 1956. He was awarded the Pulitzer Prize in Drama for *Death of a Salesman* in 1949. Half a century later, his works and awards continue to increase.

Detroit

EDGAR A. GUEST MIDDLE SCHOOL

10825 Fenkell. (313) 873-9460.

This school serving students in grades five through eight is named for a man who was born in England but who attended public school in Detroit. Edgar A. Guest became a successful poet and newspaperman in Detroit.

East Lansing

EDGAR A. GUEST IN HALL OF FAME

Michigan State University Communi-

cation Arts and Sciences Building. (517) 353-6430.

Syndicated poet and columnist Edgar A. Guest (1881–1959) is included here in the Michigan Journalism Hall of Fame. A permanent display of the inductees is in the lobby of the building's first floor. *Detroit Free Press*, where Edgar A. Guest worked for 60 years, published his dialect verse in weekly and daily columns for more than three decades. His works include the poetry collection, *A Heap o' Living*. Called "America's Best Loved Poet of the Newspaper Age," Edgar A. Guest was selected for Michigan's Journalism Hall of Fame in 1997.

———MINNESOTA———

Mankato

MAUD HART LOVELACE WING

Minnesota Valley Regional Library. 100 E. Main St. Hours: Mon.–Thur.: 9:30–8; Fri.–Sat.: 9:30–5; Closed Sun. and holidays. (507) 387-1856.

The 1977 dedication ceremony honored Maud Hart Lovelace (1892–1980). Her popular "Betsy-Tacy" novels are based on the childhood and youth of the author and her friends in Mankato. Prominent in the Lovelace Wing is a mural of her fictional Deep Valley with scenes from her books. Also featured are framed original Lois Lenski illustrations for the Lovelace books. An autographed collection of Lovelace works includes the series of ten "Betsy-Tacy" books, three other novels for young people, and six historical novels for adults. Memorabilia and audio-visual presentations complete the display.

TACY'S HOUSE

332 Center Street. (507) 345-8103.

The Betsy-Tacy Society has purchased the Kenney house, immortalized in the series as the home of Tacy. The little girl was the best friend and neighbor of Betsy, whose prototype was the author, Maud Hart Lovelace. Still undergoing restoration, the house is used by the Society for meetings and literary events. The Betsy-Tacy Society was founded in Mankato in 1990.

MAUD HART LOVELACE EXHIBIT

Heritage Center, Blue Earth County Historical Society, 415 E. Cherry. Open Tues.–Sat. 10–4, Closed Sun. and holidays. Admission: $4. (507) 345-5566.

A permanent display commemorates Maud Hart Lovelace. Included is the Betsy Bride Doll, inspired by *Betsy's Wedding* (1955) the final book in the Betsy-Tacy series.

Maud Hart Lovelace Memorial Bench

Corner of Center and Lewis Streets.

Dedicated in 1989, this bench replaces the original one featured in the Betsy-Tacy books.

Lovelace Grave Site

Glenwood Cemetery, 711 Glenwood Ave.

The grave of Maud Hart Lovelace is in the cemetery's old section, where the author strolled as a child. It is now the site of pilgrimages by her fans.

New Ulm

The Wanda Gag House

226 N. Washington. Open Sat.–Sun. summer afternoons; other times by ap-

pointment. Admission: free will donations. (507) 359-2632.

Wanda Gag (1893–1946), author and illustrator of children's books, was three years old when her family moved to this Queen Anne house, built in 1894. It was placed on the National Register of Historical Places in 1980. Large windows, two skylights, and an artist's studio are its unique characteristics.

Influenced by her artist father, Anton Gag, Wanda grew up drawing and painting here. In the parlor are copies of Mr. Gag's oil paintings, and his stenciled and free-hand painted ceiling border. Some of the many lithographs by Wanda Gag are exhibited in the dining room. She won international acclaim for her lithographs. After the death of both her parents, the house was sold in 1918. Ten years later her classic, *Millions of Cats*, was published. The Wanda Gag House Association purchased the house in 1988 for

Wanda Gag, author and illustrator of the children's classic, *Millions of Cats*, grew up in this house. It became a museum in 1988, 70 years after the Gags sold it.

preservation and as a center to interpret Wanda Gag, her artistic family, and her New Ulm surroundings. The Association also promotes literature and arts in the community.

Northfield

ROLVAAG MEMORIAL LIBRARY

St. Olaf College. (507) 646-3224.

Ole Edvart Rolvaag (1876–1931), American novelist and professor of Norwegian, taught at his alma mater, St. Olaf College, from 1907 until his death. The building which bears his name opened in 1942. As the first secretary and archivist of the Norwegian-American Historical Association, Ole Rolvaag laid the ground for the library's archives of Norwegian-American life. Rolvaag's classic novel, *Giants in the Earth*, explores the hardships faced by Norwegian settlers in the Midwest during the late nineteenth century. The English translation of *Giants in the Earth*, first published in Norwegian, appeared in the United States in 1927.

St. Paul

THE MAUD HART LOVELACE HISTORY PLAYER

History Center, Minnesota Historical Society, I-35E and I-94, corner of Kellogg and John Ireland Blvd. Hours: Mon. (July–Labor Day only), Wed–Sat. 10–5, Tues. 10–8, Sun. 12–5. Free admission. (800) 657-3773.

In the Families exhibit a costumed historic interpreter portrays writer Maud Hart Lovelace. Through a dramatic performance as well as informally interacting with the audience, she brings to life a segment of history. The interpreter wears a reproduction of the outfit Mrs. Lovelace wore at a military review in her honor at Fort Snelling in

1929. That recognition was for historical accuracy in her novel *Early Candlelight*, set at the Minnesota military fort.

Sauk Centre

SINCLAIR LEWIS BOYHOOD HOME

Sinclair Lewis Ave. and Main St. Open: Memorial Day–Labor Day, Mon.–Sat., 9:30–5, Sun. 10:30–5. Admission: Adults: $3, Sr.: $2.50, Students: $2, Children: $1.50.

With the help of the Minnesota Historical Society, the Sinclair Lewis Foundation has restored this home of the Lewis family from 1899 to 1926. It opened in 1970, the fiftieth anniversary of the publication of *Main Street*, the most famous novel by Sinclair Lewis (1885–1951). The book's setting is Gopher Prairie, a fictional name for Sauk Centre. Among the family items on exhibit at the house is Lewis' narrow wooden bed. The house is a national and a state historic site.

The author's birthplace, directly across the street, is also owned by the Foundation but is not open to the public. Several other sites commemorating Sauk Centre's famous native son include the Sinclair Lewis Park and The Sinclair Lewis Arch. A reference to his novel, *Main Street*, appears on Lewis'

Great Americans Issue, 1985.

Sinclair Lewis Home

Sauk Centre, MN

In 1885 Sinclair Lewis was born in this Sauk Centre, Minnesota, house. He received the Nobel Prize for literature in 1935, the first American recipient of the award.

tombstone in Greenwood Cemetery, east of town.

SINCLAIR LEWIS INTERPRETIVE CENTER

Hwy. 71 and 194S. Open: Memorial Day weekend through Labor Day, Mon.–Fri., 8:30–3, Sat.–Sun., 9–5. Winter hours: Mon.–Fri. 8:30–3. Free admission. (612) 352-5201.

This museum tells the story of Sinclair Lewis, America's first Nobel laureate in literature. A video presentation traces the life of the Sauk Centre native. Among the exhibits on the self-guided tour is a complete set of the 23 Sinclair Lewis novels, signed by the author. A bronze bust, cast for the Sinclair Lewis Centennial, is also on display at the Interpretive Center.

Walnut Grove

LAURA INGALLS WILDER MUSEUM

330 Eighth St. Open Memorial Day–Labor Day, 10–7; May and Sept. 10–5. Free admission. (507) 2358, 2155.

As a child *The Little House* author lived in Walnut Grove. The television series based on the books is set in Walnut Grove. The museum displays mementos from the show. A quilt made by Laura is also on exhibit. The Ingalls dugout and other Laura sites are marked around town. The places are included in Wilder's book, *On the Banks of Plum Creek*.

WALNUT GROVE'S LAURA INGALLS WILDER PAGEANT

Presented each summer in Walnut Grove. (507) 859-2174.

——— MISSISSIPPI ———

Hattiesburg

THE DE GRUMMOND COLLECTION

McCain Library and Archives, University Libraries, The University of Southern Mississippi. (601) 266-4349.

A leading research center in the field of children's literature, the de Grummond Children's Literature Collection was founded by Dr. Lena de Grummond, children's author and librarian, in 1966. The focus of the Collection, which represents more than 1,200 authors and illustrators of children's books, is American and British children's literature, historical and contemporary. Historical and contemporary periods are also represented in the collection's magazine section.

Among the programs of the de Grummond Collection are special exhibits and the annual Children's Book Festival. The festival's highlight is the presentation of the University of Southern Mississippi Medallion to an author or illustrator who has made outstanding contributions to children's literature. Since 1968 when the recognition began, these ten recipients have been among those honored: Lois Lenski (1969), Barbara Cooney (1975), Scott O'Dell (1976), Madeleine L'Engle (1978), Ezra Jack Keats (1980), Maurice Sendak (1981), Beverly Cleary (1982), Katherine Paterson (1983), Charlotte Zolotow (1990), and Richard Peck (1991).

Jackson

EUDORA WELTY LIBRARY

300 N. State St. Open: Mon.–Thurs. 9–9, Fri. and Sat. 9–6, Sun. 1–5. Jackson Hinds Library System. (601) 968-5811.

Eudora Welty, novelist, short story writer, and photographer, was honored in 1986 by the naming of the headquarters library in her honor. Miss Welty (1909–) is a native of Jackson. She received the 1973 Pulitzer Prize for her novel, *The Optimist's Daughter*. Eudora Welty is featured in the library's Mississippi Writers Room. Among its exhibits is Welty's *One Time, One Place: Mississippi in the Depression: A Snapshot Album.* The book contains her photographs of Mississippi life. Other exhibits relate to the annual Eudora Welty Film and Fiction Festival.

Eudora Welty's portrait, a study for one in the National Portrait Gallery in the Smithsonian, hangs in the library. Miss Welty was awarded the French Legion of Honor in 1996. Closer to home, her name, through her story, "Why I Live at the Post Office," inspired a computer program. Eudora Welty's birthplace in Jackson will soon become the centerpiece for an international writers' center called the Eudora Welty Writers Center.

MARGARET WALKER ALEXANDER LIBRARY

> 2525 Robinson Rd. Open: Mon.–Fri. 10–7, Sat. 10–6. Jackson/Hinds Library System. (601) 354-8911.

Margaret Walker Alexander (1915–1998), poet, novelist, and educator, is honored here by the city where she lived and worked. The library's Margaret Walker Alexander Collection advances understanding of the African-American experiences by providing services for the public on the culture and history of people of African descent. Margaret Walker's internationally known novel, *Jubilee,* was published in 1966.

MARGARET WALKER ALEXANDER RESEARCH CENTER

> Ayer Hall, Jackson State University, Prentiss St. (601) 968-2055.

Dr. Alexander is honored here on the campus where she taught. The center is a national resource for collecting, preserving, and interpreting twentieth century African American History. Its resources include oral history, archival records, and material culture.

Oxford

ROWAN OAK, HOME OF WILLIAM FAULKNER

> Old Taylor Road, off S. Lamar. Open: 10–12 and 2–4 Tues.–Sat., 2–4 only on Sun., closed Mon. Free admission. Owned by U. of MS; Curator, Department of English. (601) 234-3284.

William Faulkner (1897–1962), novelist, bought this house in 1930, the year after he published his novel, *The Sound and the Fury*. Built in 1848, the Greek Revival house sits at the end of a lane lined with tall cedars and oaks. The house's name comes from a legend that the rowan oak brings security and peace, and Rowan Oak was Faulkner's refuge until his death. In 1973 Ole Miss bought the property from the Faulkner family. Rowan Oak was designated a national historic landmark in 1977. Today it appears much as when the author lived there.

Faulkner's office, added in 1950, is a highlight of the house tour. His old Underwood typewriter rests here. Still here is the one-week plot outline, Sunday through Saturday, that Faulkner printed across two walls, for his novel, *A Fable*. Faulkner's first Pulitzer Prize was awarded for that book in 1954; the other was for *The Reivers* (1962). The Nobel Prize came in 1949 and was presented in 1950, before either Pulitzer was awarded.

The grounds still reflect Faulkner's handiwork. He built a stable for his horses and designed the formal garden. As fame grew, his attempts at privacy included a brick wall and a leafy retreat. In his 19 novels and 80 short stories, Faulkner created his little postage stamp of native soil, as he termed it.

In Oxford, Mississippi, tall cedars and oaks line the lane leading to Rowan Oak, Faulkner's home. It is named for a legendary tree, symbol of security and peace.

His mythical Yoknapatawpha County and its county seat, Jefferson, have their counterparts in LaFayette County and Oxford, where Faulkner lived all his life. Settings in Faulkner country are clearly paralleled in Oxford's surroundings. Today a number of sites in the city are Faulkner memorials.

FAULKNER STATUE ON THE COURTHOUSE SQUARE

To mark the Faulkner centennial, a bronze life-size statue of the writer was dedicated here on September 25, 1997. The sculpted Faulkner, holding his pipe and wearing his familiar jacket and hat, sits on a park bench in front of City Hall.

ANNUAL FAULKNER AND YOKNAPATAWPHA CONFERENCE

Since 1974 the Department of English at the University of Mississippi has sponsored this summer event, drawing global participation. (601) 232-7439.

THE FAULKNER COLLECTION

Archives and Special Collections, John Davis Williams Library, Second Floor. Hours: Mon.–Fri. 8:30–5 when university is in session. Closed Sat. and Sun. (601) 232-7408.

The exhibition room displays Faulkner materials in exhibition cases. Among them are items from Faulkner's student days at Ole Miss. Faulkner's Nobel Prize medal and diploma are there along with a number of other international awards. Movie posters on the walls represent the Faulkner novels adapted to the screen, often with the novelist as screen writer. Among them are *Sanctuary* and *Intruder in the Dust*.

The Rowan Oak Papers, discovered in a Rowan Oak broom closet, are a major manuscript find of the twentieth century. The papers contain over 1,800 pages of hand and typewritten drafts of Faulkner's works from 1925 to 1939. Acquired by the University, the Rowan Oak Papers are now the cornerstone of the Faulkner Collection.

Literary Arts Series, 1987.

WILLIAM FAULKNER'S GRAVE

St. Peter's Cemetery, E. 16th St. and Jefferson Ave.

Shaded by ancient oaks, the Faulkner plot is at the foot of a steep hill. A nearby state historical marker erected by the Oxford Rotary in 1990 points to the site:

> William Faulkner
> The Creator of Yoknapatawpha County,
> whose stories about his people
> won him the Nobel Prize, is buried
> twenty steps east of this marker.

Also in St. Peter's Cemetery is the grave of the nurse to William Faulkner and his brothers. Called Mammy Callie by the Faulkners, Caroline Barr, who was born in slavery, lived from 1840 until 1940. Her epitaph is inscribed: "Her white children bless her." Faulkner dedicated *Go Down, Moses* to Caroline Barr, paying tribute to her fidelity and devotion.

Starkville

JOHN GRISHAM ROOM

3100A Mitchell Memorial Library, Mississippi State University. Open: 8–5, Mon.–Fri. (closed 11:30–12:30 and university holidays). (601) 325-2559.

Novelist John Grisham (1955–   ) is honored by his alma mater on the third floor of the Mississippi State University library. Established soon after the appearance of Grisham's first novel in 1989, the room holds the only complete collection in the country of his papers and publications. Manuscripts of *A Time to Kill*, the first of the writer's numerous best-selling novels, are exhibited in Grisham's handwriting. Even index card drawings sketching the book's carefully crafted plot are on display. Drafts of other novels, including *The Client and the Firm*, are also to be seen, as well as all of Grisham's books in both hardback and paperback, translated into 36 languages. Magazine and newspaper articles on display in this spacious room trace John Grisham's astounding writing career.

This passage from Faulkner's Nobel Prize Acceptance Speech in 1950 is on the University of Mississippi library wall in Oxford, Mississippi. It has been moved to an inside wall.

MISSOURI

Branson

THE SHEPHERD OF THE HILLS HOME-STEAD AND OUTDOOR THEATRE

5586 West Highway 76. Open late Apr.–Late Oct. Guided homestead tours: 10 A.M. and 12, 4, and 5:30 P.M. Outdoor Drama: 8:30 nightly, 7:30 after Labor Day. Rates: Adults $19, Children 16 and younger, $9. Homestead Tours: Adults $15, Children Free. (417) 334-4191.

Harold Bell Wright (1872–1944), minister and author, published *The Shepherd of the Hills* in 1907. Phenomenally popular as novel and movie, the story is based on the lives of Wright's Ozark neighbors. Public interest in the people and places of Wright's book began area tourism. By the 1920s the restored Old Matt's Cabin, as the Ross cabin was called in the novel, had become a museum exhibiting furniture and memorabilia associated with the Rosses and Wright. In 1960 performances of an outdoor historical drama based on *The Shepherd of the Hills* began at an amphitheater on the homestead. Its name emphasizes its historical and literary significance as the site of the legend Harold Bell Wright created.

Columbia

THE JOHN G. NEIHARDT COLLECTION

Western Historical Manuscript Collection, 23 Ellis Library, University of Missouri. (573) 882-6028.

Old Matt's Cabin in Branson, Missouri, is the center of The Shepherd of the Hills Homestead and Outdoor Theatre. Harold Bell Wright's 1907 novel began it all.

The papers of writer John G. Neihardt (1881–1973) cover the years from 1908 to 1974, and are composed of two series: correspondence and miscellaneous. The correspondence includes family letters and letters relating to Neihardt's career as teacher and writer. The miscellaneous section includes newspaper clippings covering 60 years, research materials, photographs, drawings, and manuscripts. Neihardt was an instructor and poet in residence at the University of Missouri from 1949 until 1966.

Hannibal

MARK TWAIN PROPERTIES

Hours: June–Aug. 8–6 daily; May 8–5 daily; Apr., Sept. and Oct. 9–5 daily; Nov.–Feb. Mon.–Sat. 10–4, Sun. 12–4; Mar. 9–4 Sat.–Mon., Sun. 12–4. Admission. Mark Twain Home Foundation. (573) 221-9010.

The Mark Twain Boyhood Home and Museum. 208 Hill Street. Associations with Samuel Clemens/Mark Twain (1835–1910) are all around, particularly at this small clapboard house. It was built by his father, Judge Clemens, in 1844, and the family lived here until 1853. Because Twain modeled Aunt Polly's home after this house, *Tom Sawyer* immortalizes several rooms including Tom's bedroom and the dining room. The desk where Twain wrote the classic is also on display. The house was given to the city in 1911.

Next door is the Mark Twain Museum. The stone building, a WPA project, opened in 1937. For sixty years until 1997 when the New Mark Twain Museum opened, its limited quarters overflowed with Twain arti-

Mark Twain Boyhood Museum is in Hannibal, Missouri. The house is the model for Aunt Polly's house in *Tom Sawyer*.

facts, first editions, and memorabilia. Among Twain's personal items exhibited are a famous white suit worn by Mark Twain and the academic gown worn at Oxford when an honorary degree was conferred. Members of the cast of the 1937 David Selznick film, *Tom Sawyer*, attended the museum's opening ceremony.

The New Mark Twain Museum. 120 North Main Street. This modern new facility opened in stages. On July 4, 1997, the second floor area opened, followed by the mezzanine replica of a pilot house in October. In April 1998, the first floor exhibit opened. Initially temporary displays were used while permanent exhibits were planned to be put in place by the summer of 1999. Two themes are the focus of the new museum, Tom Sawyer and Mark Twain.

This bust of Mark Twain is in The Mark Twain Boyhood Home and Museum in Hannibal, Missouri.

Fifteen oil paintings by Norman Rockwell commissioned for special editions of *Tom Sawyer* and *Huckleberry Finn* are on permanent exhibit. Rockwell painted them in Hannibal in 1936. The pilot house exhibits relate to Sam Clemens' career as a riverboat pilot, the basis for his book, *Life on the Mississippi*. The author's pen name, "Mark Twain," a river term meaning two fathoms, or safe water, came from that experience.

Judge Clemens Law Office. Sam's father, John Marshall Clemens, was a justice of peace who presided over court cases here in the early 1840s. One hundred years later the building was saved from destruction and moved to its present site as a gift of appreciation to the city from Warner Brothers Studio. The courtroom inspired the setting of the trial scene in *Tom Sawyer*.

Pilaster House. Corner of Main and Hill Streets. This Greek Revival house is named for its rectangular exterior columns. It was erected in 1836 by the town's first mayor. Dr. and Mrs. Grant lived on the second floor. When the Clemens family lost their home, they lived here a year with their friends, the Grants. Judge Clemens died in the house in 1847. Later the family was able to move back home.

Grant's Drug Store. The Pilaster House's first floor housed Dr. Grant's office and his drug store. Its stock of patent medicines were of the type Aunt Polly relied on in *Tom Sawyer*. In later years the author related some of his mischievous adventures in this house and in his father's law office as well as in his own home. Those escapades were echoed in *Tom Sawyer*.

Becky Thatcher House. 211 Hill Street. This house is directly across the street from the Clemens house. Laura Hawkins lived here in the 1840s. Although Mark Twain said later that she was one of many little girl friends of his early years, he did confirm that she was a model for Becky Thatcher in *Tom Sawyer*. The parlor and a bedroom are restored, and there is a first floor bookstore.

HUCK AND TOM STATUE

At the end of Main Street, a block from the Mark Twain Home and Museum.

Dedicated in 1926, the Frederick Hibbard sculpture is believed to be the world's first statue dedicated to fictional characters. In 1985 the bronze was restored to its original color. The character Huck Finn was partly inspired by a neighborhood boy. Plans are underway to rebuild his home on North Second Street.

Becky Thatcher in *Tom Sawyer* was modeled after a girl who lived in this house across the street from the home of Samuel Clemens in Hannibal.

MARK TWAIN STATUE, RIVERVIEW PARK

North edge of Hannibal.

A statue of Mark Twain stands at Inspiration Point. Also sculpted by Frederick Hibbard, it was given to the city by the state of Missouri. Dedicated in 1913, the bronze statue was restored to its original color in 1987.

MARK TWAIN CAVE

Highway 79 South, 2 miles south of Hannibal. (573) 221-1656.

Settlers had known of the cave's existence since the winter of 1819-20, and it had undergone several name changes before its present one. Although Twain called it McDougal's Cave in his books, it began to be called by the author's name about 1880 after the publication of *Tom Sawyer* in 1876. Visitors then and now want to see the cave where Tom and Becky were lost, and where Injun Joe hid a treasure. Informed guides lead a one-hour tour pointing out places mentioned in Mark Twain's writings. The cave is a registered U.S. Natural Landmark with special historic or scientific significance.

Mansfield

LAURA INGALLS WILDER–ROSE WILDER LANE HISTORIC HOME AND MUSEUM

3068 Highway A, 1 mile east of town. Open: Mar. 1–Oct. 31, Mon.–Sat. 9–5, Sun. 12:30–5:30; June–Aug. open daily until 5:30. Adults $6, Seniors, $5, Students $3, Under 6 free. The Laura Ingalls Wilder Home Association. (417) 924-3626.

This white farmhouse, home of children's author Laura Ingalls Wilder for 63 years, is just as she left it. It began as two rooms built by Laura and Almanzo Wilder in 1895. Here at age 65 Mrs. Wilder began publishing her series of nine internationally famed *Little House* books.

Next door is the Laura Ingalls Wilder–Rose Wilder Lane Museum, full of the Wilders' personal belongings and many items mentioned in the *Little House* books, including Pa's fiddle and Ma's sewing machine. One area focuses on the life and work of Rose Wilder Lane (1886–1968). *Let the Hurricane Roar* is the best known work of the Wilder daughter's varied writing career.

Other Mansfield points of interest are the Laura Ingalls Wilder Library and the Mansfield cemetery, where Laura, Almanzo, and Rose are buried. Related interests in the area include the pageant, *Little House Memories,* which recreates scenes from the series, presented weekends in August through September in Dogwood Valley Park on Highway A.

In 1902 Mark Twain dedicated the plaque that is still seen on the front of the house. In 1936 it opened as the Eugene Field House and St. Louis Toy Museum.

St. Louis

EUGENE FIELD HOUSE AND ST. LOUIS TOY MUSEUM

634 S. Broadway, I-40 Broadway Exit. Open: Wed.–Sat. 10–4, Sun. 12–4. Closed Mon.–Tues., and national holidays. Open Jan. and Feb. by appointment only; Admission: Adults $3, Ages 12–18 $2, Under 12 $.50. The Eugene Field Foundation, Inc. (314) 421-4689.

Eugene Field (1850–1895), the Children's Poet, was born in this federal-style row house and lived here until 1864. The building was then part of a 12-unit structure known as Walsh's Row built in 1845. Mr. Walsh had leased the land from the city school system. In 1902 Mark Twain dedicated a plaque identifying the house as the birthplace of the poet. The plaque is still in place out front. When Walsh's Row was to be razed in 1934, public outcry saved the house. The Board of Education preserved this one unit of the 12. In 1936 the house became a museum after St. Louis public school children raised money for restoration. The museum was operated by the School Board until 1968.

Today the museum exhibits artifacts from Eugene Field's personal collections of pipes, toys, china, and curios. Rotating displays from the museum's large collection include toys from several centuries. Not all are antique, however, as the exhibit of robots, rockets, and space ships attests. Great varieties of dolls make up the permanent displays in the second floor Toy Room. Although Eugene Field became widely known as the "Father of the Personal Newspaper Column," his lasting fame is in keeping with the toy museum aspect of his birthplace. He is best known for his poems for children, including "The Sugar Plum Tree" and "Little Boy Blue."

The Eugene Field House and St. Louis Toy Museum was a new house in 1850 when Field was born here. Today it is a historic treasure in downtown St. Louis, Missouri.

THE ST. LOUIS WALK OF FAME

6200-6400 Delmar Blvd. in the University City Loop, centrally located in the St. Louis area. Open all year. Free. Businessman Joe Edwards is the founder and director of the non-profit organization based at 6504 Delmar. (314) 727-7827.

Four city blocks of large brass stars are embedded in the sidewalk on both sides of the street. Each star bears the name of an individual who has had an impact on the nation's cultural heritage. Each inductee was either born in the city or spent formative or creative years in the area. A wide cross-section of St. Louisans comprise the selection committee. Brief biographies on bronze plaques accompany the stars. Founded in 1988, the walkway glistened with 80 stars by 1998. Sixteen of them represent these individuals who have achieved in literature or journalism:

Maya Angelou was born Marguerite Johnson in St. Louis in 1928. The best-known of her dozen works of prose and poetry is *I Know Why the Caged Bird Sings.* Ms. Angelou's screenplay, *Georgia, Georgia,* was the first by an African American woman to be filmed. Her star is at 6337 Delmar.

William Burroughs was born in St. Louis in 1914. Burroughs was instrumental in shaping the beat generation. His highly influential novel, *Naked Lunch,* was published in 1960. William Burroughs' star is at 6362 Delmar.

Kate Chopin was born Katherine O'Flaherty in St. Louis in 1851. With her marriage came an introduction to the Creole culture, the setting for many of her stories. Her early feminist work, *The Awakening,* is a classic novel. Her star is at 6310 Delmar.

T.S. Eliot was born in St. Louis in 1888 and became a Nobel laureate in 1948. He was awarded the American Medal of Freedom in 1965. Among his well-known works are *Murder in the Cathedral* and *The Wasteland.* Eliot's star is at 6525 Delmar.

Stanley Elkin was born in 1930 and joined the Washington University faculty in 1960. Elkin's well-known novella, *The Bailbondsman,* became a movie. His star is at 6275 Delmar.

Literary Arts Series, 1986.

The St. Louis Walk of Fame is composed of stars and accompanying plaques for honorees. A criterion is that inductees be native St. Louisans, like Burroughs.

Eugene Field was born in St. Louis in 1850. He became a newspaper reporter in the city and then an outstanding Chicago newspaper columnist. Field is best-known for his children's verses including "Wynken, Blynken, and Nod." His star is at 6315 Delmar.

William Gass was born in 1924 and joined the Washington University faculty in 1969. His volumes of critical essays received distinguished recognition. The best-known work by Gass is *In the Heart of the Heart of the Country*. His star is at 6632 Delmar.

A.E. Hotchner was born in St. Louis in 1920. He is best-known for the biography, *Papa Hemingway*, and the novel, *King of the Hill*, which also became a movie. Hotchner's star is at 6608 Delmar.

William Inge was born in 1913. While teaching at Washington University, Inge wrote *Come Back, Little Sheba*, his first play. He received a Pulitzer Prize in drama for *Picnic*, and an Academy Award for his screenplay, *Splendor in the Grass*. Inge's star is at 6624 Delmar.

Marianne Moore was born in St. Louis in 1887. She became the editor of *The Dial*, the most prestigious literary magazine of its time. Moore received the Pulitzer Prize for *Collected Works*, one of her many acclaimed volumes of poetry. Her star is at 6625 Delmar.

Howard Nemerov was born in 1920. He became professor of English at Washington University in 1969. *The Collected Poems of Howard Nemerov* received the 1978 Pulitzer Prize. He was appointed Poet Laureate of the United States in 1988. Nemerov's star is at 6500 Delmar.

Joseph Pulitzer was born in 1847. Before founding the *St. Louis Post-Dispatch*, he was a St. Louis reporter and a Washington correspondent. He left a bequest to create

"OUR REPUBLIC AND ITS PRESS WILL RISE OR FALL TOGETHER"

1847 1947
JOSEPH PULITZER

3¢ UNITED STATES POSTAGE

Joseph Pulitzer Issue, 1947.

the Poet Laureate of the United States in 1992. Her star is at 6273 Delmar.

Tennessee Williams was born in 1911. He attended St. Louis high schools and Washington University. Williams was awarded the Pulitzer Prize in drama for *A Streetcar Named Desire* and *Cat on a Hot Tin Roof.* His star is at 6500 Delmar.

awards honoring advancement in American literature. Accordingly, the Pulitzer Prize was established. Mr. Pulitzer's star is at 6515 Delmar.

Irma Rombauer was born in St. Louis in 1877. Her 1998 induction to the Walk of Fame was for achievement in journalism literature. Her cook book, *The Joy of Cooking,* has become an American kitchen classic. Mrs. Rombauer's star is at 6636 Delmar.

Sara Teasdale was born in St. Louis in 1884. Her volume of poetry, *Love Songs,* received the 1918 Pulitzer Prize for poetry. Teasdale is credited with being a voice for women's achievement. Her star is at 6603 Delmar.

Mona Van Duyn was born in 1921 and moved to St. Louis in 1950. Her seventh book of poetry, *Near Changes,* received the 1991 Pulitzer Prize for Poetry. Mona Van Duyn became

MONA VAN DUYN

BORN MAY 9, 1921

Sidewalks in the University Loop of St. Louis, Missouri, are lined with Walk of Fame stars. A criterion is that inductees live creative years in the city, as Van Duyn has.

Stoutsville

SAMUEL L. CLEMENS BIRTHPLACE

Hwy. 107 and Route U. *(The village of Florida existed here in 1835. Today its mailing address is Stoutsville.)*

A Missouri red granite monument marks the original location of the small cabin where Samuel Langhorne Clemens (Mark Twain) was born on November 30, 1835. The cabin has been moved one-fourth of a mile away to the museum at the Mark Twain State Park. The monument has also been moved. In 1914 it was erected at the intersection of Main and Mill streets, main thoroughfares in the village of Florida. Today the village is almost deserted; only the concrete platform which originally supported the monument marks the intersection, one-half block north of the birthplace. In 1964 concern for the preservation of the granite monument with its bronze bust of Mark Twain resulted in its removal to the nearby museum. Two years later the granite marker was again relocated, this time to the actual site of the author's birth. It is inscribed:

> In this village was born
> November Thirtieth
> 1835
> Samuel Langhorne Clemens
> Mark Twain
> He cheered and comforted a tired world

MARK TWAIN BIRTHPLACE, MARK TWAIN MEMORIAL MUSEUM, MARK TWAIN STATE PARK AND HISTORIC SITE

Off Missouri Hwy. 107. Open: Daily except New Year's Day, Easter, Thanksgiving, and Christmas; Hours: Mon.–Sat., 10–4, Sun. 12–6 (12–5 from Nov. 1–Mar. 31). Admission: Over Age 12,

This granite marker stands at the exact location of the cabin where Mark Twain was born in Florida, Missouri. The frontier village had 20 other houses then.

$2., 6–12, $1.25, Under 6, free. (573) 565-3449.

Samuel L. Clemens (1835–1910) was born in this two-room cabin, then located nearby in the village of Florida. After the cabin was restored, it was moved in 1930 to the Mark Twain State Park established here in 1924. It is now sheltered in the Mark Twain Birthplace Museum, built in 1960. The cabin in furnished in frontier Missouri style. A plaque at the front door reads:

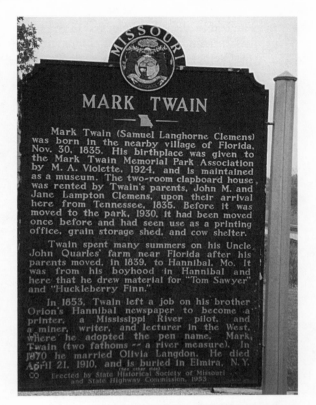

> Into the narrow limits of this
> Cabin was born Samuel Clemens, who,
> As Mark Twain, lived to cheer and
> Comfort a tired world.

Among the museum's exhibits is a collection of Mark Twain's books translated in approximately 60 languages, an exhibit on early steamboats and one on Twain's inventions. There is also an exhibit devoted to Jane Clemens, Samuel's mother. Her rocking chair and other artifacts are displayed.

Top: This historical marker stands in the Mark Twain State Park. The park was established in the 1920s through efforts of the Mark Twain Memorial Park Association. *Bottom:* The Mark Twain birthplace cabin has a kitchen (right side) and a bedroom. The large Clemens family lived here only a few months before seeking a bigger home.

The bed in the cabin belonged to her family. Numerous paintings and photographs of the Clemens family are in evidence. The Hartford Furniture Collection is made up of seven pieces of furniture from Twain's Connecticut home. They were purchased from his daughter Clara in 1951. In the 1920s this only survivor among the three Clemens daughters gave singing concerts to benefit the establishment of the Mark Twain Memorial. A museum highlight is the 1876 manuscript of *The Adventures of Tom Sawyer* for English publication.

MONTANA

Choteau

A.B. GUTHRIE, JR. EXHIBIT

> Old Trail Museum, 823 N. Main. Hours: Summer, Daily May 15–Sept. 15; Winter Tues.–Sat.; Sept. 15–May 15, 10–3. Admission: Adults $2, Children $.50. (406) 466-5332.

A.B. Guthrie, Jr. (1901–1991), novelist, is remembered here in his home town by an exhibit reflecting highlights of his life and work. After *The Big Sky*, the first of Guthrie's sweeping novels about Montana, was published in 1947, the author returned to Choteau to live and write near what he called the Rocky Mountain Front. The museum display includes the old typewriter Guthrie used to write his epic works. Photographs are here, too, along with his books and stories. Guthrie received the 1950 Pulitzer Prize for *The Way West;* he also wrote acclaimed screenplays for *Shane* and *The Kentuckian*. A scrapbook represents his journalism career in Lexington, Kentucky. The newspaper publications reflect Guthrie's 20-year absence from Choteau. Guthrie's regard for Montana was mutual. The state changed its nickname from "Treasure State" to "The Big Sky" and gave him the Governor's Award for Lifetime Achievement in the Arts.

NEBRASKA

Bancroft

THE NEIHARDT CENTER

> Corner of Elm and Washington streets, 2 blocks W. of Main Street. Hours: Mon.–Sat. 9–5, Sun. 1:30–5. Call to verify winter weekend hours. (402) 648-3388.

Dedicated in 1976, the Neihardt Center memorializes John G. Neihardt (1881–1973), Nebraska's Poet Laureate. Neihardt lived in Bancroft from 1900 until 1920. The center houses a museum, library, and research facility as well as the Neihardt Study. The building, erected at this site in the 1890s, was rented by Neihardt from 1911 to 1920. Here he began his epic poem, "A Cycle of the West." The Neihardt Study was entered in the National Register of Historic Places in 1970. Exhibits at the center relate the story of the poet's appreciation for Indian culture, evident in his book, *Black Elk Speaks*. The John G. Neihardt State Historic Site is a branch museum of the Nebraska State Historical Society.

Chadron

Mari Sandoz Heritage Room

10th and Main St., Chadron State College Administration Bldg., Rm. 225. Hours vary. By appointment. Mari Sandoz Heritage Society. (308) 432-6276.

The life and work of Mari Sandoz (1896–1966), biographer, historian, and novelist, is traced through displays and archives of the Sandhills author. Historical items and memorabilia reflect her focus on the High Plains, especially the western Nebraska homesteaders and Native Americans. Mari Sandozs' books, the most famous of which is *Old Jules*, are there, also. The Mari Sandoz Heritage Society will begin construction in September 2000 of the Mari Sandoz High Plains Center. It will be housed in the 1929 Chadron College library and

will also be a research repository for the region.

Elmwood

The Bess Streeter Aldrich House and Museum

The Elms, 204 East "F" St., and Bess Streeter Aldrich Museum, 124 West "D" St. Hours for both sites: Wed., Thur., Sat. and Sun., 2–5; other times and groups by appointment. Admission: Adults: $3, Children 6–12: $2, Family rate: $10. (404) 994-3855.

Bess Streeter Aldrich (1881–1954), novelist and short story writer, lived at The Elms from 1922 until her death. Here she was widowed shortly before her second book was published, and here she continued to write while rearing her four children. The house, containing the Aldrich furniture and

Trees like the one to the left inspired the Aldrich home's name, The Elms, and the town, Elmwood. Aldrich set many stories in Elmwood, calling it by other names.

memorabilia, opened to the public in 1992. In the study, Mrs. Aldrich, an O. Henry Award winner, wrote her 14 books. Throughout her home are evidences of the intertwining of Mrs. Aldrich's writings and her surroundings. A quilt embroidered with the title of her first novel, *The Rim of the Prairie,* features a scene from the story. Visitors hear of the link between a displayed Mason Family flour sack and Aldrich's first book, *Mother Mason,* a collection of short stories.

The Bess Streeter Aldrich Museum was dedicated in 1990. Among the displays of memorabilia are magazines carrying Aldrich stories. They demonstrate her popularity with such leading publications as *Ladies' Home Journal.* The cover of the December 10, 1938, edition of *The Saturday Evening Post* announces the beginning of the serialization of Aldrich's *Song of Years.* Copies of all of the Aldrich books are available at the museum. The Bess Streeter Aldrich Foundation, which owns and operates the home and the museum, annually hosts *Bess Streeter Aldrich Remembrance Day* and *Rim of the Prairie Day.*

Gordon

MARI SANDOZ ROOM

117 Main St. Open Mon.–Fri. 9–5, Sat. 9–12. Free. (308) 282-9972.

This museum honors author Mari Sandoz, who wrote about growing up on a ranch nearby. In addition to an extensive display of Sandoz memorabilia, free pamphlets are available, pointing out local Sandoz connections.

MARI SANDOZ GRAVE

South of town on a hillside overlooking her father's Sandoz Sand Hill ranch.

MARI SANDOZ MUSEUM AND RESEARCH LIBRARY

South and east of Gordon. (308) 282-1687.

This bust of Mari Sandoz is in the Nebraska Hall of Fame at Lincoln, Nebraska. Sandoz is known as the Storycatcher of the Plains.

Memorabilia and research materials are maintained in the home of Mari Sandoz's sister.

Lincoln

NEBRASKA HALL OF FAME

State Capitol Building, second floor.

The Hall of Fame's bronze busts and accompanying plaques memorialize Nebraskans in varied walks of life. Every two years, the Nebraska Hall of Fame Commission nominates one person for induction. Three Nebraskan writers honored by induction into the Hall of Fame are Willa Cather (1962), Bess Streeter Aldrich (1971), and John Gneisenau Neihardt (1974).

WILLA CATHER GARDEN

University of Nebraska campus.

This garden at Willa Cather's alma mater commemorates her centennial (1873–1973). By quoting Cather's *My Ántonia*, a plaque set into the garden walkway pays tribute to the writer. She is acknowledged as the first author to celebrate Nebraska.

Omaha

WILLA CATHER BRANCH

Omaha Public Library, 1905 S. 44th St. Hours: Mon.–Wed. 12–8; Thurs.–Sat. 10–5:30; Sun. 1–5. (402) 444-4851.

Top: This bust of Willa Cather is in the Nebraska Hall of Fame in Lincoln, Nebraska. The tribute reads: "The life of pioneers she described, a literature of Nebraska she created." *Bottom left:* This bust of Bess Streeter Aldrich stands in the Rotunda of the State Capitol in Lincoln, Nebraska. *Bottom right:* This bust of John Gneisenau Neihardt is in the Nebraska Hall of Fame in Lincoln, Nebraska. The tablet calls him "Epic poet of the West, historian, philosopher, friend of the American Indian."

A portrait of Willa Cather hangs in this library named for the novelist.

Red Cloud

WILLA CATHER PIONEER MEMORIAL

State Historic Site, 326 N. Webster. Open: Daily 8 A.M.–5 P.M., Tours: 9:30, 11, 1:30, 2:45, 4. Admission. Owned and maintained by the Nebraska State Historical Society. (402) 746-2653.

Much of this Webster County town where novelist Willa Cather (1873–1947) grew up is a memorial to her. In 1965 the state legislature proclaimed the western half of the county Catherland. The Willa Cather Memorial Prairie borders Red Cloud, Cather's home town. Founded in 1955, The Willa Cather Pioneer Memorial (WCPM), has restored five buildings closely associated with Cather's life and writing. Tours begin at the WCPM offices and bookstore downtown on Webster Street. An introductory film explores Red Cloud's close connection with Cather, beginning with her childhood bond with the pioneer country and her eventual role as Nebraska's interpreter to the world.

The Willa Cather State Historic Site is a branch museum of the Nebraska Site Historical Society. It is housed next door in the Farmers and Merchants Bank Building. Exhibits include photographs, Cather's high school diploma, and her desk. Academic regalia and certificates mark Cather's honors from numerous universities. The Willa Cather Archives are housed here, as well.

Willa Cather's childhood home, the jewel of the restored buildings, contains Cather family furniture and memorabilia. In the parlor the family Bible where Willa changed her birth year from 1873 to 1876 can be seen. Of special interest is Willa's upstairs bedroom, still with the wallpaper and

Willa Cather's childhood home is the centerpiece of the Willa Cather Pioneer Memorial in Red Cloud, Nebraska. Cather used the house as a setting for several stories.

The plow logo on this sign is inspired by *My Ántonia*. Ántonia is a hired girl, patterned after a friend of Cather's. She worked at this house, near Cather's home.

a magic lantern she took as pay at her schoolgirl job at the drug store. The Cather house appears in *The Song of the Lark*, "Old Mrs. Harris," and "The Best Years."

Four other buildings are included in the Willa Cather Pioneer Memorial. One is the Burlington Depot, a scene in several Cather short stories. Two restored properties are church buildings, St. Juliana Catholic Church, a significant setting in *My Ántonia*, and Grace Episcopal Church, where Cather was a member. The last, currently undergoing restoration, is the Red Cloud Opera House, where Willa Cather graduated and gave the valedictory address. Six of Cather's twelve novels used Red Cloud as a setting and were inspired by Cather's experiences growing up here. The preserved sites are woven into the tapestry of *A Lost Lady*, *One of Ours*, *Lucy Gayheart*, *The Song of the Lark*, *O Pioneers!*, and, particularly, *My Ántonia*.

The WCPM also operates a bookstore carrying all of the books written by Willa Cather and a large number of works written about her. Maps are available here for walking tours of Red Cloud and driving tours of the surrounding countryside. Both guides are dotted with sites closely related to Cather's novels, especially *My Ántonia*. A Cather Country sign identifies the farm home of Willa Cather's uncle, whose house and family are the inspiration for Cather's Pulitzer prize winning novel, *One of Ours*. The WCPM sponsors Willa Cather conferences, which annually attract international visitors to possibly the most described village in literature.

NEVADA

Reno

NEVADA WRITERS HALL OF FAME

University Library, University of Nevada.

Two Nevada writers are inducted annually into the Writers Hall of Fame begun in 1988. The names of all members are prominently displayed on the wall of the University Library's Hall of Fame alcove. There a Smithsonian-style display features the honored writers and their literary works. One of the first inductees was Walter Van Tilburg Clark (1909–1971). He became a national literary figure with the 1940 publication of his novel *The Ox-Bow Incident*. Another prominent inductee is Will James (1892–1942). He is best known for *Smoky, The One Man Horse*, which won the 1927 Newbery Medal.

—NEW HAMPSHIRE—

Derry

FROST FARM

1 and ¾ miles S. of the Derry Circle on Rt. 28 Open: Spring and Fall, Sat.–Sun. 10–6; Summer, Thurs.–Mon. 10–6. Last tour at 5. Admission: Adults $2.50. New Hampshire Division of Parks and Recreation. (603) 432-3091, 271-3556.

Robert Frost (1876–1963) moved to this white clapboard farmhouse with his wife and infant daughter in 1900. The last three children were born in this house built in 1885. The farm his grandfather bought for him gave the young, unpublished poet a place to hone his craft. He combined farming, poetry writing, and teaching at nearby Pinkerton Academy. His textbook for teaching sophomore English at the academy is here. During his ten years on the farm, Frost wrote many of the poems in his first three volumes; the first two volumes were published in England, where the Frosts moved in 1912.

In the barn a video narrated by Mr. Fred Rogers of PBS and Lesley Frost Ballantine, Frost's oldest child, guides viewers through the house and comments on the family's life here. Frost's unorthodox farming methods, such as putting the cows on a midnight milking schedule and the chickens in cages on wheels, are explored.

Long after the Frost years in Franconia, this property became a commercial garage and auto graveyard called Frosty Acres.

The plaque at Frost Farm in Derry, New Hampshire, states that the poet owned the farm from 1900–1911 and developed there the poetic voice that would win him four Pulitzers.

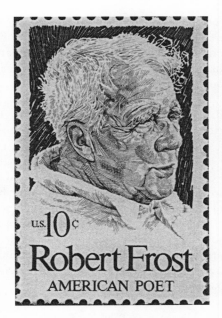

Robert Frost Issue, 1974.

Mrs. Frost's dry soapstone sink is here, rescued from the junkyard. Her wedding china is in the dining room. An upstairs attic area was the bedroom of a summer farm hand who inspired "Death of the Hired Man." The site became a registered national historic landmark in 1968.

Frost's neighbor here insisted on the ritual of spring mending time. From that experience came the famous "Mending Wall." The rock fence is still standing. Close by is the "West Running Brook." The introductory video shows the poet reading "The Road Not Taken." At this farm he took the road which was to win him four Pulitzer prizes and world renown. In 1961 Frost recited his "The Gift Outright" at the Kennedy presidential inauguration.

Restored in the 1960s under the guidance of the Frost daughter, the house now looks as it did when the poet lived here, even down to a 1902 red wallpaper pattern from Sears.

Franconia

THE FROST PLACE

Ridge Road. Directions: I-93 N., Ex. 38, Rt. 116 S for 1 mi. Signs mark the

The Frost Place in Franconia is the second New Hampshire farm owned by Robert Frost. Three hours north of Boston, it is in the White Mountains.

way to the Frost Place. Open: Memorial Day to end of June: Sat. and Sun. 1–5; July 1 to Columbus Day: every day except Tues., 1–5. Admission: Adults $3, Seniors $2, ages 6–12 $1.25, Under 6 free. Owned and operated by the town of Franconia. (603) 823-5510.

Robert Frost (1876–1963) lived with his family in this 1859 farmhouse from 1915 to 1920. Exhibits feature Frost family photographs and memorabilia. Mrs. Frost's marble kneading board is here. Beside a worn leather Morris chair is displayed an article from the *Boston Post*, February 14, 1916, picturing the poet seated in that chair. Frost's practice of composing Christmas card poems for special friends began here in 1915 with "Christmas Trees." Some poems from the Christmas series are displayed. *Mountain Interlude* contains the poetry Frost wrote while living here in the White Mountains.

Behind the house is The Henry Holt Center, built in 1976 as a memorial from the Frost publisher. It exhibits Frost-related photographs and memorabilia. A video shown here provides an overview of Frost's life and works, concentrating on the Franconia years. That era began when the Frosts returned from England where his first volumes, *A Boy's Will* and *North of Boston*, were published. This place was selected so that he could write while farming. In *New Hampshire*, Frost includes a piece about buying the farm.

On the half-mile poetry trail, plaques of Frost poems are attached to trees. Frost wrote "Goodbye and Keep Cool" after he had finished planting the orchard where the poetry trail ends today. The Frost Place is also a center for the arts. Its summer resident crafts poetry and gives readings in the timbered barn. The Frost Place is on the National Register of Historic Places.

OLD MAN OF THE MOUNTAIN—
GREAT STONE FACE

Franconia Notch, I-93 S, Ex. 2. The Old Man of the Mountain Museum

Discovered in 1805, this rock profile in Franconia Notch, New Hampshire, became famous with Hawthorne's 1850 story, "The Great Stone Face."

and Preservation Association, Division of Parks and Recreation.

Twelve hundred feet above Profile Lake in the White Mountains, a rock profile is clearly visible. Two of the five ledges which form the profile are anchored deep in the cliff and support the two above. The profile measures 40 feet from chin to forehead. In 1955 a United States commemorative postage stamp was issued to mark The Old Man of the Mountain's sesquicentennial. A plaque at Profile Lake provides this tribute to Nathaniel Hawthorne:

It was Nathaniel Hawthorne's beautiful tale, "The Great Stone Face," written in 1850 that immortalized the Old Man of the Mountain.

Jaffrey Center

Willa Cather Grave

The Old Burying Ground, behind the Meeting House, off Rt. 124.

A glass-enclosed sign beside the Meeting House explains Willa Cather's connection with the place. Beginning in 1917 Cather spent summers in Jaffrey for 20 years. She stayed in the old Shattuck Inn, high up in a dormer room. Her Pulitzer Prize novel, *One of Ours*, drew upon the wartime diary of a Jaffrey Center physician.

The grave of novelist Willa Cather (1873–1947) is in the shaded southwest corner of the aged cemetery. The epitaph reads:

THE TRUTH AND CHARITY OF HER GREAT SPIRIT WILL LIVE ON IN THE WORK WHICH IS HER ENDURING GIFT TO HER COUNTRY AND ALL ITS PEOPLE

"…that is happiness to be dissolved into something complete and great"
From *My Ántonia*

Willa Cather's grave is at the Old Burying Ground, Jaffrey Center, New Hampshire. Some of the graves here date back to the Revolutionary War.

Portsmouth

THE THOMAS BAILEY ALDRICH MEMORIAL

Strawberry Banke Museum, I-95 Exit 7. Follow the green signs 1.7 mi. to the waterfront. The entrance is located on Hancock Street. Hours: mid–Apr. to Nov. 1, 10–5 daily. Admission: Adults $12, Seniors $11, Youths (7–17) $8, 6 and under free. (603) 433-1106.

Thomas Bailey Aldrich (1836–1907), author and editor, lived in this house during the formative years of his boyhood, from 1849 until 1852. Owned by Aldrich's grandfather, Thomas D. Bailey, the house was built in 1798. It has changed very little, architecturally, in two hundred years. Bailey recorded his experiences while living in this house with his grandfather in *The Story of a Bad Boy*, the most famous of his numerous books. Published in 1870, it introduced an innovative approach to children's stories.

After Aldrich died, his family repurchased the house and restored it as a memorial to him. The possessions of the drawn-from-life characters in *The Story a Bad Boy* are on exhibit. Grandfather Nutter, Aldrich's name for his grandfather; Miss Abigail, who managed the household; Kitty Collins, the Irish maid; and Tom Bailey, the author himself, are all represented. This house on Court Street was one of the first in the country to be restored to a specific era and for a specific purpose. Mark Twain, whose *Tom Sawyer* was influenced by *The Story of a Bad Boy*, attended the 1908 dedication. The house was operated by the Thomas Bailey Aldrich Memorial Association until it became a part of Strawberry Banke in 1979.

——— NEW JERSEY ———

Camden

WALT WHITMAN HOUSE

330 Mickle Blvd. Access is from Rt. 30 in Camden which is across the river from Philadelphia. Open Wed.–Sun. No fee. State of New Jersey. (609) 964-5383.

This two-story wood frame house was the poet's home from 1884 until his death in 1892. It is the only house the "Good Gray Poet" ever owned. The townhouse with modest Greek Revival details contains some furniture which belonged to Whitman along with a number of his personal artifacts and his copies of his published works. The house is operated by the New Jersey Division of Parks and Forestry. A National and State Historic Site, the 1845 house has recently undergone complete restoration.

WALT WHITMAN ASSOCIATION

326 Mickle Blvd., open by appointment. (609) 541-8280.

The Association maintains the Walt Whitman Research Library and offers literary and historical programs.

WALT WHITMAN CULTURAL ARTS CENTER

2nd and Cooper streets. (609) 964-8300.

Dedicated to promoting the poet's legacy of artistic excellence.

CAMDEN CITY HALL

Sixth Street between Federal and Market streets.

Around the top of this 1929 Art Deco building is inscribed the city's unofficial

Left: **Walt Whitman House in Camden, New Jersey, was the poet's last home. Although afflicted by strokes, he continued here to perfect his poetic opus,** *Leaves of Grass.* **Right: A marker at Whitman's tomb in Harleigh Cemetery, Camden, New Jersey, identifies him as author of** *Leaves of Grass,* **a "most extraordinary piece of wit and wisdom."**

motto, "In a dream I saw a city invincible"—Whitman.

WALT WHITMAN'S TOMB

> Harleigh Cemetery, Vesper and Haddon Ave. (609) 963-0122.

This 70-ton granite family crypt was designed by Whitman, who had his parents and other family members re-interred here. A plaque identifies Walt Whitman as the author of *Leaves of Grass.* The tomb is a pilgrimage site, especially on Whitman's birthday, May 31.

New Brunswick

THE JOYCE KILMER BIRTHPLACE

> 17 Joyce Kilmer Avenue. Open weekdays by appointment 9–3. Free. Joyce Kilmer Centennial Commission. (800) 572-0524.

This frame house in the vernacular Greek revival style is the birthplace of poet Joyce Kilmer (1886–1918). The oldest section of the house is a Dutch farmhouse built about 1780. After the local American Legion Post bought the house in 1929 for its headquarters, the upstairs front bedroom where Kilmer was born was dedicated as the *Joyce Kilmer Shrine*. Kilmer, who enlisted in World War I and was killed in action in France, is best-known for his poem, *Trees*. Cut down in 1963, the area's ancient "Kilmer Oak" may have inspired the 1913 poem. The Kilmer birthplace is now owned by the city. In addition to the street where the house is located, other area memorials include Joyce Kilmer Park and Camp Kilmer. Brooklyn's Kilmer Square and Joyce Kilmer Memorial Forest in North Carolina are two of numerous other Kilmer memorials.

Princeton

THE MANUSCRIPTS ROOM

Firestone Library, Princeton University.

The Manuscripts Room is dedicated to the memory of historical novelist, James Boyd, Class of 1910. Boyd's words are inscribed on a silver tablet:

> The Belief that leads to a democracy is this: that every man has something sacred about him. This sacredness is held to be inherent and perpetual: no ruler, no religion, no group of men, no government is justified in violating it. It is the first principle of man's life and nothing takes precedence over it.

Rutherford

WILLIAM CARLOS WILLIAMS CENTER FOR THE PERFORMING ARTS

Park Avenue at Williams Plaza. (201) 939-2323.

This center honors Dr. William Carlos Williams (1883–1963), poet and physician. He maintained his medical practice in Rutherford while writing some forty vol-

umes of poetry. It has been said that Williams delivered more babies than any other poet who ever lived. An imagist, he was one of the twentieth century's most influential poets. Possibly his most famous poem is "The Red Wheelbarrow." The Williams Center provides children's theater, lectures, musical events, and drama. Dr. Williams' photograph hangs in the center's lobby.

FREE PUBLIC LIBRARY

150 Park Avenue. (201) 460-3033.

The William Carlos Williams Collection here is housed in its own room. Memorabilia, books, and papers were collected by the Williams family and by townspeople acquainted with him. Although the collection focuses on Williams as a physician and citizen of the community, his desk and chair and tapes of the poet are here. Williams' Pulitzer Prize diploma is on display. That 1963 award for poetry was for *Pictures from Breughel and Other Poems*.

Wayne Township

TERHUNE SUNNYBANK MEMORIAL PARK

East shore of Pompton Lake in Passaic County. Maintained as a Wayne town park.

Sunnybank, home of novelist Albert Payson Terhune (1872–1942), was featured in many of his dog stories. The most famous collie, Lad of Sunnybank, is buried with other dogs on the estate with headstones marking their graves. Called "The Place" in Terhune's books, the house built by his parents in 1861 was torn down in 1969, unsalvageable. A park entrance sign identifies Terhune as a world famous author of dog stories.

NEW MEXICO

Cimmaron

SETON MEMORIAL LIBRARY AND PHILMONT MUSEUM

Philmont Scout Ranch. Open daily June–Aug.; Mon.–Fri. Sept.–May. (505) 376-2281.

Ernest Seton (1860–1946), author, artist, and naturalist, helped to organize the Boy Scouts of America in 1910. As First Chief Scout, he wrote the first American Scout manual. Included in the museum collections are many of his over 40 major books on wildlife and nature. His best known work is *Wild Animals I Have Known*. Seton's art work, mammal skins, and Indian artifacts are exhibited. The site was dedicated in 1967.

The Seton Memorial Library and Philmont Museum is at Philmont Scout Ranch, Cimmaron, New Mexico. Ernest Seton, author and Boy Scouts founder, is memorialized here.

NEW YORK

Austerlitz

STEEPLETOP, THE MILLAY COLONY FOR THE ARTS

Three hours north of NYC in eastern New York. Not open to the general public. (518) 392-3103.

This 600-acre farm estate was the home of Edna St. Vincent Millay (1892–1950). Since 1973, the Millay Colony for the Arts has provided residencies to talented writers, composers, and visual artists. The Millay Colony for the Arts is supported by private individuals and foundations as well as by the New York State Council on the Arts and the National Endowment for the Arts.

Cooperstown

FENIMORE HOUSE MUSEUM

Rt. 80, Lake Road. Open Apr.–Dec.; Apr.–May, Tues.–Sun., 10–4 (Closed Mon.—except Memorial Day); June–Sept., Daily, 9–5; Oct.–Dec., Tues.–Sun., 10–4 (Closed Mon., Thanksgiving and Christmas). Admission: Adults $9, children 7–12 $4, 6 and under free. NY State Historical Association. 1-888-547-1450.

The Cooper Room on the museum's first floor is devoted to America's first novelist, James Fenimore Cooper (1789–1851). On exhibit are furnishings from Cooper's home, portraits and memorabilia of the author and his family, and exhibits of scenes from his novels. His most famous novels, *The Leatherstocking Tales*, were inspired by his growing-up years on the frontier. Many sites around Otsego Lake still bear the names given them in Cooper's books. From 1813 to 1817 Cooper and his wife lived in a small farmhouse called Fenimore on this site. The farmhouse was torn down in 1932, and replaced with this Neo-Georgian mansion, which became a museum in 1945.

East Hampton

HOME SWEET HOME MUSEUM

14 James Lane, Open: Mon.–Sat., 10–4 Sun. 2–4. Admission: Adults, $1.50, Children, $1. (516) 324-0713.

This saltbox farmhouse circa 1660, childhood home of author, actor, and playwright John Howard Payne (1791–1852), commemorates his life and work. The museum takes its name from Payne's famous song, "Home Sweet Home." The house contains furnishings from various periods as well as textiles and English ceramics. The village has owned and operated the house as a museum since 1928. Tours provide information on the collections and on John Howard Payne.

Elmira

SAMUEL CLEMENS GRAVE SITE

Woodlawn Cemetery, north end of Walnut Street.

MARK TWAIN EXHIBIT

Chemung County Historical Society, 415 E. Water St. Open: Tues.–Sat.

ELMIRA COLLEGE SITES

Open daily in summer, rest of the year by appointment. Free. (607) 735-1941.

Mark Twain Exhibit. Hamilton Hall. Includes memorabilia and a 20-minute video.
Mark Twain Study. Park Place.

Home Sweet Home Museum occupies this 1660 salt box house in East Hampton, New York. The museum's name is from a song by John Howard Payne, born in the house.

Designed as a replica of the pilot house of a Mississippi River steamboat, the study was given to Elmira College in 1952. Twain wrote here often.

Quarry Farm. Twain's summer home.

Huntington Station

WALT WHITMAN BIRTHPLACE STATE HISTORIC SITE AND INTERPRETIVE CENTER

246 Old Walt Whitman Road, West Hills, Huntington. Open all year, Wed.–Fri. 1–4, and 11–4 on Sat. and Sun. From Memorial Day to Labor Day, open daily 11–4. Closed holidays. Group Tours Mon.–Sat., 9–5 by appointment. Free. Call (516) 427-5240.

The Visitors Interpretive Center provides an in-depth look at Walt Whitman (1819–1892), one of America's leading poets.

Exhibits include numerous portraits of Whitman as well as original letters and manuscripts. Significant artifacts on view are the desk which Whitman used as a young schoolteacher on Long Island and first editions of his brilliant book of poetry, *Leaves of Grass*, and his autobiographical *Specimen Days*.

A multi-media area features a video about Whitman and a recording of his voice.

Behind the Interpretive Center is the house where Walt Whitman was born. Built by the poet's father, the two-story cedar-shingled house is constructed of hand-hewn beams connected by wooden pegs. Several other unusual features of construction and architecture characterize the house, which is on the National Register of Historic Places.

The birthplace of Whitman, the Good Gray Poet, was built in 1819. Its innovative features include a corbeled chimmey and large twelve-over-eight pane windows.

Malone

THE WILDER FARMHOUSE

> Open: Memorial Day weekend to Labor Day, Tues.–Sat. 11–4, Sun. 1–4, other times by appointment. Admission: Adults $3, Students $1.50. (518) 483-1207.

This is the childhood home of Almanzo Wilder, husband of Laura Ingalls Wilder. Her book, *Farmer Boy*, one of the *Little House* series, takes place here. Appearing just as described in the book, the Wilder home has been almost completely restored.

New York City— The Bronx

THE HALL OF FAME FOR GREAT AMERICANS

> Campus of Bronx Community College of the City University of New York— University Avenue and West 181 Street. Open daily 10 A.M. to 5 P.M. Free admission. For directions and reservations for guided group tours, call (212) 220-6003.

Founded in 1900, this original Hall of Fame in America is a National Landmark. The principal feature is the 630-foot-long, open-air Colonnade, which encircles three neoclassic buildings including the circular Gould Memorial Library. The granite Colonnade houses the bronze portrait busts of the approximately 100 honorees. They are

American men and women whose lives contributed significantly to human advancement. A multi-million dollar restoration program has now been completed, and plans are underway to reopen the election process. Twenty-three writers of the eighteenth and nineteenth century have been inducted into the Hall of Fame. The Gallery of Authors is the section of the Colonnade where most of these writers are honored. Bronze tablets recessed in the wall beneath the busts carry inscriptions of significant statements by those honored. A printed tour guide provides the following biographical data. The number before each name designates the location of the bust in the Colonnade.

25. Thomas Paine (1737–1809) Elected 1945
His pamphlets, *Common Sense* and *The Crisis,* were significant in the cause of the American Revolution.

26. Benjamin Franklin (1706–1790) Elected 1900
Although honored as printer, diplomat, scientist, statesman and inventor, his writings, especially *Poor Richard's Almanack*, are classics.

59. Henry David Thoreau (1817–1862) Elected 1960
Essayist, philosopher and poet, author of *Civil Disobedience*, an essay which has influenced world leaders in challenging injustices.

61. Stephen Collins Foster (1826–1864) Elected 1940
Composed popular ballads and songs including "O Susanna" and "Old Folks at Home."

76. Booker T. Washington (1858–1915) Elected 1945
First head of Tuskeegee Institute, author of *Up from Slavery.*

81. Phillips Brooks (1835–1893) Elected 1910
Wrote the words to "O Little Town of Bethlehem"; Episcopal bishop and renowned preacher.

86. Walt Whitman (1819–1892) Elected 1930
The poet of democracy. His most famous works are *Leaves of Grass* and his elegies for President Lincoln including "O Captain, My Captain."

87. Sidney Lanier (1842–1881) Elected 1945
Poet, musician, and literary critic in the post–Civil War South.

88. James Fenimore Cooper (1789–1851) Elected 1910
Creator of epic tales of American frontier life. Best known for the Leatherstocking Tales, including *Last of the Mohicans*.

89. Harriet Beecher Stowe (1811–1896) Elected 1910
Author of antislavery novel *Uncle Tom's Cabin*, which influenced the coming of the Civil War.

90. John Lothrop Motley (1814–1877) Elected 1910
Historian whose books compared political freedom and tyranny.

Left: **Prominent Americans Issue, 1968.** *Right:* **Walt Whitman, Famous Americans Issue, 1940.**

91. Samuel Langhorne Clemens, Mark Twain (1835–1910) Elected 1920
Writer, lecturer, and humorist whose works expressed uniquely American outlook.

92. Francis Parkman (1823–1893) Elected 1915
Historian who wrote of the American frontier in richly descriptive narratives including *The Oregon Trail.*

93. Edgar Allan Poe (1809–1849) Elected 1910
Poet, critic, and short-story writer. Innovator in detective story genre and tales of horror and the supernatural.

94. George Bancroft (1800–1891) Elected 1910
Historian whose ten-volume *History of the United States* saw American history as progressing from despotism to democracy.

95. William Cullen Bryant (1793–1878) Elected 1910
Poet, editor of *The New York Evening Post.* Favored workmen's rights, opposed slavery, and helped found the Republican party.

96. John Greenleaf Whittier (1807–1892) Elected 1905
Poet who wrote "Snowbound"; journalist who wrote fiery abolitionist articles. Devout Quaker whose poems have become church hymns.

97. Oliver Wendell Holmes (1809–1894) Elected 1910
Poet, essayist, and physician; renowned for his poem, "Old Ironsides."

98. James Russell Lowell (1819–1891) Elected 1905
Poet, editor, teacher, diplomat, and po-litical satirist, a foremost man of letters, editor of *The Atlantic Monthly*; author of *The Biglow Papers.*

99. Ralph Waldo Emerson (1803–1882) Elected 1900
Poet, essayist, lecturer, and the outstanding American philosopher of his day; a founder of American transcendentalism.

100. Nathaniel Hawthorne (1804–1864) Elected 1900
Novelist and short-story writer. His writings consider the human tragedy that results from radical social change.

101. Washington Irving (1783–1859) Elected 1900
Satirist, historian, and ambassador; America's first man of letters to achieve international prominence.

102. Henry Wadsworth Longfellow (1807–1882) Elected 1900
First American author to support himself through poetry; "The Courtship of Miles Standish" and other epic poetry celebrated America.

EDGAR ALLAN POE COTTAGE

Poe Park, The Grand Concourse and East Kingsbridge Rd. Open: Sat. 10–4, Sun. 1–5, Weekdays by appointment. Admission: $2. Administered by The Bronx County Historical Society in arrangement with NYC Department of Parks and Recreation. (718) 881-8900.

Left: **Prominent Americans Issue, 1967.** *Right:* **James Russell Lowell Famous Americans Issue, 1940.**

In 1846 Poe, seeking healthful surroundings for his ill wife, rented this rural farmhouse. The room
and bed where she died and Poe's rocking chair are all here.

Poe lived in this last home from 1846
until his death in 1849. Here he wrote several of his famous poems including "Annabel
Lee" and "The Bells." To introduce the
guided tour, a film set against the backdrop
of nineteenth century New York City presents Poe's life and literary career. Exhibits
about Poe and his wife Virginia are on display, along with furniture of the 1840s including pieces belonging to Poe. Visitors to
the cottage learn that poverty required Poe's
mother-in-law to sell the furniture for the
Poes' funeral expenses. Fortunately, it has
been retrieved. In 1902 the city of New York
created Poe Park directly across from the
Cottage. In 1913 the city bought the 1812
cottage and moved it to Poe Park. The national historic landmark has been a museum
since 1917.

Brooklyn

Ezra Jack Keats Memorial

Prospect Park—Imagination Play-
ground, off Ocean Ave., south of Lincoln Road. For directions call (718)
965-8952.

Brooklyn-born Ezra Jack Keats (1916–
1983), children's author and illustrator, is
honored here by a bronze statue commemorating three of his books, *The Snowy Day*,
Whistle for Willie, and *Peter's Chair*. Atop a
large boulder, the sculpture depicts Peter sitting on the ground reading a book while
reaching down to pet the nose of his dog,
Willie. Three carved steps make the statue
easily accessible to children, and a child-
sized chair awaits a young reader just below
the boulder. The sculpture was commissioned by the Ezra Jack Keats Foundation so

that children can find a space at the park dedicated to storytelling and reading. The sculpture is the first public statue to honor the African American child.

CLEMENT CLARK MOORE TRIBUTE

Trinity Cemetery, Broadway and 155th Street.

Clement Clark Moore (1779–1863), professor and author, is honored each year at Christmas at his grave site. The New York Institute for Special Education sponsors the event, a reading of Moore's famous poem, *A Visit from St. Nicholas*. Begun in 1911, the commemoration is the oldest continuous holiday tradition in New York City.

New York City— Manhattan

AMERICAN MUSEUM OF NATURAL HISTORY

Central Park W. at 79th St. Hours: Sun.–Thur. 10 A.M.–5:45 P.M., Fri. and Sat. 10 A.M.–8:45 P.M. Closed Thanksgiving and Christmas. For tour information, directions, and admission rates call (212) 769-5100.

The Isaac Asimov Fund supports an annual Isaac Asimov Memorial Lecture at the museum's Hayden Planetarium. Asimov (1920–1992) wrote over 500 books spanning the realm of human knowledge, especially science. Topics for the memorial lectures include astronomy, astrophysics, and humanity's place in the universe. Through the memorial lectures, the legacy of Asimov's contributions to public science education at the Museum will continue.

A permanent exhibit devoted to John Burroughs, naturalist, is also at the museum. The American Museum of Natural History's Margaret Mead Film and Video Festival was organized in 1977 to honor Margaret Mead's pioneering use of film in documenting cultures. Margaret Mead served as curator of ethnology at the museum.

OSCAR HAMMERSTEIN II CENTER FOR THEATRE STUDIES

Columbia University School of the Arts, Morningside Heights, Upper Manhattan.

This artistic and production arm of the Division of Theatre Arts was named for the renowned playwright, lyricist, Oscar Hammerstein II (1895–1960). He was an alumnus of Columbia University, where he also studied law. At Columbia Hammerstein wrote and acted in several student plays.

COUNTEE CULLEN REGIONAL LIBRARY

104 West 136th Street. (212) 491-2070.

In 1941 one of the oldest New York Public Library branches moved to its present location. The branch library building was a new construction on the site of the home of A'Lelia Walker, a patron of the arts during the Harlem Renaissance. In 1951 the library was renamed for the Harlem poet, Countee Cullen (1903–1946). Cullen was a teacher, neighbor and long-time friend of the branch library.

The library is the permanent home of a monument to Countee Cullen composed of two portraits of the poet. The "bronze" Countee Cullen reaches out to a bust of himself created in the classical mode for a poet, a white marble-like bust crowned with a laurel wreath. The monument rests on a base inscribed with lines from Cullen's poetry.

JAMES WELDON JOHNSON COMMUNITY CENTERS, INC.

2201 First Ave. (212) 860-7250.

Founded in 1948, this East Harlem settlement house is named for the African-American poet, novelist, journalist, civil rights leader, and diplomat. Before Johnson (1871–1938) achieved recognition in these and other fields, he was an educator; a middle school in Jacksonville, Florida, also bears his name. The JWJ Community Center focuses on children and youth.

New York City—Queens

LANGSTON HUGHES COMMUNITY LIBRARY AND CULTURAL CENTER

The Queens Borough Public Library, 100-01 Northern Boulevard, Corona, NY. Hours: Mon. and Fri. 10–6, Tues. 1–6, Wed. and Thurs. 1–8, Sat. 10–5. Closed Sun. (718) 651-1100.

In 1969 the library's doors were officially opened to the public. Langston Hughes, the well-known black poet and playwright, became the library's namesake. The library's archives document the African-American experience. Cultural celebrations are regular features at the library. The Annual Langston Hughes Celebration Day at the library honors the poet's life and legacy.

Roslyn

THE KNOTHOLE MUSEUM

Christopher Morley Park, Searington Road, North Hills. Open May–Aug. weekends, 12–4. Also July and Aug., Wed.–Fri. 10 A.M.–2 P.M. Maintained by Nassau County Department of Parks and Recreation. (516) 571-8130.

The Knothole is the name Christopher Morley (1890–1957) gave his studio on the grounds of his home in Roslyn Estates. In 1934 the literary columnist, novelist, and poet built the pine cabin as a writing place and retreat. Already a well-established writer, lecturer, and editor, he produced a variety of additional works at the Knothole. After Morley's death, the Christopher Morley Knothole Association was formed to buy, restore, and maintain the Knothole as a memorial to house Morley memorabilia. Morley's cabin is hospitable with its built-in bunks, cheery fireplace, and reading area. Morley's books and papers are on exhibit. A very early pre-assembled bathroom is a unique feature of the Knothole. It and the studio were designed by the famed Buckminster Fuller.

Roslyn Harbor

CEDARMERE, HOME OF WILLIAM CULLEN BRYANT

225 Bryant Avenue. Open weekends May through early Nov., Sat. 10 A.M.–4:45 P.M. and Sun. 1 P.M.–4:45 P.M. Free admission. Maintained by Nassau County Department of Recreation and Parks, Division of Museum Services. (516) 571-8130.

This large house was the Long Island home of the prominent nineteenth century poet, civic leader, and editor of the *New York Evening Post*. Bryant (1794–1878) purchased the house in 1843 as a rural haven away from the stress of the city. The original farmhouse dates to 1787. Bryant made a series of enlargements and renovations to the house during the years he lived there. He designed the showplace gardens. Bryant's grandson added a sunken garden and a stone bridge to the grounds. A plaque featuring Bryant's picture is set in a wall of the sunken garden. In 1975 Bryant's great-granddaughter gave the seven-acre estate to Nassau County to preserve as a memorial to William Cullen Bryant. Cedarmere is on the National Register of Historic Places.

Roxbury

THE JOHN BURROUGHS NATURE CENTER

Catskill Mountains. Open summer

weekends and for planned programs. Operated by Woodchuck Lodge, Inc.

John Burroughs (1837–1921) is America's most famous literary naturalist. He was born on his family's farm near Woodchuck Lodge. At age 73 Burroughs took the lodge, now a museum, as his summer home. When Burroughs was a youth, his favorite place on the farm was Boyhood Rock, where he sat and studied nature around him. His volumes of philosophical nature essays heralded the modern conservation movement.

When Burroughs left Woodchuck Lodge for what was to be the last time on October 26, 1920, he noted the date in pencil on a porch siding, and added the words "Leave today." Visitors see the lodge much as he left it. On his eighty-first birthday, Burroughs was buried at the foot of Boyhood Rock on the hill above Woodchuck Lodge. Burroughs Memorial Field, including the gravesite, is a New York State Historic Site.

Top: This plaque of William Cullen Bryant's visage is set into a garden wall at Cedarmere, his home at Roslyn Harbor, New York. *Bottom:* Cedarmere was William Cullen Bryant's home the last 35 years of his life. It sits on Bryant Road in exclusive Roslyn Harbor on Long Island.

Seneca Falls

THE NATIONAL WOMEN'S HALL OF FAME

76 Fall Street. Open: May–Oct., Mon.–Sat. 9:30–5; Nov.–Apr., Wed.–Sat. 10–4; Sun., Year Round, 12–4. (315) 568-2976.

Created in 1969, the National Women's Hall of Fame honors women citizens whose contributions in a wide variety of areas have benefited America. Fifteen inductees are well known as writers:

Louisa May Alcott (1832–1888)
Her *Little Women* and other books were the first books readily available for young girls. Her experiences as a volunteer Civil War nurse were published as *Hospital Sketches*. She used her pen to support women's rights.

Maya Angelou (1928–)
She has written poetry, fiction, and plays. The title of her popular autobiography, *I Know Why the Caged Bird Sings*, emphasizes the restrictions of the black artist's spirit. At the inauguration of President Clinton in 1993, Angelou read her poem, "On the Pulse of Morning," which celebrates America.

Gwendolyn Brooks (1917–)
Poet and novelist. When Brooks received the Pulitzer Prize in 1949, she was the first African-American recipient.

Pearl S. Buck (1892–1973)
First woman to receive the Nobel Prize for literature and the first woman to receive both the Nobel and Pulitzer. A humanitarian, she fostered a bridge between American and Asian cultures with her novel, *The Good Earth,* and with her founding of international organizations to benefit orphaned children.

Rachel Carson (1907–1964)
Marine biologist whose books on the sea brought knowledge of the oceans to the public. An environmental activist, Carson warned of dangers of indiscriminate use of pesticides in her landmark 1962 book, *Silent Spring.*

Willa Cather (1873–1947)
Her novels immortalized the pioneer experience in Nebraska. She was awarded the Pulitzer Prize in 1923 for *One of Ours,* which provides a graphic picture of the First World War.

Elizabeth Jane Cochrane (1864–1922)
Better known as Nellie Bly, America's best reporter, this trail-blazing journalist pioneered investigative reporting.

Emily Dickinson (1830–1886)
Virtually unpublished during her lifetime, Dickinson is now considered one of the world's great lyric poets. She developed poetic techniques widely used in the twentieth century.

Margaret Fuller (1810–1850)
Author, early literary critic, and first foreign correspondent. Her *Woman in the Nineteenth Century*, a classic of feminism, helped arrange the Seneca Falls Women's Convention in 1848.

Julia Ward Howe (1819–1910)
Suffragist and author of "The Battle Hymn of the Republic."

Zora Neale Hurston (1891–1960)
Author and anthropologist who contributed much to preserving the African-American heritage with her factual and fictional accounts.

Helen Keller (1880–1968)
Author, humanitarian and lecturer. Left blind and deaf from illness when a young child, she supported legislation to protect newborns from blindness.

Margaret Mead (1901–1978)
World-renowned anthropologist; a trailblazer in the study of child-rearing practices and the first to conduct psychologically oriented field studies. Her *Coming of Age in Samoa* had a great impact on the study of adolescence.

Harriet Beecher Stowe (1811–1896)
Mrs. Stowe was the first American woman to earn a living by writing. Her concerns about slavery resulted in her best-selling novel, *Uncle Tom's Cabin* (1852). The book is considered influential in starting the Civil War.

Edith Wharton (1862–1937)
First woman recipient of the Pulitzer Prize (1921); first woman to receive a Yale honorary doctorate, and one of the few civilians to receive the Chevalier of the Legion of Honor for her humanitarian work in France in World War I.

Staten Island

EDWIN MARKHAM LIBRARY AND MANUSCRIPTS COLLECTION

Horrmann Library, 1 Campus Road.
Wagner College, 631 Howard Avenue.

The poet Edwin Markham (1852–1940) bequeathed his personal papers and library of 15,000 volumes to Wagner College, where his son was on the faculty. The strengths of the collection are in literature, the social sciences, religion, and philosophy. Included in Markham's manuscripts are letters from well-known political and literary figures of the early twentieth century. The poet's best-known work is "The Man with a Hoe," protesting exploitation of the downtrodden. The 1899 poem is said to be the single most commercially successful poem ever published.

Tarrytown

SUNNYSIDE, WASHINGTON IRVING'S HOME

Hudson River shore, W. Sunnyside Lane, off Rt. 9. Open: Jan.–Mar., Sat. and Sun., 10–4; Apr.–Dec., Wed.–Mon., 10–5. Admission. Owned and operated by Historic Hudson Valley. (914) 332-6659.

Sunnyside is the three-dimensional autobiography of Washington Irving (1783–1859). In 1835 after Washington Irving completed his diplomatic career as Minister to Spain, he bought a 1690 cottage, remodeled, and enlarged it. Above the front door, he mounted a tablet inscribed to his *bouwmeester*, the Dutch word meaning architect. The Romantic style house reflects aspects of the writer's varied interests and experiences. Irving, born in Dutch New York, built his

Sunnyside, Washington Irving's romantic stone cottage at Tarrytown, New York, incorporates his interests in Dutch, Scottish, and Spanish history.

This bust of Washington Irving stands at Sunnyside, his home at Tarrytown, New York.

reputation as a writer on the history and legends of early Dutch settlers, including the famed *Legend of Sleepy Hollow* and *Rip Van Winkle,* hence the stepped parapet and the weathervanes, reflective of Dutch architecture. Irving added the fanciful date, 1656, high on the west side.

The house incorporates influences of Irving's almost 20 years of living abroad. Sir Walter Scott had helped him begin his literary career in Europe. He also influenced Irving architecturally. Among the similarities between Scott's Abbotsford and Irving's Sunnyside are steeply pitched roofs and cluster-columned chimney stacks. The tower Irving added to his house was inspired by monastery towers in Spain, where Irving served as Minister to Spain for four years. His book, *The Alhambra,* draws on his experiences in that country.

Costumed guides point out Irving's landscape designs, including ivy and wisteria planted by the author. Visitors hear the story of America's first successful, internationally known author and his architecturally unique house. Irving's study, a highly documented period room, is just inside the front door. Its furnishings belonged to Irving as did many of the others throughout the house. The oak partners desk was a gift from his publisher upon the completion of his monumental biography of George Washington, the pinnacle of Irving's writing career. Visitors to Sunnyside hear of Irving's being presented to George Washington, his namesake, as a young child. Everywhere at Sunnyside are signs of the bachelor owner's creativity and hospitality to friends and to his big extended family. Various brothers and their children made their home at Sunnyside.

In 1945 the Irving family sold Sunnyside to John D. Rockefeller, Jr., who acquired it for Historic Hudson Valley, and in 1947 the National Historic Landmark was opened to the public. Careful and authentic restoration of house and grounds continues. Among the numerous special events at Sunnyside is the annual celebration of Washington Irving's birthday. When Irving died, Tarrytown schools and businesses closed for his funeral. He had asked to be buried with the Bible of his young fiancée who died suddenly. Visitors see her miniature which Irving always carried with him. Irving is buried at Sleepy Hollow Cemetery, Tarrytown.

West Park

SLABSIDES AND JOHN BURROUGHS SANCTUARY

> Open House at Slabsides is held twice a year, the third Saturday in May and the first Saturday in October. Owned and maintained by the John Burroughs Association.

John Burroughs, the famed naturalist and essayist, built this rustic retreat. He named it Slabsides because the outer walls were slabs, the first cut—including the bark—from the log. Burroughs wrote that his purpose was "a fresh cut at life."

West Point

THE WARNER HOUSE

Constitution Island (part of United States Military Academy) across the Hudson River from West Point. Open: June–Sept., Wed.–Thur. Boat leaves West Point South Dock at 1 and 2 P.M. Admission: Adults $9., Sr. and 6–16 $8, age 5 and under, $2. For reservations, call (914) 446-8676.

The two-hour tour of the site includes a boat ride on the Hudson River to the island and an escorted tour of the Warner House. The oldest part of the 17-room Warner House was built in 1774 and includes a thick stone wall dating to Revolu-

tionary War days. The eight-room Victorian Wing was built in 1836.

The two daughters of the family, Susan Bogert Warner (1819–1885) and Anna Bartlett Warner (1827–1915), were well-known writers in the nineteenth century. Susan, who used the pseudonym Elizabeth Wetherell, wrote the best-seller, *The Wide, Wide, World,* published in 1850. Anna is best-known for writing the words to the children's song, "Jesus Loves Me." Using the penname Amy Lothrop, she also wrote books for juveniles and on religion and gardening. The Anna B. Warner Memorial Garden on the site is planted with the same flowers Anna Warner described in her 1872 book, *Gardening by Myself.*

The Constitution Island Association, organized in 1916 to preserve the Warner House and its family furnishings, still maintains the living museum's artifacts and the award-winning old-fashioned garden. The federal government maintains the building

Warner House on Constitution Island, West Point, New York, is the home of two nineteenth century writers, Anna and Susan Warner.

and grounds. Tours of 15 rooms of the house are conducted by guides in Victorian-style costumes. The site is a National Registered Landmark.

——NORTH CAROLINA——

Asheville

THE THOMAS WOLFE MEMORIAL

Thomas Wolfe Memorial Plaza, 52 N. Market Street. Open: Apr. 1–Oct. 31, 9–5 Mon.–Sat., 1–5 Sun.; Nov. 1–Mar. 31, Tues.–Sat. 10–4, Sun. 1–4, Closed Mon. Admission: Adults $1, Children $.50. NC Department of Cultural Services. (828) 253-8304.

During the years that novelist Thomas Wolfe (1900–1938) was growing up in this rambling Victorian house, it was operated by his mother as a boarding house, named "Old Kentucky Home." In his autobiographical novel, *Look Homeward, Angel* (1929), Wolfe immortalized the house, which he called "Dixieland." A number of the house's 29 rooms are described in the work. When the house became a memorial in 1947, the original Wolfe family furnishings and photographs were intact, arranged much as Thomas Wolfe knew them. A 1998 fire forced an interruption of interior tours. Restoration is projected to require three years. In the interim, visitors can still tour

Thomas Wolfe grew up in this house in Asheville, North Carolina. During that time it was a boarding house owned by his mother. Wolfe used it as a setting for his novels.

the exterior and see the bronze cast of Wolfe's large shoes in the yard.

The Visitors Center, directly behind the house, was dedicated in 1997. It features an audio-visual overview of Wolfe's family and his childhood in Asheville, the inspiration for his stories. The exhibit hall presents Wolfe's life and works. A highlight of the self-guided tour is the display of furnishings from Wolfe's New York apartment, including the desk and typewriter where he wrote his massive novels. Two of the four works have the word "home" in their title. The Thomas Wolfe Memorial became a state historic site in 1976.

THOMAS WOLFE GRAVE

Riverside Cemetery, 53 Birch Street, Hours: Mon.–Fri. 8–4. (828) 258-8480.

Thomas Wolfe is buried here in the family plot. His gravestone is inscribed with passages from two of his novels. A plaque on the gate of this historic cemetery also commemorates Thomas Wolfe. Given by the Thomas Wolfe Society in 1988, the memorial plaque is inscribed with a passage from *Look Homeward, Angel*.

WILLIAM SYDNEY PORTER GRAVE

Riverside Cemetery.

The final resting place of William Sidney Porter (1862–1910) is an almost obscure grave. The short story writer, who became famous as O. Henry, spent time in Asheville for his health during the last years of his life. His second wife was an Asheville native.

Chapel Hill

PAUL GREEN THEATRE

Country Club Rd., University of North Carolina campus. (919) 962-7529.

This plaque is on the gate of Riverside Cemetery in Asheville, North Carolina.

Paul Green (1894–1981), dramatist, was honored in 1976 by the university where he was an alumnus and professor. The theatre named for him is near the site where Green's freshman play was presented. It earned the first of countless honors awarded to this distinguished writer. Among them are the 1927 Pulitzer Prize, Dramatist Laureate of North Carolina, and posthumous induction into the Theatre Hall of Fame. *The Lost Colony* is the first of Green's 20 outdoor historic dramas staged annually across the country.

THOMAS WOLFE COLLECTION

North Carolina Collection, Wilson Library, University of North Carolina. (919) 962-1172.

Thomas Wolfe was graduated from the University of North Carolina in 1920. In 1950 his family donated materials which began The Thomas Wolfe Collection. It now includes Wolfe manuscripts, correspondence, clippings, photographs, original illustrations, and recordings. Use of parts of the Collection requires prior permission, but the North Carolina Collection's Reading Room exhibits selected Wolfe items.

Flat Rock

CARL SANDBURG HOME NATIONAL HISTORIC SITE

1928 Little River Road, I-26 Upward Rd. exit, or US Hwy. 25 to Little River Rd. Hours: Daily 9–5, except Christmas Day; Fee: $3 for guided house tour, age 16 and under free. National Park Service. (828) 693-4178.

This 240-acre farm, Connemara, was the last home of Carl Sandburg (1878–1967), poet and Lincoln biographer. The family moved to this 22 room antebellum house in 1945. By then Sandburg had already been awarded the Pulitzer Prize in history for *The War Years*, the last four volumes of his six-volume Lincoln biography. Six years after moving to the farm in the western North Carolina mountains, Sandburg received

Connemara was Carl Sandburg's home at Flat Rock, North Carolina, for his last 22 years.

Sandburg played the guitar as a young man traveling the country. In 1953 at his 75th birthday party in Chicago, he entertained the guests with his guitar music.

another Pulitzer, this time in poetry for his *Complete Poems*. Here he also wrote his autobiography, *Always the Young Strangers*.

Today Connemara looks just as the Sandburgs left it. The first two floors reflect the family's simple lifestyle. The dining room also served as the family gathering room. Floor to ceiling bookcases are filled with many volumes of the Sandburgs' library. Of special interest is the downstairs study filled with the writer's papers, books, and personal belongings, the trademark cap, bandanna, and cigar. Orange crates serve as bookcases and typing table. In the living room the family enjoyed music. Sandburg's guitar here is a reminder of his love of folk songs. He performed them publicly, and he collected them into two volumes of *The American Songbag*. Sandburg's third floor office and adjoining bedroom are not accessible to visitors, but photographs are shown while the tour guide narrates.

A video tour of the house and video interviews with Mr. and Mrs. Sandburg are also available. At the barn visitors see the remnant of Mrs. Sandburg's prize-winning Chikaming goat herd bred and raised on the farm with the help of the three Sandburg daughters. For guests, Sandburg sometimes wrote out by hand a copy of his famous little poem, "Fog." Today visitors often leave Connemara with a printed copy from the bookstore in hand.

FLAT ROCK PLAYHOUSE, THE STATE THEATRE OF NORTH CAROLINA

2661 Greenville Highway, across the road from the Carl Sandburg Home. NHS park amphitheater. (828) 693-6795.

This summer stock theatre performs plays based on Sandburg's life and works, including Norman Corwin's *The World of*

Carl Sandburg and Sandburg's *Rootabaga Stories.*

Greensboro

O. HENRY EXHIBIT

Greensboro Historical Museum, 130 Summit Ave. Hours: Tues.–Sat. 10–5, Sun. 2–5, Closed Mon. Admission: Free. (336) 373-2043.

William Sydney Porter (O. Henry) was born in 1862 near Greensboro. This year-round highlight features memorabilia from the popular short-story writer. His works are also the subject of occasional lectures and special events at the museum.

RANDALL JARRELL LECTURE HALL

University of North Carolina—Greensboro, Walter Clinton Jackson Library, 1000 Spring Garden Street.

Randall Jarrell (1914–1965), poet, professor, and critic, taught at Women's College of the University of North Carolina from 1947 until his death. The ceremony for the dedication and naming of this auditorium was held in 1970.

THE RANDALL JARRELL COLLECTION

University of North Carolina–Greensboro Walter Clinton Jackson Library Special Collections and Rare Books Division. (336) 334-5246.

In the 1950s Jarrell began donating his manuscripts to the library. Through other donations, the collection has expanded to include literary and biographical materials and a collection of news clippings about the poet.

LOIS LENSKI COLLECTION

Walter Clinton Jackson Library, Special Collections and Rare Books Division, University of North Carolina–Greensboro. (336) 334-5246.

Lois Lenski (1893–1974) donated to the library her manuscripts and illustrations of her early American children's books from 1958 until 1968. Lenski stated that she chose the institution as a repository because of an affection for North Carolina she developed while writing *Blue Ridge Billy* in the state. In 1962 the University of North Carolina at Greensboro conferred an honorary doctorate upon Lois Lenski.

Southern Pines

THE BOYD HOUSE

Weymouth Center for the Arts and Humanities, 555 East Connecticut Avenue. Open: The Boyd House is open Mon.–Fri. 10–4. Gardens and grounds open daily. (910) 692-6261.

In the 1920s James Boyd (1884–1944), historical novelist, renovated and expanded a portion of his grandfather's 1904 home, Weymouth. During the construction, the Boyds lived in a gatehouse on the property. There Boyd wrote his first and most successful book, *Drums.* The Boyd house became a gathering place for literary guests in the 1920s and 1930s. The Friends of Weymouth purchased the estate in 1979 to establish a cultural center. The Weymouth Lectures and Writers-in-Residence are two of the center's year-round programs. The Boyd house is listed on the National Register of Historic Places.

THE NORTH CAROLINA LITERARY HALL OF FAME—BOYD ROOM, WEYMOUTH

In 1996 The North Carolina Writers' Network established this program. It is housed at Weymouth in the upstairs room that was the study of novelist James Boyd. Visitors see a framed photograph of each inductee and take home individual flyers for each writer. Plans are underway to provide further information through taped recordings.

The 1998 induction ceremony expanded the membership of the North Carolina Literary Hall of Fame to 26.

The Boyd Room honors all of the inductees: James Boyd, Charles Waddell Chestnutt, Jonathan Daniels, Wilma Dykeman, John Ehle, Inglis Fletcher, John Hope Franklin, Paul Green, Bernice Kelly Harris, O. Henry, George Moser Horton, Harriett Jacobs, Randall Jarrell, Gerald Johnson, John Charles McNeill, Joseph Mitchell, Pauli Murray, Guy Owen, Frances Gray Patton, Sam Ragan, Louis Rubin, Thad Stem, Jr., Richard Walser, Jonathan Williams, Manly Wade Wellman, and Thomas Wolfe.

NORTH DAKOTA

Medora

THE MALTESE CROSS RANCH CABIN

Theodore Roosevelt National Park.

This Maltese Cross Ranch cabin belonged to Theodore Roosevelt (1858–1919). Now at the park's south entrance, it was originally located seven miles south of Medora. Built to Roosevelt's specifications in 1884, the one and one-half story pine log cabin was exceptional for its time with its wooden floors and three separate rooms. Theodore Roosevelt owned a number of items in the cabin today, including the rocking chair and a wicker-lined canvas clothing trunk.

In this ranch cabin, years before he became President, Roosevelt wrote several volumes beginning with reminiscences of his life in the Badlands. At the living room desk, a fold-out writing table in the hutch, he wrote *Hunting Trips of a Ranchman* in 1884–85, followed by another book on ranch life and hunting. During his years as a rancher, he also completed a biography of Thomas Hart Benton, and *The Winning of the West* in two volumes. Roosevelt remained a lifelong prolific writer, completing some 20 volumes in all. In 1947 the 70,000-acre national park was established commemorating America's twenty-sixth president.

OHIO

Cincinnati

HARRIET BEECHER STOWE HOUSE

2950 Gilbert Ave., State Route 3 and US Route 22. Open: Tue.–Thur. 1–4, Closed, Fri.–Mon. and holidays. Free admission. Ohio State Historical Society. (513) 632-5120.

Before her marriage, Harriet Beecher Stowe (1811–1896), moved with her father to this house in 1833. It had just been built for the president's residence at Lane Seminary. Here Stowe first heard tragic stories of slaves seeking freedom. These experiences helped to inspire *Uncle Tom's Cabin*, published in 1852. The Stowe House is a museum leased by the Citizens' Committee on Youth. The organization operates the house as a cultural and educational center which promotes black history and oversees Stowe Park.

Clyde

CLYDE PUBLIC LIBRARY

222 W. Buckeye.

A collection of books by Sherwood Anderson (1876–1941) and a short documentary video are available here. Clyde is the pattern for *Winesburg, Ohio*, Anderson's 1919 classic. Anderson grew up here in the 1880s and 1890s in two houses which are still standing but without identifying markers. They are identified on a pamphlet that also points out sites of numerous scenes described in the novel. The pamphlet is available at the library.

Columbus

THE JEROME LAWRENCE AND ROBERT E. LEE THEATRE RESEARCH INSTITUTE

1430 Lincoln Tower, 1800 Cannon Drive, Ohio State University. Hours: Fall, Winter and Spring Quarters, 9–5, Closed weekends and holidays. (614) 292-6614.

Founded in 1951, the institute was renamed in 1986 for Ohio-born playwrights Jerome Lawrence (1915–) and Robert E. Lee (1918–1994). The collaborators have received many prestigious awards in the theatre. Acclaimed as modern classics, their works include *Inherit the Wind*. The institute's microfilm archives the Western world's theatre history. Holdings include copies of rare documents, posters, playbills, and costume and scene designs.

The Thurber House in Columbus, Ohio, is the setting for "The Night the Ghost Got In" and other Thurber essays. Thurber was at OSU when he lived here from 1913 to 1918.

THURBER HOUSE MUSEUM

77 Jefferson Ave., 1 block W. of I-77 and Broad St. Open: 12–4 year-round except legal holidays. Admission: Free; Guided tours, Adults: $2, Seniors and students: $1.50, under school age: free. Docent guided tours include a reading and are by appointment and on Sun. from 12–4. (614) 464-1032.

James Thurber (1894–1961), writer and cartoonist, lived in this house with his parents, brothers, and a slew of family dogs. During Thurber's years here, from 1913 to 1918, he was a student at Ohio State University. He immortalized the house with his essays in *My Life and Hard Times*. Listed on the National Register of Historic Places, the 1873 Victorian home was restored and opened in 1984 as a literary center and museum of Thurber materials. The Thurber Country Bookstore occupies the former dining room, the setting for "The Night the

Literary Arts Series, 1994. (Based on drawing by Thurber.)

Ghost Got In." Among the programs of the Thurber House and the Thurber Center next door are a Writer-in-Residence program and a number of literary activities featuring nationally known authors. The Thurber Prize for American Humor encourages the art of humor writing.

Between the two buildings is the Centennial Reading Garden, where sculptures of Thurber dogs greet visitors. Thurber introduced them in his cartoons and writings. Nearby is another sculpture, *The Unicorn in the Garden*, which Thurber fans will recognize from one of the Thurber pieces about the battle of the sexes. The Thurber House is part of the Jefferson Center for Learning and the Arts.

JAMES THURBER GRAVE

> Green Lawn Cemetery, 1000 Green Lawn Avenue. The tombstone is inscribed with Thurber's illustration for *The Last Flower*, his poignant parable.

THURBER THEATRE

> Located in the Drake Union at 1849 Cannon Drive, Ohio State University.

For the opening of this 600-seat Continental theatre, Lawrence and Lee wrote the opening play, *Jabberwock: Improbabilities Lived and Imagined by James Thurber in the Fictional City of Columbus, Ohio*. Thurber himself contributed to the performing arts. He co-authored a play, *The Male Animal* and wrote the award-winning revue, *A Thurber Carnival*. His *My World and Welcome to It* became a television show, and his celebrated story, "The Secret Life of Walter Mitty" became a movie. Although Thurber never earned a degree at Ohio State University, he was awarded one posthumously in 1995.

Dayton

PAUL LAURENCE DUNBAR STATE MEMORIAL

> 219 N. Paul Laurence Dunbar St., 4 blocks east of US 35. Open: Memorial Day–Labor Day, 9:30–5, Wed.–Sat., 12–5, Sun.; Sept.–Oct. 9:30–5, Sat., 12–5, Sun.; Nov.–May, by appointment Mon.–Fri. Admission: Adults: $3, Children 6–12: $1.25, age 5 and under free. (513) 224-7061, 224-5625.

American Arts Series, 1975.

Paul Laurence Dunbar (1872–1906), poet, purchased this house upon returning to his native city in 1903 and lived here until his death. His mother continued to live in it, preserving her son's possessions, until her death in 1934. Two years later, Dunbar House became the first state memorial to honor an African American when the state bought and dedicated it. The Ohio Historical Society, delegated to administer the memorial, opened it in 1938. Dunbar's study is preserved. The bicycle built by the Wright Brothers and given to Dunbar, their former classmate, is on exhibit, as is a ceremonial sword, the gift of President Theodore Roosevelt. The House hosts programs on Dunbar, his legacy as a voice for black dignity, and African-American history.

Lucas

MALABAR FARM STATE PARK

4050 Bromfield Road. Admission: Adults $3., Children $1. Big House Tours: May 1–Memorial Day 10–5,

Above: Malabar Farm at Lucas, Ohio, the home of author Louis Bromfield, became an international showplace. The Big House is of Western Reserve architecture. *Inset:* Bogart and Bacall were married at Malabar's Big House in 1945. One of its 32 rooms was their honeymoon suite. Malabar is an Asian word for beautiful valley.

closed Mon.; Memorial Day–Labor Day, Daily 10–5; After Labor Day–Oct. 31, 10–5, closed Mon. and holidays; Nov. 1–Dec. 1, 11–5, closed Mon. and holidays. (419) 892-2784.

This 900-acre farm was the home of Louis Bromfield (1896–1956), Pulitzer Prize winning author and agriculturist. Malabar, named for India's Malabar Coast, the setting for Bromfield's novel, *The Rains Came*, became an international showplace in the 1940s. Also popular with Hollywood celebrities, the farm was the setting for the Bogart-Bacall wedding. The Big House, a blend of colonial and Victorian styles, is the 32 room main residence. The house contains the Bromfields' furniture, paintings, and custom wallpaper.

A smoke house, dairy barn, and a number of other farm buildings are a part of the working farm. In addition, the site includes a youth hostel, a farmhouse, and the cemetery where Bromfield and his family are buried. In 1972 the property was deeded to the state of Ohio with the agreement that it would continue to operate as a working farm emphasizing agricultural conservation.

Norwich

NATIONAL ROAD/ZANE GREY MUSEUM

8850 E. Pike, US Rt. 40. Open: Mar.–Apr., Wed.-Sat.: 9:30–5, Sun. and holidays: 12–5; May–Sept., Mon.–Sat.: 9:30–5, Sun. and holidays: 12–5; Oct.–Nov., Wed.–Sat.: 9:30–5, Sun.: 12–5, Closed Holidays. Admission: Adults $5, Children 6–12 $1.25. The Ohio Historical Society. (740) 872-3143, (800) 752-2602.

Zane Grey (1872–1939), premier Western novelist, was born and lived his first 17 years at Zanesville, ten miles east of this site. In 1973 this museum opened on the National Road which Zane Grey's ancestor had helped to begin. A wing of the museum is

devoted to Zane Grey. His study is recreated at the museum. Many of Grey's manuscripts and first editions, including *Riders of the Purple Sage*, are exhibited along with a collection of his trophies and other memorabilia.

Oxford

McGUFFEY MUSEUM

Oak and Spring Streets. Open: Sat. and Sun. 2–4 P.M. Closed in August. Administered by Miami University Art Museum. For tours call (513) 529-2232.

William McGuffey (1800–1873), educator and textbook author, built this house in the early 1830s while a professor at Miami University. Hanging in the parlor are portraits of McGuffey and his wife, painted during his tenure on the faculty here (1826–1836). The library exhibits a collection of McGuffey Eclectic Readers. Eighteen thirty-six marked the beginning of the series of these famous books for the first six grades of elementary school. Millions of copies had been sold by 1920. Professor McGuffey's lectern, traveling three-part secretary/bookcase, and his octagon table are displayed in a room added to the original house. McGuffey Museum is a registered National Historic Landmark.

Westerville

HANBY HOUSE

160 West Main Street. Open: May–Oct., Sat. 10–4, Sun. 1–5, Groups by appointment. Admission: $1.50 adults, $.50 children 6–12, Under five, free. Maintained and operated by Westerville Historical Society under agreement with Ohio Historical Society. (614) 891-6289.

Benjamin Russell Hanby (1833–1867), composer, lived in this house, which was then on Grove Street. In the 1920s it was renovated and moved to its present location. Hanby House was opened to the public in 1937. It contains five rooms of Civil War era antiques, including a walnut desk made by Hanby. Hanby's piano and a large collection of his sheet music are on exhibit. Also dis-played are the original plates for the first edition of Hanby's "Darling Nelly Gray," one of the most popular songs of the Civil War. His most enduring song, "Up on the Housetop," is still popular.

OKLAHOMA

Chandler

LINCOLN COUNTY HISTORICAL SOCIETY MUSEUM OF PIONEER HISTORY

717–719 Manvel. Museum Hours: 9:30–4, Mon.–Fri. Free admission. (405) 258-2425.

The museum maintains files and changing exhibits honoring Oklahoma writers associated with Lincoln County. One exhibit highlights a writers' circle of the Fallis community in the 1930s and 40s. Nationally recognized Fallis writers included Blanche Seale Hunt (1912–1972), Jennie Harris Oliver (1866–1942), and Beulah Rhodes Overman (1894–1990). Mrs. Hunt wrote the *Little Brown Koko* children's books. That series is on exhibit along with a collection of dolls representing its characters.

The Hoffman Library in the museum's North Gallery contains the 30 western novels of Vingie Roe (1879–1958). Another exhibit prominently features Alberta Wilson Constant (1908–1981) and her book about the settling of Chandler, *Oklahoma Run*. In 1998 Lincoln County Historical Society reprinted that historical novel with a foreword by Anna Myers, Chandler author of award-winning historical novels for children. Also on display at the museum are Mrs. Myers' works. Several, including *Red-Dirt Jessie* and *Fire in the Hills*, have Oklahoma settings.

Claremore

THE LYNN RIGGS MEMORIAL

Lynn Riggs Park, 121 N. Weenonah. Open: Mon.–Fri. 9–12, 1–4; also summer weekends, 1–5. Free admission. (918) 627-2716.

Lynn Riggs (1899–1954), poet, playwright and screenwriter, is honored at this city-owned site. A Kellstone statue of Riggs stands at the entrance. His most famous play, *Green Grow the Lilacs,* is about real people in his native Verdigris valley. It became the basis for the musical *Oklahoma!* by Rodgers and Hammerstein. Among the memorial's exhibits are two props from the *Oklahoma!* movie, the "surrey with the fringe on top" and Laurey's honeymoon dress. Lynn Riggs was born, reared, and buried in Claremore. The portion of the historic highway Route 66 that is within the Claremore city limits is named for him.

WILL ROGERS MEMORIAL MUSEUM

1720 West Will Rogers Blvd. Open year-round, 8–5. Admission by voluntary contribution. (800) 828-9643, (918) 341-0719.

Will Rogers (1879–1935), columnist, humorist, and author, is commemorated by an eight-gallery museum. Built in 1938 of limestone quarried nearby, the museum was financed by state funds. Additional state funding added the east wing in 1982. A three-million dollar renovation completed in 1995 was provided by private and public sources. The museum's library houses more than 2,000 volumes by, about, or referencing Will Rogers. Rogers wrote six books in addition to over 4,000 syndicated newspaper columns. The museum archives protect thousands of photographs, original manuscripts, and papers documenting Will Rogers' celebrated life and variegated career.

Will Rogers' birthplace at nearby Oologah, Oklahoma (918) 341-0719, is also open to the public as is his Santa Monica Ranch, Pacific Palisades, California (213) 454-8212.

Oklahoma City

RALPH ELLISON LIBRARY, METROPOLITAN LIBRARY

2000 NE 23rd St. at Martin Luther King Ave. (405) 424-1437.

Ralph Ellison (1914–1994), African-American author, is honored at this branch library bearing his name. A metallic wall sculpture of Ellison is the centerpiece of the library's foyer exhibit. A wall plaque in the foyer shrine to Ellison states:

> Ralph Ellison was born in Oklahoma City in 1914. His novel, INVISIBLE MAN, was chosen the most distinguished American novel published between 1945 and 1965.

Another part of the exhibit is a tablet inscribed:

> Who knows but that, on the lower frequencies, I speak for you?
> last line of *Invisible Man*, 1952

Ripley

THE WASHINGTON IRVING TRAIL MUSEUM

Southeast of Stillwater. Hours: 10–5, Tue.–Sat., 1–5, Sun.; Winter hours

The Washington Irving Trail Museum near Ripley, Oklahoma, is located on the site where Irving camped in 1832 during a trip he recorded in *A Tour on the Prairies*.

Famous Americans Issue, 1940.

(Nov. 1–Apr. 1) 10–5, Thu.–Sat., 1–5 Sun. Free.

Washington Irving, America's first internationally acclaimed author, camped at this site on his western tour with the U.S. Rangers in 1832. A first-edition copy of his resulting book, *A Tour on the Prairies* (1835) is exhibited at the museum. Other exhibits highlight early Oklahoma and the writers who have chronicled it, including Glenn Shirley of Stillwater. Shirley, an authority on law enforcement in the Old West, has written 24 books and hundreds of articles and stories during his nearly 60-year career. The museum is headquarters for the Glenn

Shirley International Fan Club. The Payne County and Central Oklahoma Museum Association sponsors this museum.

Sallisaw

SEQUOYAH'S CABIN

3 miles north of town on St. Hwy. 59, then east on St. Hwy. 101. Open year round Tues.–Fri. 9–5. Sat. and Sun. 2–5. Closed Mon. Free admission. (918) 775-2413.

Sequoyah (1776–1843), Cherokee soldier and teacher, built this log cabin home in 1829, a year after he moved to Oklahoma. Not a writer in the traditional sense, Sequoyah is, nevertheless, a man of letters. His invention of the Cherokee alphabet for his people is a unique contribution. After 12 years of studying the Cherokee language, he devised a system of 86 characters to symbolize every sound in the language. Within a few years, thousands of Cherokees learned to read and write in their own language. His cabin contains many artifacts related to his remarkable achievements. The Reader's Choice Book Award selected by Oklahoma school children is named for Sequoyah. The giant redwood trees of California also perpetuate his name.

OREGON

Forest Grove

HARVEY W. SCOTT MEMORIAL LIBRARY

Pacific University, 2043 College Way. (503) 359-2204.

Harvey W. Scott (1838–1910), editor

and author, was awarded the university's first baccalaureate degree in 1863. He became editor of *The Portland Oregonian,* now the state's largest newspaper. Scott's myriad articles on Oregon history constitute the six-volume *History of the Oregon Country,* published in 1924. The library honoring Scott's legacy at his alma mater was built in 1967.

PENNSYLVANIA

Doylestown

JAMES A. MICHENER ART MUSEUM

138 South Pine Street. Open: Tues.–
Fri., 10–4:30; Sat.–Sun., 10–5; Closed
Mon. General Admission, $5. Seniors,
$4.50, Students, $1.50, Under 16 free
on Sat. l0–1; Children under 12 are ad-
mitted free but must be accompanied
by adult. The museum is a private, in-
dependent, and non-profit cultural institution. Listed on the National Register of Historic Places. (215) 340-9800,
ext. 126.

James A. Michener (1907–
1997) lived in this eastern Pennsylvania town all of his boyhood
and much of his adult life. In 1988
The James A. Michener Art Museum, housed in the old Bucks
County Prison, opened. The 1884
stone structure was saved by a
group of townspeople who peti-
tioned the state for it and then
raised two million dollars to con-
vert the prison to an art museum.
The Michener estate endows it
now, as well.

Just inside the renovated
prison is a room devoted to the exhibit, James A. Michener: A Living Legacy. Michener's Bucks
County office, complete with his
desk and chair, typewriter, and dictionary, has been moved to this
room. The exhibit celebrates the
Pulitzer Prize–winning novelist's
career as writer, philanthropist, and
public servant. Michener's Presidential Medal of Freedom, pre-

sented in 1977, is on display. Original manuscripts and memorabilia from his more than
forty books can be seen. Michener began his
phenomenal career in 1947 with *Tales of the
South Pacific*, following it with *The Bridges
at Toko-Ri, Hawaii, Centennial, Texas,* and
many others, totaling an estimated sales of
75 million copies worldwide.

The museum was expanded in 1996
when an addition funded by the author's late
wife's will was opened. The Mari Sabusawa
Michener Wing houses a permanent exhibit,
Creative Bucks County: A Celebration of
Art and Artists. The 7,400 square foot wing

**The James A. Michener Art Mu-
seum in Doylestown, Pennsylvania,
is housed in the old stone prison. The
Michener room exhibit celebrates the
novelist's life and works.**

also includes a featured artist exhibition, a video theater and an interactive artist database. Quotations from the works of renowned world authors are prominent throughout the area. In addition to several painters honored in this exhibit, seven famous American writers are commemorated creatively through photography, biographical sketches, and varied mementos of their writing careers. For at least part of their careers, the writers all lived and wrote in Bucks County, Pennsylvania. Like the museum's namesake, Michener, almost all of the writers commemorated here are also recognized for their humanitarianism.

Pearl S. Buck (1892–1973)

Befitting America's first woman to receive both the Nobel and Pulitzer prizes in literature, a prominent spot is devoted to this author of more than a hundred books. She lived the first half of her life in China, the setting of her famous novel, *The Good Earth*. In 1935 she moved to Bucks County, her home until her death. Mrs. Buck's Green Hills Farm was often the gathering place for the artists who lived and worked in Bucks County. In this museum exhibit, photographs of her international family of adopted children are on display, and her humanitarian work is highlighted. In addition to her efforts on behalf of children worldwide, Mrs. Buck worked for improvement in the areas of civil and women's rights, mental retardation, and East-West relations.

Oscar Hammerstein II (1895–1960)

The museum's exhibit allows visitors to experience some of this great lyricist's greatest works. One of them is *Showboat*, written with Jerome Kern. Others represented in the exhibit are from his long collaboration with Richard Rodgers: *Oklahoma!*, *Carousel*, *South Pacific*, and *The Sound of Music*. All of these hit musicals were born in Bucks County. In 1940 Hammerstein purchased Highland Farm, near Doylestown, where he lived and worked for the rest of his life. Productions written in Bucks County earned 26 Tony awards and 14 Oscars. At Highland Farm Hammerstein was also mentor to the young Stephen Sondheim, who was to write the next generation of classic Broadway musicals.

Moss Hart (1904–1961)

A special exhibit at the museum features Hart and Kaufman, the premier writing team of the 1930s. An old Silvertone radio permits listeners to hear a previously unreleased work, *The Play's the Thing*. The famous team recorded it in 1939. Their first play was the satire, *Once in a Lifetime*, a hit in 1930. On opening night Kaufman gave the majority of the credit for the play to Hart. The pair received the Pulitzer Prize for *You Can't Take It with You* in 1937. After he bought a country manor near New Hope in Bucks County, Moss Hart wrote two plays with Kaufman inspired by their Bucks County experiences. Hart wrote the screenplay for the Oscar-winning *Gentlemen's Agreement*. He also won acclaim as a play director for *My Fair Lady* and *Camelot*.

George S. Kaufman (1889–1961)

The other half of the Hart-Kaufman team featured in the museum's special exhibit is identified there as "a founding father of the American popular theater." Although he wrote only eight plays with his favorite collaborator, Moss Hart, he collaborated with other playwrights on all but one of his 40 plays. Shortly after he purchased Barley Sheaf Farm in Holicong, Bucks County, *Stage Door*, his collaboration with Edna Ferber, opened. He won the Pulitzer for the political satire, *Of Thee I Sing*, his collaboration with Ryskind and Gershwin. He also successfully directed such hits as *Guys and Dolls*.

Dorothy Parker (1893–1967)

This famous wit's living room at her country manor in Pipersville, Bucks County, is reproduced here in its ten shades of red. Museum visitors who pick up her red telephone hear Parker's recorded voice. As a poet, drama critic, and short story writer, Dorothy Parker was associated with *Vogue*, *Vanity Fair* and *The New Yorker* magazines. She received the O. Henry Short Story Award for *Big Blonde*. Parker was also a Spanish Civil War correspondent and a Hollywood screenwriter. Her obituary in *Time* magazine stated: "Hers was the tongue heard round the world."

S.J. Perelman (1904–1979)

The humorist excelled in writing parody and satire. He wrote the scripts for several Marx Brothers films and received an Academy Award for his collaboration

Literary Arts Series, 1992.

on *Around the World in Eighty Days*. His essays appeared in *The New Yorker* for nearly 50 years. His estate in Bucks County was named Eight Ball Farm.

Jean Toomer (1894–1967)
His fame rests primarily with his passionate and realistic portrayal, *Cane*, published in 1923. Each individual page of this 239 page work is displayed in the museum. The book consists of prose sketches, stories, poems, and a one-act play. All these separate entities are united with the theme that blacks are most free when they celebrate their heritage. The book is considered one of the most significant creations of the Harlem Renaissance. Toomer owned Mill House, a farmhouse near Doylestown where he self-published some of his writings under the *Mill House* imprint.

Lackawaxen

ZANE GREY MUSEUM

Open: 12–4, Sat. and Sun. in May, Sept. and Oct.; Fri.–Sun in June–Aug.; Admission: $2. Adults, $1. Youth, Children free; Administered by the National Park Service. Call (570) 685-4871 for directions and current hours.

Zane Grey (1872–1939), prolific western author, moved to this area in 1905 and to this house in 1914. By 1915 Grey had published 15 books including his most famous novel, *Riders of the Purple Sage*.

In 1918 when the Greys moved to California, they retained the house until 1945. From 1948 until 1973 the new owners operated it as the Zane Grey Inn. From 1973 to 1989 they converted the inn to the Zane Grey Museum using the rooms which had been the author's office and study for exhibits. There they displayed Zane Grey's photographs, books, and memorabilia collected through the years. The site is a national historic landmark.

In 1989 the museum was sold to the National Park Service. Because of Zane Grey's long association with the Delaware River and its creative influence on the young writer, the park service included the museum in its holdings called the Upper Delaware Scenic and Recreation River. The ashes of Zane Grey and his wife Dolly were interred in a nearby cemetery.

Perkasie

GREEN HILLS FARM, PEARL S. BUCK HOUSE

520 Dublin Rd.—an extension of Maple Ave., which begins at Rt. 313 in Dublin, PA. Open for guided tours: Tues.–Sat. 11 A.M., 1 and 2 P.M. Sun. 1 and 2 P.M.; Closed Mon., major holidays, and Jan.–Feb. General Admission: Adults: $5, Seniors and Students: $4, Under six: free, Families: $12. The Pearl S. Buck Foundation (800) 220-2825, (215) 249-0100.

Pearl S. Buck (1892–1973) bought this 1835 farmhouse and 60 acres in 1935 after returning from China to live permanently in this country. She had received the Pulitzer Prize in 1932 for *The Good Earth*, set in China where she had been reared by missionary parents. The farmhouse was expanded to accommodate the large family of children adopted by Mrs. Buck and her

husband, publisher Richard Walsh. The original part of the house, built in 1740, was used for her husband's office. Green Hills Farm became a National Historic Landmark in 1980.

Throughout the house Pennsylvania antiques blend with the author's Chinese carpets and other Oriental accessories. The hand-carved Chinese hardwood desk where she wrote her classic novel may be seen in the house's large library. The Awards Room exhibits mementos of the many honors Mrs. Buck received, including the 1938 Nobel Prize. On display is the academic regalia she wore to receive 13 honorary degrees, as well as the keys to several cities where she was honored.

Fifteen thousand annual visitors learn that the living legacies of the author/humanitarian are Welcome House, an international adoption agency, and The Pearl S. Buck Foundation, which assists children and families worldwide to gain the necessary skills to improve their lives. The Pearl S.

Top: Green Hills Farm, home of Pearl S. Buck from 1935 to 1973, is near Perkasie, Pennsylvania. The author of 300 published works, Buck received the Pulitzer and Nobel prizes. *Bottom:* Pearl S. Buck's grave at Green Hills Farm faces east toward her beloved China, her home for 40 years. China is the setting of her classic novel, *The Good Earth.*

This statue symbolizes Pearl S. Buck's dedication to disadvantaged children. It stands at Buck's home, Green Hills Farm, near Perkasie, Pennsylvania.

Buck Woman's Award is presented annually to a woman who has distinguished herself in her career, in her devotion to her family, and in her pursuit of humanitarian ideals.

The Foundation's offices are located on the grounds, and there is also a statue of Mrs. Buck standing with a small child. The 1827 barn houses the Pearl S. Buck Cultural Center and the International Gift Shop. Mrs. Buck's grave is at a quiet place on the grounds of her home of 38 years.

Philadelphia

THE FRANKLIN INSTITUTE SCIENCE MUSEUM

Benjamin Franklin Parkway at 20th St. Open: Mon.–Thurs., 9:30–5, Fri.–Sat. 9:30–9, Sun. 9:30–5. Fee. Call (215) 448-1208.

A 30-ton marble statue of Benjamin Franklin (1706–1790) set in a marble rotunda pays tribute to this remarkable American. There is also a fine collection of Franklin artifacts including his printing press, his musical invention, bifocals, and writing desk. The Franklin Institute Library owns over 500 titles of books by and about Benjamin Franklin. These holdings include the most complete collection to date of the papers of Benjamin Franklin as well as early editions of his *Autobiography*.

EDGAR ALLAN POE NATIONAL HISTORIC SITE

532 North 7th St., at the corner of 7th and Spring Garden St. Open: 9 a.m. to 5 p.m. daily, June through Oct.; Wed.–Sun., Nov. through May, except Christmas, Thanksgiving and New Year's. Free Admission. Administered by the National Park Service. (215) 597-8780.

Edgar Allan Poe (1809–1849) lived in this townhouse with his wife, her mother, and their cat, Catterina, from 1843 to 1844. It is the last of four Philadelphia houses that the writer rented during his six-year stay, the most contented and productive period of his life. This house, then in a rising suburban neighborhood, was the newest and largest home that he ever had. The building as it now stands consists of two row houses; the site's entry is into the house occupied by Poe's neighbor. It is now the visitor's center and entrance to Poe's home. In addition to an audio-visual program and a small sales facility, the center houses an exhibit area. Poe's life and times are charted here. His contributions as science fiction pioneer and

his varied works as editor, critic, poet, essayist, and writer of mystery and horror stories are also traced. Busts and paintings of Poe complete the exhibit. Special events at the house include school programs and thematic tours celebrating Poe's January birth and his October death.

Poe's house, still being restored, was authorized as a unit of the National Park Service in 1978 and opened in 1980. It is unfurnished since there is no documentation about furnishings during Poe's stay there. Just inside the east door of the building,

Top: Edgar Allan Poe Issue, 1949. *Bottom left:* Poe lived in this Philadelphia house from 1843 to 1844. Here, at age 35, he was one of America's first professional writers, and he still exerts a great international influence. *Bottom right:* A raven perches at the Poe site in Philadelphia, where "The Raven" may have been written. Published in 1845, it earned some fame but probably less than ten dollars.

stairs descend to a cellar recalling the setting of Poe's story, "The Black Cat," published while Poe lived here. On the first floor are the rooms probably used as living and dining rooms. The two second floor rooms were possibly used for the writer's study and bedroom. In one of the rooms, guides show visitors the spot under the floor which may have inspired "The Tell-Tale Heart." The top floor, the warmest part of the house, probably contained the bedrooms of Virginia, ill from tuberculosis, and her mother, Maria Clemm.

Atop a pole on the grounds a large statue of a raven symbolizes Poe's most famous poem and one of the most famous in the English language. Poe may have worked on the poem while he lived in this house. Publication of "The Raven" provided Poe with international fame, but slight financial compensation, probably only nine dollars. Three other Poe museums exist, but Congress has designated this site America's memorial to its most influential writer.

MARIANNE MOORE ARCHIVES

> The Rosenbach Museum and Library, 2010 DeLancey Place. Library is open to researchers by appointment only, Mon.–Fri. 9–4:45. Sun. 11–4. Museum Hours: Tues.–Sun. 11–4, last tour at 2:45. Closed weekends, national holidays, and from Aug. 1 through 2nd Mon. in Sept. (215) 732-1600.

The Marianne Moore Archive here is the largest single-author collection of the Modernist era. It contains all the books, letters, manuscripts, journals, and clippings preserved by the poet over a long literary lifetime (1887–1972). In the 1920s Moore edited the influential literary magazine, *The Dial*. In 1952 she received the Pulitzer Prize for her *Collected Poems*. The Rosenbach Museum's Marianne Moore Room contains the living room furniture from her Greenwich Village apartment. Her trademark cape and tri-cornered hat are also on display. The museum periodically presents an exhibition from its Moore Archives.

Literary Arts Series, 1990.

Pine Grove

CONRAD RICHTER MARKER

Conrad Richter (1890–1968) was born at 33 Mifflin Street in a house now marked with a plaque. His last residence was 11 Maple Street. A state historical marker in front of the house states:

> The novelist, born in Pine Grove, wrote about American frontier life. His books include "The Town" and "The Waters of Kronos." A recipient of the Pulitzer Prize and National Book Award, Richter lived and worked in this house, 1950–1968.

After success with western settings while living in New Mexico, Richter returned to Pine Grove to write his award-winning books set in his native region. Six of his fourteen novels were adapted for movies, *The Light in the Forest* the best known. Richter is buried in the Lutheran cemetery on a hill overlooking Pine Grove. His tombstone is inscribed with this line from his writing: "Little grasses, you are taller now than me."

Pottsville

Home of John O'Hara

John O'Hara (1905–1970), novelist, changed Pottsville's name to Gibbsville when he used it as a setting for his works reflecting social mores. *Ten North Frederick* received the National Book Award, and several of his novels, including *Butterfield 8* and *From the Terrace* became successful films. In 1982 a Pennsylvania historical marker was erected in front of his home at 606 Mahantongo Street, now an apartment house.

The marker reads in part:

> This was the home, from 1916 to 1928, of one of America's best-known novelists and short-story writers. Born at Pottsville in 1905, he used the anthracite region as a setting for several of his major works.

Springdale

Rachel Carson Homestead

613 Marion Avenue, near intersection of PA 76 and Rt. 28. Homestead Tours: Sat. 10–4, Sun. 1–5, year-round. Admission: Adults: $4, children 4–18: $2.50, children 3 and under free. Rachel Carson Homestead Association. (724) 274-5459.

Rachel Carson (1907–1964), marine biologist, ecologist, environmental activist, and nature writer, was born in this five-room mid-nineteenth century farmhouse. Her childhood here nurtured a love and respect for nature which influenced the rest of her life. Carson's 1962 book, *Silent Spring*, initiated the modern environmental movement. Since 1975 the Rachel Carson Homestead Association has restored, preserved, and interpreted the site. It also provides education programs advancing Carson's environmental

The Rachel Carson Homestead is the birthplace and childhood home of the ecologist. Her book *Silent Spring* launched the modern environmental movement.

Great Americans Issue, 1981.

ethic and serves as an international resource for information on her life and work. The house tour includes an exhibit on Carson's life and legacy. It traces her dual careers with the U.S. Fish and Wildlife Service and as a writer of books about the ocean. Visitors can also follow the self-guided nature trail with interpretive signs and information about Carson's childhood explorations of the woods.

OTHER RACHEL CARSON MEMORIALS IN PENNSYLVANIA:

The Rachel Carson Trail. Thirty-four mile hiking trail in Allegheny County.
Rachel Carson State Office Building. 400 Market Street, Harrisburg.

——— R H O D E   I S L A N D ———

Providence

JOHN HAY LIBRARY

Special Collections, Brown University, 20 Prospect St. (at corner of College St.). Open to any researcher with valid ID. Hours: Mon.–Fri. 9–5. (401) 863-2146.

The Library is named for John Hay (1838–1905), statesman, author, and Brown alumnus. In addition to filling appointments to high positions in government service, Hay wrote editorials for the *New York Tribune*. Along with several volumes of poetry and essays, he published *Pike County Ballads*. The climax of Hay's writing career was his ten volume *Lincoln: A History*, published from 1886 to 1890. He had served on Lincoln's staff. At the Brown University library named for Hay, his collected papers include correspondence with a number of leading writers of his time.

John Hay Library is the repository for the extensive Harris Collection of American Poetry and Plays. Linked with the field of American literature is another comprehensive collection, the archives of small presses and little magazines. The Broadsides Collection also includes items relating to literature and theatre. The public is invited to frequent exhibitions that John Hay Library mounts from its collections.

──SOUTH CAROLINA──

Charleston

DuBose Heyward and William Gilmore Simms Memorials

The Footlight Players, 20 Queen Street. (803) 722-4487.

A bust of DuBose Heyward (1885–1940), poet, novelist, and playwright, is displayed in the lobby of the state's oldest community theatre. Heyward, who wrote about his native Charleston, served on the theatre's board of directors. He and his wife, Dorothy Hartzell, adapted his novel, *Porgy*, to a folk drama. George Gershwin's later operatic version, *Porgy and Bess*, has become a classic.

A 9 × 18 feet mural painted on the theatre's east wall in the 1940s depicts actors, playwrights, managers, and critics associated with Charleston's long theatrical history. DuBose Heyward is represented on the mural, as is William Gilmore Simms (1806–1870). Four of Simms' plays were produced at Charleston theatres. One was adapted from his novel, *Guy Mannering*. A bust of Simms is at White Point Park on the Charleston Battery.

The Timrod Memorial

Washington Square, 80 Broad Street, at Broad and Meeting streets.

Henry Timrod (1829–1867), called the Laureate of the Confederacy, is memorialized here by a large monument A bust of Timrod is supported by a pedestal inscribed on its four sides. Timrod's poem, "At Magnolia Cemetery," is engraved on the north panel. The poem was read at the 1866 Memorial Day services at Magnolia Cemetery and annually since then.

McClellanville

Hampton Plantation, Home of Archibald Rutledge

1950 Rutledge Rd., U.S. Hwy. 17 to S. Santee Rd. (SC 857). Left 2 mi. Open: Thurs.–Mon. 9–6, house open 1–4. Admission $2 adults, $1 for age 6–16. (803) 626-7444.

This ancestral home of Archibald Rutledge (1883–1973), author of poetry and prose, was built around 1750. The house and plantation suffered decline following the Civil War. After Rutledge became South Carolina's first poet laureate, he returned home in the 1930s to begin returning the

Archibald Rutledge was born and died at Hampton House in McClellanville, South Carolina. His book *Home by the River* discusses the restoration of his ancestral mansion.

mansion to its former glory. Rutledge's most famous work, *Home by the River,* describes his restoration efforts. Another of his works is the collected stories in *Hunting and Home*

in the Southern Heartland. In 1971 Rutledge sold the house and land to the state. He is buried in the family cemetery at Hampton Plantation.

SOUTH DAKOTA

De Smet

LITTLE HOUSE ON THE PRAIRIE SITES

Tours begin at the Gift Shop 105 Olivet Ave. June–Aug. 9 A.M.–7 P.M.; Sept. Mon.–Sat. 9–4, Sun. 12–4; Oct., Apr., May, Mon.–Sat. 9–4; Nov.–Mar. Mon.–Fri. 9–4. Admission: Adults $5, Children $2. The Laura Ingalls Wilder Memorial Society. (800) 880-3383.

Two houses associated with *The Little House on the Prairie* series by Laura Ingalls Wilder (1867–1957) are open to the public: the Surveyor's House, setting of *By the Shores of Silver Lake,* and the Ingalls Home, de-

scribed in *On the Way Home* and *A Little House Sampler.* Both houses display artifacts from the Ingallses and Wilders.

Six Laura Ingalls Wilder books are set in De Smet. Visitors see 18 sites the author included in those books along with the cemetery where her family is buried.

THE LAURA INGALLS WILDER PAGEANT

1 mi. southeast of De Smet on Hwy. 14, last weekend in June and the first two weekends in July, Fri., Sat., and Sun. 9 P.M., Adults $5, Children $2; The Laura Ingalls Wilder Pageant Society. (605) 692-2108.

TENNESSEE

Henning

ALEX HALEY HOUSE MUSEUM

200 S. Church St. Hours: Tue.–Sat. 10–5, Sun. 1–5

Alex Haley (1925–1992), Pulitzer Prize winning author of *Roots,* grew up in this home of his maternal grandparents, Will and Cynthia Palmer. The ten-room bungalow, as it was called, retains its 1920s appearance. Haley memorabilia and family artifacts are on exhibit. Visitors may also listen to audio tapes of the author. In this house he heard the family stories which were to inspire his most famous book. *Roots* received a

special citation from the Pulitzer committee in 1977. It became a very popular television production soon afterward. The front lawn is the writer's final resting place.

Memphis

HALLIBURTON MEMORIAL TOWER

Rhodes College campus, 2000 N. Parkway. (901) 843-3000.

Richard Halliburton (1900–1939), adventurer, author, and lecturer, is memorialized here by a 140-foot tall tower, given by his parents. Dedicated in 1962, the Halliburton

Tower was added to the National Register of Historic Places in 1978. A world traveler, Halliburton wrote about his experiences in such books as *New Worlds to Conquer* and *Seven League Boots*. He died in a Pacific Ocean venture. A five-ton, seven-foot bronze bell in Halliburton Tower sounds the hour and half-hour. Inscribed on the bell are two inscriptions characterizing Halliburton's approach to life. One of them quotes Shakespeare's *King John*: "The day shall not be up so soon as I / To try the fair adventure of tomorrow."

Nashville

ROBERT PENN WARREN CENTER FOR THE HUMANITIES

Vaughn House, Vanderbilt University. (615) 343-6060.

The Center promotes interdisciplinary research and cultural studies. This Victorian building, once a faculty residence, was established as a humanities center under the sponsorship of the College of Arts and Science in 1987 and renamed in 1989 to honor Robert Penn Warren. As both a Vanderbilt student and professor, Warren was a part of an influential literary group.

JOHN CROWE RANSOM PAPERS

Special Collections, Heard Library, Vanderbilt University, 419 Twenty-first Ave. S. (615) 322-2807.

The collection is primarily the correspondence and manuscript poetry and prose of John Crowe Ransom (1888–1974) during his retirement years (1959–1974). Ransom graduated from Vanderbilt in 1909 and taught at the university from 1914 until 1937. During his Vanderbilt faculty years he published four volumes of poetry and a book of prose.

Knoxville

ALEX HALEY STATUE

Morningside Park, 1600 Dandridge. (423) 215-2090.

Alex Haley (1925–1992), author of *Roots*, is commemorated here with a 12-foot bronze statue. Haley was associated with the University of Tennessee for a time.

Del Rio

CHAPEL HOLLOW MEMORIALS TO CATHERINE MARSHALL'S CHRISTY

I-40E exit 435 to Rt. 321 N. At Newport follow Hwy. 25 S to Del Rio Post Office. Turn onto Hwy. 107 to the Chapel Hollow community. Settings in "Cutter Gap," the name for nearby Chapel Hollow in the novel *Christy*, are identified by signs.

This rural mountain region is immortalized in *Christy*, the book by Catherine Marshall (1915–1983). It is the true story of her mother's experience as a young teacher in the area. Numerous markers in the community identify significant settings. Included are the sites of the historic mission house and the church/school building as well as several cabins.

Norris

CHRISTY EXHIBIT AND APPALACHIAN HALL OF FAME

Museum of Appalachia. I-75, Exit 122, then 1 mile east; 16 miles north of Knoxville. Open: Daylight hours all year except Christmas; Admission: Adults $7, Children $4.

Among the many points of interest in this 65-acre museum dedicated to preserving the region's past is the *Christy* exhibit. It focuses on the television series, some scenes

The Appalachian Hall of Fame at the Museum of Appalachia in Norris, Tennessee, is devoted to the region's outstanding individuals. Several authors are featured there.

of which were filmed at museum sites. Numerous articles and artifacts from the CBS series are displayed at the museum. The show was based on the book *Christy* by novelist Catherine Marshall.

The Appalachian Hall of Fame, housed in a graceful, three-story museum building, spotlights four authors connected with Tennessee. Exhibited photographs, memorabilia, and other related items commemorate their life and works.

James Agee (1909–1955)
This poet, novelist, and journalist, was born at nearby Knoxville and educated at an Appalachian boarding school. His books, including the Pulitzer-winning *A Death in the Family* and *Knoxville Summer 1915*, describe a Tennessee boyhood.

Frances Hodgson Burnett (1849–1924)
As a teenager this famous children's author moved from England to rural New Market. She considered her true home to be the Tennessee mountains. *The Secret Garden, The Little Princess,* and *Little Lord Fauntleroy* are her classic works.

Alex Haley (1925–1992)
The author and scriptwriter grew up in Tennessee. In the 1980s he built a house across the road from the Museum of Appalachia. Haley is best known for *The Autobiography of Malcolm X* and *Roots,* which received a Pulitzer Prize. Haley was cochairman of *Tennessee Homecoming '86,* a year-long celebration in the state.

Tennessee Williams (1911–1983)
Born Thomas Lanier Williams, the South's greatest playwright adopted the

Literary Arts Series, 1995.

name "Tennessee" because of career and family ties to the state. *A Streetcar Named Desire* and *Cat on a Hot Tin Roof* earned Williams two Pulitzer Prizes for drama.

Pulaski

RANSOM AND DAVIDSON STATE HISTORICAL MARKER

Giles County Courthouse.

John Crowe Ransom (1888–1974) and Donald Davidson (1893–1964), Fugitive Poets and Giles County natives, are honored by a Tennessee historical marker erected on the courthouse south lawn in 1996. At Van-

derbilt University the two young men were leaders in producing the significant poetry magazine, *The Fugitive*. They were later a part of The Agrarians. This group of writers produced a symposium of essays entitled *I'll Take My Stand: The South and the Agrarian Tradition*. The 1930 collection urged the region to retain its economic, moral, and social independence in the prevailing climate of industrialism. Davidson became known for his literary criticism, historical studies, and composition textbooks. Ransom was an outstanding critic, editor, and poet. Another Tennessee historical marker honoring the Fugitive group stands at the Jim Frank home in Nashville, a meeting place of the writers.

TEXAS

Austin

O. HENRY MUSEUM

409 East Fifth St. Open 12–5, Wed.–Sun. Free. (512) 472-1903.

William Sydney Porter (1862–1910), famous as O. Henry, the master of the short story, rented this 1886 Queen Anne–style cottage from 1893 to 1895. After it was given to the city, the house was moved a few blocks to its present site, restored, and opened in 1934 as a museum. The house's exterior, tan with blue trim, looks much as it did when the Porters lived here. The original pine floors have been preserved, and four brick chimneys missing for 60 years were put back in place during restorations begun in 1994.

Furniture belonging to the Porters and other period pieces are on display. Visitors see Porter's writing desk and his swivel

chair from his bank teller's position at Austin's First National Bank. Embezzlement charges against Porter by this bank led

This marker at the O. Henry Museum in Austin, Texas, reviews O. Henry's fame. Another memorial is the prestigious national O. Henry Short Story Award, begun in 1918.

In Austin, Texas, William Sydney Porter lived in this house from 1893 until 1895. Now the O. Henry Museum, it preserves the writer's story "The Gift of the Magi" and encourages young writers.

to his imprisonment, where he began writing short stories in earnest. Two wicker chairs in the bedroom are sometimes called "The Magi" chairs because they are thought to have inspired the O. Henry classic, "The Gift of the Magi." Porter's wife was ill from tuberculosis. When he tried to cheer her by giving her money to attend the Chicago World's Fair, she selflessly bought curtains and the wicker chairs for their home instead.

In addition to presenting Porter's story, the museum sponsors the O. Henry Writing Clubs for Austin school children. It also hosts the popular O. Henry Pun-Off, a word-play tournament begun in 1977. Listed on the National Registry of Historic Sites, the house is administered by the City of Austin, Parks and Recreation Department. The Austin Convention and Visitor's Bureau (800) 926-2282 offers a map and brochure of Austin's O. Henry Trail.

THE O. HENRY ROOM

Austin History Center, 9th and Guadalupe streets. Open: Mon.–Thur. 9–9, Fri.–Sat. 9–6, Sun. 12–6. (512) 499-7480.

The O. Henry Room is filled with displays, photographs, and paintings related to William Sydney Porter (O. Henry), especially his Austin years. Photographs show Porter behind the teller's window at the First National Bank and as part of the popular Hill City Quartet. Paintings inspired by O. Henry stories, including "The Ransom of Red Chief," are on the walls. A collection of early printings of "The Gift of the Magi," O. Henry's best-known story, is in an exhibit case. O. Henry's 14 volumes of short stories are there, too.

TEXAS STATE CEMETERY

Main entrance on Comal St., Visitor Information Center, 201 E. 2nd St. Hours: Mon.–Fri. 8–5; Sun. and holidays 9–6. (800) 926-2282, (512) 478-0098.

These three Texas writers have been interred here by Governor's Proclamation:

James Frank Dobie (1888–1964). Headstone Text: Storyteller of the Southwest, Presidential Medal of Freedom

Fred Gipson (1908–1973). Headstone Text: His books are his monument.

Walter Prescott Webb (1888–1963). Headstone Text: Historian, University of Texas 1918–1963.

Zilker Park

PHILOSOPHERS' ROCK

Barton Springs Pool, Barton Springs Road. (512) 867-3080.

A large sculpture of three Texas writers, Roy Bedichek (1878–1959), J. Frank Dobie (1888–1964), and Walter Prescott Webb (1888–1963) stands at the entrance to Barton Springs Pool. Dobie and Webb frequently swam at the pool. Bedichek, as de-

picted in the sculpture, did not swim. The sculpture presents the friends and colleagues deep in conversation. Professors at the University of Texas, this legendary triumvirate is credited with establishing Texas literature. Examples of their works are Bedichek's *Adventures with a Texas Naturalist*, Dobie's *The Longhorns*, and Webb's *The Texas Rangers*.

Mason

FRED GIPSON EXHIBITION AREA

Mason County M. Beven Eckert Memorial Library, 410 Post Hill. Hours: Mon.–Wed. Noon–7 P.M., Thur., 1–5:30, Fri., 9–1:30, Sat., 10–12. (915) 357-5446.

Fred Gipson (1908–1973), novelist, is memorialized here in the town where he was born. The extensive Fred Gipson Exhibit

Philosophers' Rock in Austin, Texas, is at Barton Springs Pool, a favorite gathering spot of its subjects, J. Frank Dobie, Walter Prescott Webb, and Roy Bedichek.

dominates the library's central foyer. A life-size bronze statue of "Old Yeller" is a focal point. When Gipson died, three million copies of *Old Yeller* had been sold, and it had become a popular movie. The writer's life is chronicled here through displays of personal memorabilia, his typewriter, and literary awards earned in a career yielding 12 books, numerous periodical articles, and six screenplays and television scripts. Along with photographs of Gibson, this quotation is prominently displayed: "A simple tale about a boy and a dog is all there is to *Old Yeller*, all that I ever meant for it to be."

A life-size bronze sculpture, *Old Yeller*, is at the M. Beven Eckert Memorial Library in Mason, Texas. Fred Gipson, a native of Mason County, wrote *Old Yeller*.

UTAH

Salt Lake City

WALLACE STEGNER COLLECTION

University of Utah, J. Willard Marriott Library, Photograph Archives. (801) 581-8558.

This collection contains about 130 photographs taken from the 1920s to 1994 of Wallace Stegner (1909–1993) and the people and events associated with his life. A 1930 graduate of this university, Stegner also was an instructor here from 1933 to 1934. Stegner received recognition for his work as novelist, educator, historian, and environmental activist. From the appearance of his first important novel, *Big Rock Candy Mountain*, until his death 50 years later, Stegner was a part of the national scene. The University Library also became the repository for the Wallace Stegner Papers in 1995.

WALLACE STEGNER CENTER FOR LAND, RESOURCES AND THE ENVIRONMENT

University of Utah College of Law.

Launched in 1996, the Stegner Center honors university alumnus Wallace Stegner. Embracing its namesake's views on the responsibility of the West, the center's mission is to achieve equitable and feasible solutions to environmental problems, local to international.

VERMONT

Ferrisburgh

ROKEBY MUSEUM

Route 7. Open: mid–May to mid–Oct., Thurs.–Sun. Guided tours at 11, 12:30, and 2. Admission: $4 Adults, $3 seniors and students, $1 under 12. (802) 877-3406.

Rowland E. Robinson (1833–1900), author of sporting and nature books, died in the same room in which he was born on the farm occupied by his family for four generations. The house, a late eighteenth century Vermont cape with a federal-style addition, is a national historic site. The museum displays varied collections and contains an immense library. Its holdings include 10,000 family letters and hundreds of family books, pamphlets and periodicals. The Archives have the complete manuscripts of Rowland E. Robinson's published works including *Forest and Stream Fables* and *Vermont: A Study of Independence.*

Rokeby, a documented Underground Railroad stop, maintains a collection of nineteenth century anti-slavery newspapers, including *The Liberator.* The church journals received by this Quaker family are also preserved. New England's social history from the 1790s to 1961 is interpreted at this Vermont Time Capsule.

Old Bennington

ROBERT FROST GRAVE

Old First Congregational Church Cemetery.

Rokeby, the Robinson family museum in Ferrisburgh, Vermont, preserves 200 years of the region's social history. Rowland E. Robinson's art and literary works are here.

ROBERT LEE FROST
MAR. 26, 1874 — JAN. 29, 1963
"I HAD A LOVER'S QUARREL WITH THE WORLD"

HIS WIFE
ELINOR MIRIAM WHITE
OCT. 25, 1873 — MAR 20, 1938
"TOGETHER WING TO WING AND OAR TO OAR"

MARJORIE FROST FRASER
MAR 29, 1905 — MAY 2, 1934

CAROL FROST
MAY 27, 1902 — OCT 9, 1940

ELLIOTT FROST
SEPT. 28, 1896 — JULY 28, 1900

ELINOR BETTINA FROST
JUNE 20, 1907 — JUNE 21, 1907

LILLIAN LABATT FROST
NOV. 13, 1905

Directions to the grave of Robert Frost in this historic old churchyard are well marked. The gravestone is inscribed with this line from Frost's poetry: "I had a lover's quarrel with the world."

Ripton

FROST MEMORIAL

> Green Mountain National Forest Wayside, beside Route 125. U.S. Department of Agriculture and Forest Service.

Dedicated in 1964, this site commemorates Frost's years in Ripton and Vermont with a plaque and exhibits. Across the highway, the Robert Frost Trail posts seventeen of his poems along a trail which Frost often walked. The poetry, exhibited in the setting in which much of it was composed, is a tribute to New England's nature poet.

HOMER NOBLE FARM/ROBERT FROST FARM

> Robert Frost Cabin, Left onto Hwy. 396 from Rt. 125. Owned and maintained by Middlebury College. Not open to the public.

A plaque set in a rock identifies the site as a national historic landmark since 1968. A sign at the entrance states that visitors may follow the lane to view the cabin where Frost lived and worked the last years of his life. From the 1920s until his death Frost was on the staff at the Bread Loaf Writers Conference each summer at nearby Middlebury. The conference director lived in the main house on this farm, owned by Frost.

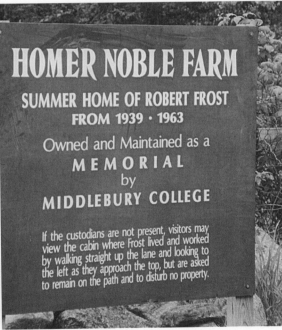

Opposite: Robert Frost's gravestone is inscribed "I Had a Lover's Quarrel with the World." After Frost's name, the names of his wife, two sons, and two daughters are listed. *Above left:* A sign at this site near Ripton, Vermont, states that Frost spent the summers of 1938 through 1962 in this area and was inspired by his wanderings through the woods and fields. *Above right:* Frost bought the Homer Noble Farm in 1939. He opted for the log cabin, and his colleague at nearby Bread Loaf Writers Conference lived in the main house.

The Robert Frost cabin is near Ripton, Vermont. While Frost was living here, he received his fourth Pulitzer Prize for *A Witness Tree* in 1942.

VIRGINIA

Alexandria

HORATIO ALGER ASSOCIATION

99 Canal Center Plaza. (703) 684-9444.

Horatio Alger, Jr. (1832–1899), wrote more than 120 books to inspire young people. Alger's poor heroes succeeded through perseverance and high ideals. International sales of these post–Civil War books total over 250 million copies. The Horatio Alger Association awards college scholarships to students who have conquered great hardship and who are committed to serving humanity. Annually, the organization honors with a bronze bust of Alger ten Americans who exemplify "the Horatio Alger story."

Big Stone Gap

THE TRAIL OF THE LONESOME PINE OUTDOOR DRAMA

June Tolliver Playhouse, Hwy. US 23 to Alt. 58 W. to Clinton Ave. June–Aug., Thur.–Sat., 8 P.M. Admission. (800) 362-0149, (540) 523-1235.

This official state outdoor drama of Virginia is adapted from the John Fox, Jr., novel. The love story of a mountain girl, June Tolliver, and a mining engineer from the East is presented against a backdrop of changes in the mountain culture forced by discovery of coal and iron ore.

JOHN FOX, JR., MUSEUM

117 Shawnee Ave. Open Memorial

Day–Labor Day. Admission. (540) 523-2747.

John Fox, Jr. (1862–1919), novelist, moved to this cedar-shingled house in the 1890s when he came to the Cumberland mountains. Here he wrote *The Little Shepherd of Kingdom Come* and other stories of the region.

Charlottesville

JOHN DOS PASSOS ARCHIVES

Special Collections Division, University of Virginia Library.

John Dos Passos (1896–1970), political novelist and non-fiction writer, chose the University of Virginia for his manuscripts and papers in 1954. After his death, letters written to Dos Passos were added to the collection as well as his letters to friends. Man-

uscripts and first editions are all part of the collection. It is a full archive of the life and writing of this influential author whose best-known work is *U.S.A.*, the 1930s trilogy.

Dumfries

WEEMS-BOTTS MUSEUM

Corner of Duke and Cameron streets. Open: Oct.–Apr., Tues.–Sat. 10–4, Sun. 1–4; May to Sept., Tues.–Sat. 10–5, Sun. 1–5; Closed Mon. all year except for holidays. Admission: adults: $3. Seniors 55+: $2. Children 6–12: $1.50. Under 6: free. Historic Dumfries Virginia Inc. (703) 221-3346.

Mason Locke Weems (1759–1825), the first biographer of George Washington, owned the oldest section of this house from 1798–1802 before selling it to lawyer Benjamin Botts. Parson Weems, as he was called, used what is now the east half of the

Weems-Botts Museum in Dumfries, Virginia, commemorates Mason Locke Weems, George Washington's first biographer. Weems lived here from 1798 until 1802.

structure for his bookstore and garret warehouse. Although he invented the story of George Washington and the cherry tree, his *Life of Washington* made the first president a permanent national hero. It was the best-selling book in America, along with the Bible, and was in print continuously from 1800 until 1927. Along with his most famous book, Weems also wrote biographies of William Penn, Benjamin Franklin, Francis Marion, and others, and he produced almanacs and sermon tracts. A number of them, as well as biographies on Weems himself, are in the museum's gift shop. In 1974 the town of Dumfries purchased the building and began its restoration.

Gore

WILLOWSHADE, WILLA CATHER CHILDHOOD HOME

> Near Winchester on Route 50. Not open to the public.

This large red brick house in the Shenandoah Valley was the home of novelist Willa Cather the first nine years of her life before her family pioneered to Nebraska. The final section of Cather's last novel, *Sapphira and the Slave Girl*, is set here. The his-

torical marker at the site provides the dates of Cather's residence there, from 1874 to 1883.

Hardy

BOOKER T. WASHINGTON NATIONAL MONUMENT

> 12130 Booker T. Washington Highway (VA # 122), 22 mi. SE of Roanoke. Open: Daily 9–5 except Thanksgiving, Christmas, and New Year's Day and other federal holidays as announced. Free admission. Administered by National Park Service. (540) 721-2094.

Booker T. Washington (1856–1915), educator, author, and lecturer, was born a slave on a tobacco farm here. In 1957 the national monument was established to commemorate his life and work. The original 207-acre plantation is almost all now a part of the national park. The Visitors Center reviews Washington's life through exhibits and an audio-visual presentation. Washington left the place in 1865 at age nine, poor, uneducated, and newly freed. In 1908 when he returned for a visit, he was a college president and the author of a number of books, including his famous autobiography, *Up from Slavery*.

Marion

SHERWOOD ANDERSON ARCHIVE

> Smyth-Bland Regional Library, 118 South Sheffey St. Open Mon.–Thurs. 9–8, Fri. 9–1 and Sat. 10–3. (504) 783-2323.

Author Sherwood Anderson (1876–1941), novelist and journalist, is commemorated by a collection of first editions, monographs, photographs, and memorabilia displayed in this rare book room. Anderson lived in the area from 1925 until his death. In 1927 he bought and became the editor of two sister newspapers in Marion. Anderson

American Arts Issue, 1973.

was already internationally famous for his novel, *Winesburg, Ohio*, published in 1919.

The Sherwood Anderson Association in Marion sponsors a yearly Sherwood Anderson Short Story Contest. Included in the ceremonies for winners is a guided tour of Ripshin, Sherwood Anderson's farm twenty miles south of Marion. It is not open to the general public.

ROUND HILL CEMETERY

Sherwood Anderson's tombstone here is inscribed "Life, Not Death, Is the Great Adventure."

Richmond

EDGAR ALLAN POE MUSEUM

> 1914–16 E. Main St., Open Tues. 10–4, Sun.–Mon. 1–4. Admission: Adults $5, Sr. $4, Students $3. The Poe Foundation. (804) 648-5523.

Since 1922 the museum has been dedicated to telling Poe's story in Richmond, where he lived longest. In this city he was reared, married, and gained recognition. The site occupies five buildings which document Poe's accomplishments through exhibits, relics, and his works.

The old stone house, Richmond's oldest standing structure, was familiar to Poe. Built about 1737, this first building of the museum houses a large-scale model of Poe's Richmond accompanied by a correlating orientation film. The Elizabeth Arnold Poe Memorial Building honors Poe's mother, who was both married and buried in Richmond. This site displays items Poe would have known, including a desk and chair from the office of *The Southern Literary Messenger*, where Poe was employed.

The Exhibition Hall is a gallery for rotating exhibits and an area recreating Poe's childhood bedroom at the home of his foster parents, the Allans. The writer's childhood bed, coverlet, and a mantle are all here. The Raven Room displays James Carling's illustrations of "The Raven." Carling devoted himself to Poe's most famous poem, one of the best-known in the English language. The Library's large collection of books and manuscripts is open to researchers.

The museum buildings open onto the Enchanted Garden, featuring flowers and other plants which Poe admired. The walled garden is also inspired by two of Poe's poems, "To Helen" and "To One in Paradise." The centerpiece is a shrine to Poe made of bricks from the building which housed the *Southern Literary Messenger*.

GLASGOW HOUSE

> One West Main St. Not Open to Public; Private residence with law offices in basement.

Ellen Glasgow (1874–1945), Southern feminist writer, lived in this house from age 13 until her death. All of her novels except one were written in her upstairs study on the northwest corner of the house. The room is still decorated with the English wallpaper she ordered during her travels. Some of her best known works are *The Battle Ground* and *In This Our Life*, for which she was awarded the Pulitzer Prize in 1942. Miss Glasgow worked for women's rights and for the cause of the destitute. Her autobiography, *The Woman Within*, was published posthumously in 1954.

Troutdale

RIPSHIN FARM

> Home of Sherwood Anderson, not open to the general public.

In 1926 novelist Sherwood Anderson (1876–1941) bought a farm in the tip of Virginia where it borders Tennessee and North Carolina. The farm, on the bank of Ripshin Creek, is named for the creek. Anderson built a house on the property, which is now a national historic site. He wrote his last works in a cabin on the place.

WASHINGTON

Seattle

THEODORE ROETHKE AUDITORIUM

Kane Hall, University of Washington, 45th and 15th streets. (206) 543-2985.

Theodore Roethke (1908–1963), poet and professor, is honored here where he was on the faculty from 1947 until his death.

Among the volumes of poetry Roethke published while teaching at the university are *The Waking*, which earned him the Pulitzer Prize, and the also highly acclaimed *Words for the Wind*. Theodore Roethke Auditorium seats 700 and is used for seminars, lectures, and concerts. It is a fitting memorial for the poet who gave frequent poetry readings in various parts of the country.

WEST VIRGINIA

Hillsboro

PEARL SYDENSTRICKER BUCK BIRTH-PLACE

US 219, about 10 mi. S. of Marlinton, in Pocahontas County. Guided Tours:

May 1–Nov. 1; Mon.–Sat., 9–5, Sun. 1–5. Open holidays except Thanksgiving, Christmas, and New Year's Day. Off season tours by appointment. Admission: Adults $4, Students $1. The Pearl S. Buck Birthplace Foundation. (304) 653-4430.

The Pearl S. Buck birthplace in Hillsboro, West Virginia, was built in 1847. Pearl S. Buck was the first American woman to receive the Pulitzer and Nobel prizes.

Pearl S. Buck (1892–1973), world famous writer and humanitarian, was born in this historic house. It was the home of her maternal grandparents, the Stultings. Today the birthplace is a fine historic house museum. Costumed guides and period rooms with some of the house's original furniture reflect the 1890s. Memorabilia associated with the author is on exhibit, along with frequent special exhibits. The Pearl Buck U.S. Postal Stamp was issued at Hillsboro.

Right: **Great Americans Issue, 1983.**

WISCONSIN

Baraboo

LEOPOLD MEMORIAL RESERVE AND LEOPOLD SHACK

12919 Levee Rd, 10 miles northeast of Baraboo. Access is by I-90/94 (east side) or Highway 12 (west side). Aldo Leopold Foundation. (608) 355-0279.

Aldo Leopold (1887–1948), conservationist and author, applied his "Land Ethic" by restoring health to the sand counties farm land he purchased in 1935. The only remaining structure, an old chicken coop, was converted to become his family's weekend home. Today the historic Shack is preserved by the Aldo Leopold Foundation to continue Leopold's tasks of ecological restoration and scientific research. Leopold's book, *A Sand County Almanac,* is a classic for environmentalists.

Edgerton

THE STERLING NORTH HOME AND MUSEUM

409 W. Rollin Street. Open: Sun. 1–5 except Jan.–Mar. Admission: Adults: $3, Students: $2, Children five and under: free. Also open by appointment. (608) 884-3074, 884-3870.

Sterling North (1906–1974), novelist, grew up in this small town, which he called "Brailsford Junction" in several of his books. From 1917 to 1918 he lived in this house with his father and pet raccoon, Rascal. The house is the setting of North's award-winning 1963 book, *Rascal: A Memoir of a Better Era.* It and North's earlier nostalgic best-seller, *So Dear to My Heart,* became successful motion pictures. North's last book, *The Wolfling,* is inspired by his father's childhood in Busseyville, near Edgerton.

In 1992 the Sterling North Society bought the author's boyhood home and opened it to the public in 1997. The house, furnished with period pieces, contains a reading/meeting room and a museum room which traces Sterling North's life through decade exhibits. The Society, dedicated to preserving and promoting the Sterling North literary heritage in the Edgerton area, is restoring a large barn on the property. It will be used to accommodate groups of visitors. The 1880s Sterling North House is listed on the National Register of Historic Places.

The Sterling North Home and Museum in Edgerton, Wisconsin, was North's boyhood home. It is the setting for his autobiographical book, *Rascal*, about a pet raccoon.

Menomonie

THE CADDIE WOODLAWN HISTORICAL PARK

9 mi. south of town, on S. Hwy. 25. Open daylight hours, spring through fall. Dunn County Historical Society. (715) 232-8685.

Carol Ryrie Brink (1895–1981), children's author, set her pioneer books in the country surrounding the present park site. Two of these acclaimed books are *The Headland* and *Four Girls on a Homestead*. Brink's most famous book, *Caddie Woodlawn*, received the 1935 Newbery Medal. The classic was inspired by the childhood experiences of her grandmother, Caroline Woodhouse, as a child on the frontier. The grandmother's childhood home has been moved to the park from a nearby farm. In 1970 the Dunn County Historical Society restored and dedicated the site.

Monona

ALDO LEOPOLD NATURE CENTER

300 Femrite Drive. (608) 221-0404.

The legacy of educator and author, Aldo Leopold, is continued here as students learn to appreciate wildlife and the land. Leopold, a University of Wisconsin professor, wrote the classic text, *Game Management*.

New Salem

HAMLIN GARLAND HOMESTEAD

357 W. Garland. Hours: Memorial Day–Labor Day, Mon.–Sat. 10–5, Sun. 1–5. The West Salem Historical Society. (608) 786-1675.

Hamlin Garland (1860–1940), short story and nonfiction writer, bought this

The Caddie Woodlawn Park near Menomonie, Wisconsin, contains the 1850s house where Carol Ryrie Brink's heroine lived. *Caddie Woodlawn* is a children's classic.

house in 1893 as a home for his parents. *Main-Traveled Roads*, the first of a series about the Midwest, had brought him early success. Garland's works chronicle the hard life of the prairie farmer he knew from his childhood on the vast plains. The Homestead, originally a log cabin, typifies the homes he knew then. *Daughter of the Middle Border* earned Garland the Pulitzer Prize for biography in 1921. The Pulitzer committee also cited Garland's *Son of the Middle Border* as significant.

The Homestead displays several pieces of original Garland furniture as well as other artifacts. It was designated a national historic landmark in 1973.

Pepin

LITTLE HOUSE IN THE BIG WOODS SITE

The Pepin Historical Museum. Open May 15–Oct. 15, Daily 10–5. (715) 442-3011.

Laura Ingalls Wilder, author of *The Little House* series, was born in Pepin in 1867. She immortalized the site in her first book, *Little House in the Big Woods*. An Ingalls cabin replica contains displays and features Laura artifacts.

Portage

ZONA GALE HOUSE

The Women's Civic League of Portage, Inc. 506 W. Edgewater St. Admission. Open by appointment. (608) 742-7744.

Zona Gale (1874–1938), novelist and playwright, built this Greek revival style house after the publication of her first novel, *Romance Island*, in 1906. The house was for the writer's parents, but two upstairs rooms were her private retreat. When Gale was in town, she stayed there until her marriage in 1928. In her upstairs study she wrote other early novels, including *Heart's Kindred*, *A Daughter of the Morning,* and *Birth*, inspired by Portage, as were most of her works. Her desk is still there, and other original furnishings are found throughout the house as are Zona Gale artifacts. When Zona Gale Breese died, her husband deeded the house to the Women's Civic League, which she had founded in 1932. The house is listed on the National Register of Historic Places.

ZONA GALE CENTER

301 E. Cook St., Hwy. 33, 1 block east of Hwy. 51. (608) 742-5655.

Constructed as a church in 1855, this site is now the center for cultural arts. Among the events scheduled here annually are the Gale Singers, other choral ensembles, opera productions, and community theatre performances. The cultural center's namesake, Zona Gale, was awarded the 1921 Pulitzer Prize for drama for *Miss Lulu Bett*.

ZONA GALE BREESE HOME

804 MacFarlane. Museum of the public library. (608) 742-4959.

During the last ten years of her life,

Zona Gale lived with her husband and family in this red brick, stucco and wood Georgian style house. For a number of years it was the Portage Free Library–Zona Gale Breese Memorial Library. Since the construction of the new public library down the street, the house has become its museum. Zona Gale's study is still there, along with part of her library. The 1912 site is a national historic landmark.

FRIENDSHIP VILLAGE ZONA GALE FESTIVAL

Third Saturday in August, Portage Chamber of Commerce. (800) 474-2525.

Since 1992 Portage has celebrated *Zona Gale Days* commemorating her birthday, August 26. Each year a local Zona Gale site is selected for the celebration headquarters and is designated the Friendship Village Station. *Friendship Village* is the title of Gale's 1908 book made up of stories set in Portage, her native city.

THE ZONA GALE GRAVE SITE

Silver Lake Cemetery, West Hwy. 16 (Wisconsin St.) to Cemetery Road.

The grave is on a knoll to the left about ¾ of a mile from the cemetery entrance.

Rhinelander

SAM CAMPBELL MEMORIAL FOREST AND HIKING TRAIL

Forest Service Rd. 2207, Nicolet National Forest. Directions from Three Lakes: Hwy. 32E to Military Rd. Then left 4.5 mi. to Old Military Rd. Take left fork 1 mi. to trail head. Trail length: 1 and ¾ mi. loop. (715) 546-2295.

Sam Campbell (1895–1962), writer and nature enthusiast, is memorialized by this trail complex developed and sponsored by the Three Lakes Historical Society in conjunction with the U.S. Forest Service. Using Campbell's writings in the *Forest Life* series, a brochure available at the trail head interprets the area. Campbell, called the Philosopher of the Forest, wrote articles on nature for newspapers and magazines and produced films on animal life. His twelve books and thousands of public lectures focused on conservation. The emphasis is continued by The Sam Campbell Memorial Scholarship Fund established by the Trees for Tomorrow Conservation Camp at Eagle River.

WYOMING

Medicine Bow

OWEN WISTER GENERAL STORE

Old Lincoln Highway (US 30).

The store was dedicated and renamed in 1981. The name change from the generic Medicine Bow General Store can be traced to a visit almost one hundred years before by Owen Wister (1860–1938). In his journal the future novelist and biographer described the experience of sleeping on the store counter on his first night in Medicine Bow. Later the incident appeared in his novel, *The Virginian*.

THE OWEN WISTER CABIN AND MONUMENT

The cabin, built in the Jackson Hole area, was the summer home and winter hunting lodge of Owen Wister. In 1976 the Medicine Bow Lions Club moved it near the

Top: The Owen Wister Cabin, built in the Jackson Hole area of Wyoming, was used by Wister, author of *The Virginian*. It is now at the Medicine Bow, Wyoming, museum. *Bottom:* The Medicine Bow Museum occupies the old train depot in Medicine Bow, Wyoming. The sign commemorates *The Virginian*, Owen Wister's novel.

Owen Wister Monument and the Medicine Bow Museum, housed in the old train depot. Erected in 1939, the petrified wood monument next door pays tribute to Owen Wister and *The Virginian.*

THE VIRGINIAN HOTEL

In 1911 this three-story, concrete block building opened. It was named for Owen Wister's 1902 book, the prototype of western novels. Completely renovated and restored in 1984, the hotel is resplendent in its Victorian decor. The Owen Wister Dining Room and Owen Wister Suite pay homage to the literary connections of the hotel, a National Historic Place.

Index